OUR JOURNEY

The Awakening

Robert W. Raine

Editing, design, typesetting and publishing by UK Book Publishing

www.ukbookpublishing.com

ISBN: 978-1-913179-82-3

Acknowledgements

I would first like to thank my family for the understanding they have shown on my journey with Spirit. Most especially, my dear wife Maureen, who has stood by me through all the bad times and the good. She has shown strength and dedication in adversity and possesses hidden strengths that are rarely appreciated by those outside our family; a true earth bound angel.

Secondly, all the friends I have in spiritualism. My first earthbound guide, mentor, and circle leader, Irene Wilson, perhaps better known as the Cinderella Medium. A special thanks also to Freeda Robson, my first encounter with a Physical Medium who took me under her wing and helped me to find my true path. To Irene Harthill, in whose house we met regularly on Friday afternoons. With her knowledge of Yoga and immense knowledge of the ways of the Yogi and the healing powers of Spirit, she was our observer, commentator, questioner, and helper.

Without the help and support of the regular members of my first circle, Donna, Sue, Margaret, Jayne, Michelle, Paul, Erika, and Leslie; whose first Nation Guide "Didi", surprised me one afternoon with his closeness and high definition appearance in full colour in my vision; I could not have continued on my journey with Spirit.

To those I have missed, I apologise sincerely, but you are all in my thoughts. May your God bless you and keep you safe always. A thought is the most powerful thing in the universe and mine are with you all.

Leaving the best until last, my grateful thanks to all the spirits that give me the privilege of conversing and channelling for guidance and help. Most remain nameless, but live on in my soul with the love, light and peace that they kindly bestowed upon me.

Spirit requested audio, video and latterly photographic evidence during all of my sessions when I started working with Freeda Robson, and they gave us some wonderful lighting effects. I will be forever grateful to these kindly souls for without their prompting to write, and the recordings they gave us, this book about my experiences on my journey would never have happened. I am truly privileged. Thank you and bless you all.

Robert William (Bill) Raine

Table of Contents

Background – A Brief Description 1

Chapter One – The Awakening 6

Chapter Two – The Development Circle 12

Chapter Three – A New Experience 30

Chapter Four – Out of Control 42

Chapter Five – Questions and Answers and "Wa-Nee-Tah" 58

Chapter Six – The Watchers and the Plane of Understanding 69

Chapter Seven – The Test and the Council of the Ancestors 81

Chapter Eight – The Power of Prayer and Love 97

Chapter Nine – The New Beginning and "Shairi - Lah" 112

Chapter Ten – Reunion. A lesson and Shairi-Lah returns 133

Chapter Eleven – "Tootsie" 161

Chapter Twelve – "Tootsie" and the Table 189

Chapter Thirteen – A New Year 229

Chapter Fourteen – Unexpected confirmation 247

Background
– A Brief Description

My name is Robert William Raine, known as Billy to family, and Bill to friends. I was born in a small mining community in County Durham called Sherburn Hill on the 2nd March 1949.

My parents lived in with my father's widowed mother. Times were hard after the Second World War. My father returned home in 1947 after serving with the RAMC in India and Palestine, now Israel, his last posting.

Within a few months of my birth, the family moved to eight, Church Villas, Shadforth, just down the road from Sherburn Hill.

In 1952, April the 19th to be exact, our family left Grandmother's house to live in a new town called Peterlee. Soon after, my grandmother moved to a one bedroomed bungalow in Sherburn village.

This is not my life story but a snapshot of my background – my parents died within eight weeks of one another in 1983, a double devastating blow.

I had got married in 1971 to Maureen, my dear wife whom I had first met in 1961. She had told her friend that I was the man she would marry, and it did happen. We have two boys, Christopher and Robert, born in 1976 and 1979 respectively.

Maureen, my wife, had finished working in May 2008 due to breast cancer. A small, pea-sized lump under her arm had quickly led to investigation. Biopsies and numerous X-rays, and scans were all to no avail in locating the prime tumour source of the disease. The only option was surgery and a lymph node clearance. Grim determination and positive thinking gave us courage and every new day was a challenge to overcome. My employers were understanding and facilitated my work commitments around Maureen's appointments until the day of surgery. I was the only person available for a two-day inspection in Cambridge, some 200 miles from home. After visiting the night before I had driven down to Cambridge to my hotel. The next day I spent working and wondering if everything was going well. I explained my position to the Engineering Manager I was working with and he gracefully allowed me to finish one hour early that day. I literally raced back up to the hospital those 200 miles for visiting time to see her. Everything had gone well, the staff informed me as I sat watching Maureen drifting in and out of awareness. The concern I had felt slowly lifted off my shoulders as she drifted off to sleep. Visiting over, I faced the return drive to Cambridge with a lighter heart.

Her acceptance of the surgery coupled with a positive outlook and her determination to beat the disease, won the day in the end. There were dark times with the pain of the surgery. Vicious chemotherapy led to hair loss, fatigue, and sickness with numerous appointments back and forth to the hospital. I think of Maureen and myself as a stereotypical northeast England family. Our area has always been hard working and relatively low paid. Coal mining, shipbuilding and steel was the mainstay of Country Durham. In the 17th and 18th century, County Durham stretched from the river Tyne in the north to the river Tees in the south. The area between was mainly poorly managed agricultural land and small embryonic industries centred around shipbuilding on the Tyne and Wear and coal supplies to the south, mainly London.

Our ancestors are a mix of the old kingdom of Northumbria that stretched down to the Humber River and the invasive Danes, the Vikings, who founded Jorvic, the present day York. Northwards to the Scottish borders and the land of the Border Reivers, a mix of Scots and English. Lawless gangs who roamed the borders stealing anything valuable; one such group using the ancient Roman fort at Housesteads as a base. Life has always been hard and shows on the faces of the older generations. Old before their time but caring and friendly in nature to each other. With Maureen and me, we just take life as it comes. The good times and the bad. We have each other. We never had any pets or any real wish to own any. Our close family unit always took priority.

Robert, my youngest son, worked at the Nissan car plant in Sunderland, a half hour drive north from Peterlee. He worked shifts and a lot of overtime to help with the buying of a very small two bedroom semi-detached house and then the required pieces of furniture and appliances to turn a house into a home. Maureen and I had helped to decorate the house from top to bottom on spare evenings and weekends before they moved in.

Robert's wife Catherine had worked as the Manager of the local Hays Travel shop in Peterlee, County Durham. Peterlee is a new town started in the North East of England in 1950, where all my family now live. The majority of housing provided was rented accommodation, reflecting the local area employment which was mainly coal mining. New factories slowly sprang up on the industrial estates added to the town as it grew.

In 2015, along came James, their first child. Catherine finished work to look after him and became a full time mother. Sleepless nights and long days with only short naps was James's routine. Maureen and I helped as best we could. Sometimes the only way to get James to sleep was walk him in the pushchair or a drive in the car to get him off to sleep almost every evening. As James grew, he became more and more active with a marginally better sleep routine. The pushchair walks or a ride in the car slowly faded out as it became easier to get him to sleep on an evening. There were still some sleepless nights of little naps followed by awkward days of the same ilk.

Their starter home was fast becoming too small with the additional items required by James. Downstairs had no entrance porch, just a front door opening straight into the living room which led into the kitchen. There was no dining room and the stairs were immediately to the right of the front door. There was just enough room for a two-seater couch against the stairs, two other chairs and a TV stand filled the small room. Twelve foot by twelve foot was about the size of the living room including the stairs and the kitchen was less, just seven feet by twelve. You can imagine the upstairs with a tiny bathroom without a window and two bedrooms where the largest just managed a standard double bed, a double wardrobe and a small chest of drawers. The second bedroom for James was even smaller with just a single bed, a built-in cupboard and a set of drawers. When James started to walk, it was eminently clear that it was time for a move to a larger house as soon as possible. This move accomplished in six months with once again; help from me, now retired, and my wife Maureen. Happily, Robert, Catherine and James had moved from the other side of town to the same estate as we lived in just a few minutes' walk away.

Just after James's second birthday in the spring of 2017, another addition to the family, Paul, arrived. A second grandson that delighted the family, especially for Robert's older brother Christopher's two daughters, Bethany and Jessica, who fussed over baby Paul like two mother hens. What joy he brought us all at that time. We were proud grandparents of two boys and two girls. Our lives were a mixture of nights in with the family and days out together. We had a few weekends away and the occasional holidays spent as one large family unit. Life was good for all of us.

It was the death of Robert's wife, Catherine, at the age of 41, on November 18th 2018, that started my quest for answers. Her passing was only three months after her cancer diagnosis and they had two boys, aged three and one. My happy, close family world had collapsed around me. This is my story of my search for answers.

Chapter One
– The Awakening

With the mind-numbing death of Catherine, we plodded on for almost four months in the fog of bereavement knowing that as grandparents we had no choice but to support our family as best we could. Robert still needed to work and the children required looking after. Close friends and family had expressed great sympathy but little compassion after the first few weeks of our loss. We had Christmas for the boys, but our hearts were broken.

Within three months, only the stalwarts remained. They helped us whenever they could by enabling us to take a breather from the new routine of looking after two houses and a small family. Our small circle was becoming a tight knit group. They know who they are and we will be forever grateful for their help and support that continues to this day. Routines were worked out and we plodded on, still numbed, and looking for an answer to why.

Six months after Catherine passed, it was late spring of 2019 when we were informed that Lee, Catherine's brother, had taken his own life. This tragedy dealt us another massive blow and once again, we found ourselves stunned and back at rock bottom.

Catherine's parents had withdrawn into themselves after Catherine's passing and this further, needless death, only compounded their sorrow, leaving them much withdrawn from us, as they still are today. Catherine was like a daughter to Maureen, my wife, and me.

We had developed a special, close relationship over the years we had known her. She was not used to as close a family as we were and marvelled at our "open house" policy to family and close friends.

When I say, close friends, there are very few. Told many years ago that you could count your true friends on the fingers of one hand, my experience has taught me that this is in fact very true for me. These friends never live in your pocket but are there when you need them, as you are for them. I was never really an English Pub person, preferring to spend time with my family. As life goes on you change close friends. They drift away as their lives change, as does yours. New interests generate new acquaintances and new friends to while away time, but rarely develop into that closeness of a true friend. At this time in my life, I have three. One has been there for almost forty years of my life. The other two replaced two that have passed. The book of life is written in your heart.

Catherine had slipped seamlessly into our lives and hearts, and bonded ever closer as a family. She had become the organiser of our days out, family celebrations and holidays. The family usually got together for a Saturday evening meal and Sunday lunch at our house, and we had many, many great nights of laughter and discussion. Happy, happy times.

I had been asking in my prayers for the reasons why she had died. I had cried and raged at God and the world in general for taking such a vibrant, young life. Why her? Why not me instead? I had not received any reply.

I had bought a new phone and joined the dreaded Facebook to keep in close contact with our small family circle and close friends. One morning on opening Facebook, I saw a message about an open circle meeting at the local Spiritualist centre. For some reason I read the details but thought nothing much about it. A couple of weeks went by and when I was in Horden, an old coal mining village next to Peterlee, I found myself driving down the street shown in the message. I thought that I would locate this Spiritualist centre, just so I knew where it was.

Sixth Street, named, as most other mining community village streets were in the east of County Durham, numbered from the first ones built, closest to the coalmine. The houses were built in the early 1900s, and mainly consisted of small terraced houses in a room configuration of two up, two down, with an outside toilet and a coalhouse at the bottom of a small enclosure behind the house termed a "yard or back yard". At the bottom of 6th street on the left, there is a grassed area. At the "T" junction with Blackhills Terrace, on the right, there are three or four shops. Opposite the junction and slightly left is the large edifice of St Mary's Church. This Church of England Church is a very large building for a colliery village and known in the area as "The Pitman's Cathedral". Coming back up 6th street fifty yards, the last terraced house has a small garden at the side of the gable end. At the end of the garden, the next building is a single storey "Temperance Hall" marked by a stone plaque above the central door with the date 1923. With a single window on either side of the door, it is easy to miss, having around thirty feet of frontage. Since the build, it has seen service as a Quaker meetinghouse, various shops, and a micro factory. It carried a sign: "Horden Spiritualist Friendship Centre".

Two weeks went by and then another Wednesday afternoon on Facebook, I saw another message about the open circle meeting. A thought flashed through my mind and I told my wife I was going that very night to seek answers to my questions.

I dressed smart casual and took the few minutes' drive to Sixth Street, Horden, not really knowing what to expect. I parked up in the narrow street where there were a couple of cars already parked on either side of the street but sufficient room to allow single file traffic to pass, which is common in these villages. Light was showing from the building but a curtain was across the inside of the door. Opening the door and I was immediately into a room that spanned the full width of the building and around twenty feet deep. On the left, centralised against the wall was a small stage, one-step high, surrounded by wood panelling with the entrance at the far side. This stage, known in Spiritualism as the "Rostrum", is akin to the basic separation of the congregation to the altar in a Christian church but without any normal religious accoutrements apart from a small lectern to the front left of the rostrum. Projecting into the room by around eight feet, the rostrum left a space on each side about six feet wide. The nearest to the door carried photographs on the wall of departed members and loved ones in the form of a cross. At some time in the past, a false ceiling had been added with recessed fluorescent lighting installed but the tubes reduced from four to two. It was still light but with a more subdued effect as the ceiling was still around ten feet high. There were no microphones, only an old home-style music centre.

The seating consisted of steel framed, stackable, office type chairs with a padded seat and small back panel, just below shoulder level. Two rows close to the walls surrounded an open space in the centre of the room with a single row that faced the centre placed in front of the rostrum. Entry was just one pound with an optional raffle ticket costing the same. I paid my fee and moved to an empty area against the far wall, near a doorway to a back room.

Irene Wilson is the Medium who runs the centre as an Independent Spiritualist Friendship Centre offering spiritualist services and healing sessions, plus a development circle for aspiring mediums. Irene Wilson is a petite woman in her seventies. Thoughtful, polite, and with a friendly caring nature, she greets attendees with a smile and small talk. The centre is a local meeting place for the community and is open for people to pop in, even for just a cup of tea and a chat on a Monday, the Reiki healing day.

It was a small place but had an atmosphere of peace. A few people turned up, a service of sorts, and a discussion took place. Greeted as a first time visitor, politely questioned as to why I had come, what had brought me there, I could not give an answer! When the circle opened, loved ones who had died passed messages through developing Mediums, to family members in the circle. The room behind, was both an office, meeting room and store room where you can sit for a chat and a cup of tea or coffee with a biscuit or some home cooked scones or cake. A central doorway led to a further room at the back of the building containing a small kitchen at one end and a toilet at the other with a small washbasin. A cup of tea and a chat, a few tears and I came back home. It had felt as if I had found a new family.

I attended a few more meetings and finally got a message. It was cryptic: but in hindsight profound. "Once I had put my problems into a locker and closed and locked that door, I would have a bunch of keys that would unlock many doors for me."

After the meeting and a chat over a cup of coffee, Irene Wilson, the medium, asked me if I would like to learn more and join the development group on a Saturday afternoon as an observer. I cautiously said yes, but with some trepidation about what this might mean or even where it might lead me.

After every meeting, Maureen, my wife, would enquire about how the meeting went and did anything happen. She was curious but reticent, as was Robert, my son, as he tried quietly and bravely to hold things together after the death of Catherine, his dear wife, to help his boys. This was the most upsetting for us all as we tried to explain to these small children that no, Mammy was not coming back, but she still loves you dearly. Many times, we desperately fought back the tears and as one of us succumbed to the grief and pain of our shared loss, quietly left the room to let it go. Let the dam burst with a flood of raw emotion. Wipe the tears, calm down and then return to face the demons once again. You drew those children close to you, holding them so tightly they could not see the silent tears that welled up and coursed down our faces. Often in these first few months, the raw emotion of remembering Catherine's life ebb away in front of me and the feeling of utter helplessness, made me wish I had never been born at all.

Yet somewhere, in the dark forgotten corners of the mind, is a spark that keeps you going. You cannot give up. Your family needs you as you need your family, trying to share the burden. You sleep eventually and tomorrow is another day on the rack of grief.

Chapter Two
– The Development Circle

30th March 2019 – Horden Spiritualist Friendship Centre.

Duly on the Saturday afternoon, I met with a few people, not as an observer on the outside, as I had first thought, but a new member of the group. We sat round as a circle of some eight or nine people with the medium (Irene) as our leader. After some small talk, prayers; then meditation began to a background of music named "Merlin's Magic". It was so surreal sitting in a chair with a group of strangers like a number in a clock face with eyes closed, listening to this rather weird background music. I had never experienced this before. Thoughts were racing through my brain; slow deep breathing, concentrating on the breath. Twice I felt a giggle coming on and just managed to supress them to a small muffled sneeze. Irene remarked afterwards that she felt, "we have a right one here".

Known as a "giggler" at school, and punished many times for laughing at the most inopportune times during my schooling, I was also quite nervous and shy and did not make friends very easily. As an only child, I have always found it somewhat difficult to talk, especially in a group of unknown people. More especially as almost all of the group were women and my secondary school was all boys.

With eyes closed for fifteen or so minutes seeing nothing but fuzzy, vague nothingness like an old TV set switched on, but with no aerial plugged in seemed so silly. Yet strangely, I was the last one to open my eyes when the music stopped. I felt quite relaxed and peaceful but had nothing for the circle and nothing else whatsoever to report when asked. Other members of the group had been on journeys through fields and woods, sandy beaches and small glades by streams. They had seen different things and faces, and some had messages for others in the group. Small details of evidence and encouragement.

This first meditation was both good yet strange. I had been nowhere, seen nothing, yet felt strangely calm and at peace. Feelings I had not had for years. The last twenty years of my working life, I had travelled everywhere by boat, aeroplane, and car. I had experienced the absolute silence of Canada's Alberta plains in the wintertime, a limitless blue sky with the snow-topped Rockies as a backdrop. Awesome, peaceful, but strangely menacing at the time. The wonders of the Taj Mahal. That magnificent edifice of a tomb with built in timelines and parallax defying inscriptions, yet surrounded by abject poverty. The spirituality of Japan and the respect for the ancestors with the tranquillity of the old wooden temples and the Samurai castles. The bustle of the Twin cities of Minneapolis and St Paul and the Mall of America, then quickly out to the countryside of White Bear Lake and an impression of temporary roots laid down with the detritus of cast off old cars slowly rotting into the landscape.

I listened to the Philosophies and a few short messages from those in the circle who could "link in". Using prompt words drawn from a bag or a circle of ribbons for inspiration leading to messages in some cases. Other more advanced members gave off short messages sometimes to more than one member of the group.

The following week I had to write a Philosophy to read from the rostrum. All week I had jumbled thoughts about the Seven Principles of Spiritualism. What would I write? Would I be able to write? The internet is a wonderful tool. Searching websites for inspiration I was gradually drawn by the following Friday to write the text below for our next meeting on Saturday the 6th April 2019.

Philosophy

Percy Bysshe Shelley was born on 4th August 1792 and died on 8th July 1822 aged 29 years. He was one of the major English romantic poets and is widely considered to be among the finest lyric poets of the English language. He is perhaps most famous for such anthology pieces as Ozymandias, Ode to the West Wind, To a Skylark, and The Masque of Anarchy. However, his major works were long visionary poems including Prometheus Unbound and the unfinished The Triumph of Life.

Shelley's unconventional life and uncompromising idealism, combined with his strong sceptical voice, made him an authoritative and much denigrated figure during his life. He became the idol of the next two or three generations of poets, including the major Victorian and Pre-Raphaelite poets Robert Browning, Alfred Lord Tennyson, as well as William Butler Yeats. Karl Marx, Henry Stephens Salt, and Bertrand Russell also admired him. Famous for his association with his contemporaries John Keats and Lord Byron, he was also married to novelist Mary Shelley.

I would just like to read a few quotes of his:-

"If he is infinitely good, what reason should we have to fear him? If he is infinitely wise, what doubts should we have concerning our future? If he knows all, why warn him of our needs and fatigue him with our prayers? If he is everywhere, why erect temples to him? If he is just, why fear that he will punish the creatures that he has filled with weaknesses?"

"What is life? Thoughts and feelings arise, with or without our will, and we employ words to express them. We are born, and our birth is unremembered and our infancy remembered but in fragments. We live on, and in living, we lose the apprehension of life. How vain is it to think that words can penetrate the mystery of our being.

Rightly used they may make evident our ignorance of ourselves, and this is much."

"Life and the world, or whatever we call that which we are and feel, is an astonishing thing. The mist of familiarity obscures from us the wonder of our being. We are struck with admiration at some of its transient modifications, but it is itself the great miracle."

A profound quote of his from Prometheus Unbound is the following lines that I remember from the mists of my youth.
"Death is the veil, which those who live call life:
We sleep, and it is lifted."

In our services, we ask that the veil be lifted, to allow communication from our loved ones through the medium.
Shelley hints at a knowledge of spirit long before spiritualism, as we know it, came about. They say that poets write from the heart as observers of life and love. They write with love, as a philosopher debates with their mind about their interpretation of all things of this earth and beyond.
When we think of the great philosophers, poets, artists, and leaders in the past, life was a little simpler then. No radio, television, few newspapers, as many could not read or write. No social media, cars, aircraft and myriad other things unknown to them. Science was in its infancy.
Hundreds of years before that we had an affinity with our surroundings. Mother Earth, the flora and fauna that we harvested for our earthly needs to survive. Come back to the present and we still harvest for our needs essentially but some for their greed to amass wealth and power. The great philanthropists of our time amassed great fortunes and gave fortunes to open museums and charities to educate the masses and help the needy who they had trampled on to amass their wealth. By their gifting to the nations,

had these people realised that their earthly life had no real purpose. Money cannot buy love. Money cannot buy understanding or truth.

What we have lost is our closeness to spirit and the understanding of our gifts from the divine. We forget to stop and marvel at nature, listen to the songs of the birds and thank our maker for these wonderful gifts to enhance our lives.

Some we say are born privileged. The most privileged are not those who are high born, nor rich, or have famous parents, but those few that have the gift of second sight from an early age. An ability to draw back the veil. To see where we have come from and where our true home is. The ability to communicate with those who have transitioned and drawn back the veil to return home.

We have almost lost this age-old ability to communicate with our ancestors. Our lives are more complicated, leaving less time for the things that really matter to our spirit. We can be distracted and wrapped up in earthly life. We have lost what we had and must regain our power of spiritual communication by training and meditation. We must spread the word of love and light, forgiveness and understanding by our actions and good deeds. We must apply our heart and soul to our quest for knowledge on this earth we have been given. Nurture and protect it, for we are bound to it in our earthly life. We should nurture our spirit with love and light to reinforce our inner self.

When we have learned to allow our spirit to communicate beyond the veil, we have gained richness beyond question. We can comfort the bereaved and give evidence and certainty to an afterlife. We can spread love and understanding to those that would listen. Best of all, we can take this knowledge with us on the next part of our journey to enlightenment. We have the love and light of spirit to show us the way. A final poem by Minnie Louise Haskins entitled "God Knows":

And I said to the man who stood at the gate of the year: "Give me a light that I may tread safely into the unknown." And he replied:

"Go out into the darkness and put your hand into the Hand of God.
That shall be to you better than light and safer than a known way."
So I went forth, and finding the Hand of God, trod gladly into the night.
And He led me towards the hills and the breaking of day in the
lone East.

So heart be still: What need our little life, our human life to know,
If God hath comprehension? In all the dizzy strife. Of things both
high and low,
God hideth His intention. God knows His will is best.
   The stretch of years, which wind ahead, so dim to our imperfect
vision,
   Are clear to God.

Our fears are premature; In Him, all time hath full provision.
   Then rest: until God moves to lift the veil from our impatient eyes,
when, as the sweeter features of Life's stern face we hail,
Fair beyond all surmise God's thought around His creatures,
our minds shall fill.

I found it fascinating how I seemed guided during the days
between Saturday development classes, as to what I would write
for the next week's philosophy. Trawling the internet on many
spiritual sites, I found a wealth of information.

Many sites encouraged you to join for a fee, or charged you for
readings or emails when you signed up. Many times after using
text from various sites, I felt encouraged to change the wording,
to delete paragraphs and substitute my own thoughts until I felt
happy with the presentation and meaning. During meditation, I
was now seeing faces.

Quick flashes of many different faces, most too quick to
recognise or even take stock of whom they might be. Sometimes
pictures came into my thoughts. Scenes of persons sitting down
or rooms with furniture.

However, I did not have a sense of my guide / gatekeeper / doorkeeper or guardian angel.

After one particular meditation, Irene was quite amused as she told me her guide had laughed as I had implored my doorkeeper for something for the circle and something for any individual. *"He does not even know his name,"* he said.

At this point Irene asked if I wanted to meet my guide to which I replied yes. Irene told me to sit opposite her in the clock position six whilst she was at twelve. I stood up, closed my eyes and breathed steadily and slowly as requested. She said she would send some energy to me and I would meet my guide.

Suddenly in front of my eyes close to my nose, there appeared an orb within an orb, slowly contra rotating within and around each other with a ragged edge around the whole. It was quite a start to my senses, as I did not know whether it would enter my nose or mouth or just into my body. This dual, contra rotating, ragged orb's slow rotation was mesmerising; fascinating; drawing me towards it. I could not take my eyes off it. I was seeing this with closed eyes!

Suddenly like the curtain parting in a theatre, the orb disappeared, and I was standing near the stern of a single masted wooden sailing vessel in a very big sea with large waves coming towards me in full colour. No sails were carried, just a pennant on the top of the single mast.

Irene asked, "Can you see anyone?"

I saw a man standing just below and in front of me. I described what I saw. A man in leather, just below the knee breeches that had cross pattern laced sides. He had a woollen shirt and a leather jacket. A blue, white spotted scarf covered his head but his hair came out of the top and was something like a ponytail. He had woollen socks and leather thonged sandals on his feet. In his right hand, he held a leather woven stock with a loop around his wrist. Leather strands hung down from the stock with knots in them. A badge of authority and discipline, although I had the impression he was a kindly man of about 54 years of age, quite stockily built and around five foot eight in height, with pain in his left leg due to a break some years before.

Irene then asked about the ship.

It was a small, wooden, single masted, coastal type vessel with a single cargo hold behind the mast. The long pennant flying from the mast top was almost straight with the wind blowing from port bow to starboard stern. The name of the ship came up like a street name but indistinct. I thought it looked like Heraklion but when I asked for clarity, it read HERMES.

A vision of the bow came to me with a large almond shaped eye and a dark eyebrow painted upon it.

Irene asked, "Are you the Captain?"

"No," I replied, *"I am the Steersman."*

"What is your name?" she asked.

"Albert," I replied.

She asked how many were on the ship.

I replied, "Four on the left side of the bow and three on the right, plus myself and one other behind me, nine souls in total."

At this, a particular set of large waves came towards me from the left front of the bow breaking on the tops and curling down onto the bow.

Irene brought me back.

I sensed I was travelling backwards and upwards from the ship as it buried itself in the waves and did not come back up. I opened my eyes to find Irene standing in front of me with a member of the class on either side, ready to catch me. A tremendous sense of loss and causing the death of my crew came to me and I wept openly.

Irene asked if I had felt a pain in my chest, but I had not.

She told me this good, kindly man had had a heart attack at the wheel, and the ship had foundered in 1758 with the loss of all hands. I asked why the class members were around me. She replied that she had never seen anyone leaning so far over without falling down. They knew by my actions, I was actually aboard that ship in a storm!

Later, while discussing my grandfather's family history with my cousin, I found out that three of my ancestors, whilst living in Memel (now Klaipeda), Lithuania, had a working title of Steurmann (Steersmen). Had I relived the death of one of my ancestors?

After this incredible experience, I was slowly improving my communication with Spirit. I often found myself flying in an evening sky during meditation. Sometimes I was under water with the water a purple colour, basking in the warmth with shapes and faces slowly passing by. I was always last to come back at the end of meditation. I asked my guide many times for fifteen minutes only, but there is no time over there. I often heard or felt a splash close to me as Irene's voice gently called me back. Irene often said I do not know where you go during meditation even though, through her guide, she could usually see where we were.

Little by little, I felt that I was making progress. In meditation, I often seemed to be flying over the world, soaring like an eagle on the currents of air. Sometimes, as if I was the pilot of a spacecraft, yet an idle passenger, just watching the world slowly go by as I proceeded on a journey of discovery. Often I would fly across cityscapes, more often at dusk with twinkling lights and a darkening sky. It was soundless and eminently peaceful. The levels change and I fly high, catching glimpses of the world unfolding as I pass the breaks in the clouds below. At lower levels, I pass through the clouds like the mist on a morning. It would become clearer, then, close in again as the mist banks slowly swirled past me with the sensation of moving forward to who knew where. Below the clouds as the perspective changed and the land, villages and cities would pass below with the blurring of early evening. A softening of the vision and the colours fading as the sky slowly darkened to night.

Other times, I floated in a pale mauve sea of coral reefs and rocky outcrops, rising from the seabed. Myriad creatures floated by in strange procession. The slow waving of seaweed and the coral polyps like wispy fans responding to unseen currents. Strange creatures floated by: indefinable shapes of light and colour, some blinking like a beacon. It was very sensual as a feeling of warmth and peace slowly pervaded my senses. There was no sensation of breathing, just a sense of the moment; being locked in the now between breaths. The world around me slowly pulsating to an unseen, unfelt rhythm. A welcome respite from the mad, frantic world I had left behind. This was only a temporary respite, savoured and enjoyed, before the signal to return; both felt and heard. The call back to a world of the grim, harsh, reality of life.

In hindsight, as I write this from memory, my philosophy of the 24th August 2019 marked a turning point in my progress. My philosophy is set out below.

Philosophy

It is six months since I first stepped through the door of this church. I rarely kept a diary during my life nor do I keep a journal of my time spent here in this church. Being an only child, I learnt how to be alone without brothers or sisters.

During my formative teenage years and in a boys-only school, I did not really learn to socialise. I was quite happy on my own, in my own bubble, observing life around me like a back seat passenger on a mystery journey. I have spent a lot of time waiting for flights in many airports. My work colleague and close friend, who I usually worked with, was also a great observer of life around him. He showed me how to read people. Not by their clothes, language, or accent, but by their actions and expressions. During his earlier years in Special Forces, his life had often depended on it. He showed me how to be relaxed, yet aware of my surroundings. How to blend in with the locals. He could read situations and say or do the right thing with uncanny accuracy. He was an observer of life and a great thinker.

The last six months here has been like starting at your first school. Everything is new and strange, yet vaguely familiar. Lessons are varied and interesting, and new friendships made. The greatest mystery is Spirit. Everyone has a different idea. Everyone has a different reason he or she became involved with Spirit, or what created the urge to follow the spiritual path.

Like the wagon ruts of the pioneers crossing the plains of America, all of us tread a different path but the end destination is the same for all. The pioneers wanted a new beginning, a new home, in a new country. As spiritualists, we know where our home is but we do not know for certain what our path will be, and what direction it will take us before we reach Home. Spirit will guide us.

We must open our minds, our hearts and souls, to communicate with Spirit. We must trust them to guide us on our journey.

Each one of us can make a difference to another by human communication of what Spirit tells us. It is not for us to reason why, or to try to interpret what Spirit tells us. We are here to pass the message on. Our spirit is but a candlelight and it is up to us to turn that candle into a beacon in the darkness of this world. Its fuel is truth, love, and trust in Spirit, with faith in God.

In the last few weeks, I have felt the energy building. It feels like there is a new urgency, a new stimulus, for us to provide the evidence of eternal life. Spirit will show us the way if we open our hearts, open our minds, and above all trust Spirit. Work with Spirit for the good of all humanity. For the plants and animals of our world, for the oceans and the air that we breathe.

Educate the children. Nurture them with love, and promote a love of nature and the world around them. Show them they have a voice. Teach them to think out of the box that we call life. Show them the wonder of our world and of the heavens above. Tell them we are never alone. Teach them kindness and respect for others' points of view. Teach them balanced thought and calm debate. Teach them peace. Tell them they are unique, a very important person. Above all, teach them truth, love, and life everlasting.

The future of their world lies in our hands. We are only the guardians of this planet and we are responsible for the legacy we leave to our children and grandchildren. As King George VI said: "The wildlife of today is not ours to dispose of as we please. We have it in trust. We must account for it to those who come after."

We are responsible for the legacy we leave to future generations and primarily, to our Maker, God.

It was around this time when I had an unnerving experience after meditation. I had given off my thoughts during meditation to the group when I felt a cold presence coming close behind me. It came very close and I felt very uncomfortable. I immediately informed

Irene who looked up and said, "Yes, I can see it. Close your eyes and ask it to step back." I did this and a strong, menacing voice said, *"You are not powerful enough"*, at which point I blacked out. I knew nothing else until I heard in the distance Irene asking me to "come back, Bill… please come back, Bill… come back please… Bill".

I came round with Irene behind me and Paul working on my chest and back, whilst Jayne was holding my left hand, as her guide had told her to. I was very, very cold and unaware of what had taken place. The circle was in quiet panic except for Donna, who asked why they had not just let the Spirit talk. Apparently, I had started shouting in Norwegian, saying *"Ok, I will go, I will go. I am going"*.

This episode really unnerved me, as I could not understand it, or give an explanation, except that it took a while to remove the uninvited entity. I still felt a presence close by for the rest of the afternoon and taking the advice of one circle member, I invoked the Archangel Michael to protect me, as I had no previous experience of personal protection. After this episode, Irene told me not to meditate at home and I was to sit next to her at all future development group's meetings. I did. I was truly frightened and seriously thought of giving spiritualism up for good.

Two weeks later, 10th July 2019, I attended a physical trance night. The Physical Medium, Freeda Robson, was the guest speaker and demonstrator; this changed my mind. I had taken my video camera and asked if I could record the proceedings, to which she agreed. It was an amazing night of physical changes to her persona and pinpoint evidence of life after death to various people in the limited audience. I copied the video to DVD and gave her a copy later.

Another trance experience at our development group was after I had given the following philosophy on Saturday 7th September

2019. Once again, this was a modified text from Internet site sources.

Philosophy

Adam was created from the dust of the earth and became a living soul. Because of this, our senses, which are contained in our souls, are attuned to the earth. That is why our feelings shift and change according to what is happening around us. Everything that is of the earth is unsteady and changeable, which is why a person who allows their soul to control their life is never at rest. Through the soul – through our senses and feelings – we have contact with people. Someone who lives according to the soul is always in unrest with regard to what other people think and say about us. Through our spirit, we are in contact with God. However, when we are soulish we live according to our understanding, our senses, which are earthly. Our human bodies are used to serve this world. Our spirit is filled with that which is of this world, with the result that we have little or no contact with God.

Belief in God is meant to change this relationship so that we become spiritual and heavenly instead of soulish and earthly. The result is a life of faith instead of a life according to our human understanding. The intention is that our spirit becomes aware so that God can speak to us; we should live for Him and heavenly things and not for earthly things. Then we find rest for our souls. The heavenly things are eternal and unchangeable. When we live before God's face, we are free from people and the unrest that comes from living in this world.

We usually judge situations according to our feelings and human reasoning; but if we have begun to seek God, we open ourselves to divine Spirit. It knows the thoughts of the heart and pierces and divides between soul and spirit – between that which is earthly (human) and which we absorb in our souls, and that which is spiritual and heavenly, which we receive into our spirit. We have to believe Spirit and be obedient to it. The words "Overcome evil with good" goes right against our human feelings and our human reasoning; but if we believe in Spirit and are obedient to it, we enter into rest. Then we will experience that Spirit's wisdom is greater than our senses. There is also the words to forgive the person who sins against you. If you are soulish, you will preserve that which is earthly, and your honour and your heart will make plans as to what you should do with such a person and you will seek the opinions of family and friends. Rather let Spirit in to pierce and divide between what you are absorbing through your senses – especially through your feelings – and the wisdom that is from Spirit, which you absorb into your spirit. Live by faith and not according to your human reasoning; then you will enter into rest and spirit communication will be opened.

While I was reading this philosophy, Jayne, one of the more advanced members, experienced in trance, was getting quite agitated. No sooner had I finished; she said her guide "Isaac" wanted to speak. She came up on the rostrum and sat down. A few moments later and her guide was with her again.

Speaking in a different voice he said, *"I was listening and I am pleased with the energy the group are generating and Spirit is pleased with your progress. However, you are wrong as Spirit and the Soul are as one."*

He thanked us for allowing him to speak and as he did not want to interrupt our class for too long he would leave Jayne, which he did almost immediately.

When I returned to the rostrum, I asked Jayne if her guide was still with her. She replied "Yes". I asked if he could clarify his statement, *"Soul and Spirit are as the same"*.

The reply he gave was, *"The Spirit is the nucleus of the Soul"*. Jayne stated she did not understand this.

My simple understanding was that I likened this statement to the nucleus (of a molecule) being the centre of the soul with atoms circling around electrically bonded to the nucleus. I likened this to the Spirit surrounded by the memory of earthly lives and the whole constituted the soul. "Isaac" immediately replied *"Yes"*.

This incredible interruption by Spirit showed myself, and the group, that Spirit are constantly listening to our thoughts and discussions about Spirit. Spirit later told me that this was indeed true!

Sunday 4th August 2019, Freeda Robson again held a service for us, but this time as a Guest speaker and demonstrator. After the service we were chatting about her trance night and the DVD I had given her. As we discussed Spirit and how they work with us. I told her about my disconcerting experience at the development group some weeks previously and she invited me to a small closed group she attended every Thursday or Friday afternoon. The proviso being, that agreement from the other two members of the group must come first.

Seven weeks later, on 20th September 2019, armed with a tape recorder she had asked me to bring, I was blissfully unaware that my introduction to channelling Spirit was about to take place.

Chapter Three
– A New Experience

On the afternoon of Friday 20th September 2019, at a circle with Freeda and Irene Harthill, a Yoga teacher and crystal healer, I experienced my first blending or channelling of Spirit. In hindsight, I feel that the Spirit I channeled was in actuality my Doorkeeper / Guardian Angel, Albert, but this information was neither asked for, nor was it offered. We did digitally record this session.

After this first session, we both audio and video recorded all sessions with the consent of Spirit, as evidence for review and further discussion.

The circle was at Irene Harthill's house in Shotton Colliery, to give it the full name, west of Peterlee. The Colliery or coalmine closed many years ago but some of the terraced rows of colliery houses remain. Locals just call it Shotton as Old Shotton, the original village, is on the southwest edge of Peterlee. Irene lives on the western edge of Shotton around ten minutes' drive from my home. Irene is a widow in her late seventies. Of short stature, just over five foot, Irene is a very slim woman showing signs of her advancing years. A vegetarian, she has two small dogs for company. The older one is a poodle and the younger a Chihuahua. She had spent time in India studying the Buddhist religion and healing. Irene follows her own path to enlightenment and is well versed in the ways of the Yogi.

Her house is in a row of detached houses with a small garden to the front and a larger one to the rear. From the front door is a small hallway with stairs to the left and a corridor through to the kitchen. Immediately right is the living room door with a bay window to the right. To the left is the main area with a walk-through arch to the dining room where we sit around the six-seater dining table for our sessions. Immediately to the left of the arch is a connecting door to the kitchen. The whole area of the living and dining area is probably forty feet long by twelve-foot wide. My first feeling was of a home with something indefinable missing. I was warmly welcomed and made to feel at home, which was nice.

Irene acts as our observer, timekeeper, and helper with breathing and meditation. No music plays during our meditation. After the Lord's Prayer, and some slow, steady breathing from Freeda and myself, Freeda's guide came through to Freeda and spoke to us to explain how the session would progress. I then had a guide who worked through me, who had some difficulty in voicing his words. His voice was quite stilted and slow. After he had gone, another female spirit came through who was very quiet in voice but spoke confidently.

Although all had some difficulty in following a clear train of thought and paused, repeated some words or hesitated and sometimes stuttered, even laughing a little, the meaning was quite clear.

To aid the reader's understanding, I have written this in script style. Using myself identified as S1 and S2 for the two Spirits, Freeda herself as F, and her guide as FG.

Transcript

F   So they, they will know we are going to do this before we
     start so will you sit there, Bill? No, I want you on the other
     side so I can hear, right? OK, thank you. So first of all, which
     you know, we do the Lord's Prayer (said together). Right,
     so. I would like to say welcome to anybody that is going to
     come through today. You will have known that we were
     going to have a meeting today so Irene, we welcome you:
     Bill, we welcome you, and of course, myself, Freeda, are
     here to be a communicator for Spirit. I do not know what
     we are going to get. All you have to do, Bill, is to do what
     you normally do. You might find I do it differently. I like to
     alter my breathing. That is the way I go into it. Like sends
     me off to sleep, so, I am quite relaxed about it. Do you have
     the tape on, Bill?
Me   Yes.
F   Right ok. It is now twenty past two. Irene, could you watch
     the clock please. I do not know. There, do you want my
     watch because, ok. I like to put a time on it, you know. You
     can start and relax, Bill. Right you got the clock there: that
     is fine. What time is it now?
Irene. Well by this, it might be a couple of minutes fast.
F   Well take us to twenty to because you know, I have to pick
     the bairns up (Children). Well, ok. So what time are we
     starting? Twenty-five past is it now?
Irene Well, yes.
F   Ok that is fine so it is a good fifteen minutes that Spirit
     can come in and join us and I would like to say welcome
     friends, Spirit guides and helpers. Please come and join us
     today. Amen.
Pause Meditation starts and Freeda's guide comes through.
FG   Some sounds from guide then "come now... We want
     to... Can you tell me why you are here today? You come
     sometimes to join us in our mind. We want you to be more

accounted, for we are with many. Sometimes we want... help.

You will help us try. Today we have come with you as you have invited us. Invitations from Spirit is very good. We cannot work unless you invite us.

You know you are in control, not us. You are the controller. You work with mind, body and Spirit. You control what we want to tell you. Sometimes things do not go right with you, but that is fine because we want to do more work on you. See, you are not working well when things are not right with you, so we know that and we try to alter things for you to join us, and help us, but you are the controller. Remember that. You are the volume, sound, everything. You are my guide: not us. We use you as a guide for us. You can tell things that we are guiding you to. If I say to you. You go into that beautiful garden and see things. You do it. So we are using you as a guide, right? Remember that. Right?

When we are helping you, we are clearing stuff like your vision, your hearing, your heart, your sound. I know Freeda is telling me mentally that I am bossy. I cannot help this. I am a very bossy man. You think... Oh, I am getting very restless. My foot hurts. Oh, oh, ow, ow, aww. Anyway I am a very bossy man but I am here as the first introduction. I work as the person who starts the show, who helps you, and then, after that, we get other people coming in. That is my first part I have to tell you, right. Freeda is trying to tell me, I do not understand it; but I know you will, right? Ok? Lovely energy. I like the energies today. Bill, why cannot you say things? You can hear: you can talk. You are seeing things and hearing things but you can do it. Just let your spirit guide come through and see what it wants to say. You are not saying it. You are holding back. Do not feel stupid, do not feel silly, just do it, right? Ok, I know I am bossy; I

know I am bossy but sometimes you need (bell heard?) a
prod in the back. Right, (Bell heard?) ok?

Me   Ok.

FG   *I am sitting back because I know there is a guide with Bill*
that wants to come through. Right!

Me   *I can feel, yes I can feel. I feel Spirit with me.*

FG   *Correct!*

Me   *A very warm feeling on me.*

F   *Good.*

Me   *Very warm. Now it is very close to me.*

F   *Keep your breathing going, Bill please. Take Spirit in more,*
into your energy field. Take Spirit in more. Breathe it in
and breathe it out. Control it. Control the flow. Your Spirit
guide is ready to talk.

S1   *Bill; does; has; not; found; no. (Bell heard) Bill does not.*

F   *Come on, get it out. Get it out.*

S1   *Under, understand his purpose. What, what, he thinks*
we, we should tell him, what, what, we want him to do.
But; but, but, we can only gi, gi, gi, give him gu, gu, guide,
guidance. He must, decide, himself what he senses; feels;
senses; what. I; find this; di, di, difficult to explain. Ahh.
He, ah, is, ah, unsure which path he should take.

F   *Keep your breathing going, Bill. Keep it going, you are doing*
well?

S1   *We, we cannot; we cannot make his choice for him.*

F   *Keep it going. It is fading, keep it going.*

S1   *We, hmm, must, hmm, talk again.*

F   *Correct! (Pause). I think he wants to go.*

S1   *Yes.*

F   *Thank you for coming. Thank you for coming. You are very*
welcome.

S1   *It's.*

F   *Bill would like to say thank you.*

S1   *It has been difficult.*

F	*Yes, we understand. We understand.*
S1	*This is the first; first time.*
F	*Yes. We understand.*
S1	*But it must, surely, get easier.*
F	*Certainly will. Certainly will.*
S1	*Must we try?*
F	*We will try.*
S1	*Without, without, without stressing this man.*
F	*Yes, Thank you. Thank you for being so considerate.*
S1	*You're, you're very welcome, Freeda.*
F	*Thank you. Thank you. Until we meet again, till we meet again.*
S1	*Good afternoon to you all.*
F	*You have done very well, thank you. Thank you very much and we will let Bill go back into his resting position now. Bill, you have a lady, who would like to come through as well, but I think it might be too much for you today right. Just rest, ok.*
Me	*(Happy sigh).*
F	*Just rest, just take your time. We are going to ask you to come back, when it is right, not just yet.*
S2	*(A different much quieter and softer voice). I am a very strong lady.*
F	*Right. Welcome friend. Welcome friend. Can you hear me? Welcome Friend.*
S2	*I can hear you.*
F	*Right, thank you. I will not shout. Sorry, I will not shout.*
S2	*It is ok.*
F	*Right. Good.*
S2	*I can hear you quite clearly.*
F	*Thank you.*
S2	*You want to ask me questions.*
F	*Yes please, yes please, thank you.*
S2	*Go ahead.*

F	*Right. How old are you?*
S2	*Very old.*
F	*Very old. A very old lady.*
S2	*In earth years.*
F	*Yes. Have you come to help Bill?*
S2	*(Musing noises) I cannot yet make my mind up.*
F	*Right.*
S2	*Does he need me?*
F	*Yes, he does need you. He needs as much help as he can. In what, in what way can this lady, which is you, be helpful to Bill? I feel you are a lady with a lot of stored knowledge. Have you come to help him a lot more? Did you used to do this kind of thing?*
S2	*(Sigh and laugh). 423 years ago.*
F	*Right.*
S2	*I was burned as a witch.*
F	*Laughs. Same as me. Ditto.*
S2/F	*(both laugh)*
F	*It is not nice, is it?*
S2	*It was rather warm (laugh).*
F	*(laugh) I did not like the smell of my hair burning. It is not nice.*
S2	*I was taken away before the pain started.*
F	*Good. Good. Good. You are a very knowledgeable lady. Right? It is nice that you have come through.*
S2	*It is increasingly difficult, for me to come down, to this level.*
F	*Yes, but good, good. I would like to say, thank you for coming. I am very much interested in the history of witchcraft, in the fact that, many people were I would say, burned wrongly. All you had was the knowledge...*
S2	*Thousands.*
F	*The knowledge you know.*
S2	*Thousands, thousands.*
F	*Dear me. It must have been terrible.*

S2	*It is superstition.*
F	*Superstition, Ridiculous. Ridiculous.*
S2	*Made by man.*
F	*Yes, definitely.*
S2	*In various theologies.*
F	*Yes, yes, I am so sorry that you had to go through that.*
S2	*All books, all books.*
F	*Oh dear.*
S2	*On religion: are tainted by man's hand.*
F	*Yes. You sound a very relaxed lady, a very knowledgeable lady, and very understanding.*
S2	*I am in the process of joining as a pure spirit.*
F	*Brilliant, Brilliant. That is a gorgeous.*
S2	*So I feel like a man and a woman.*
F	*You are so, beautiful.*
S2	*I am that I am. There is terrible times to come.*
F	*There is terrible times to come. I understand that.*
S2	*Man made.*
F	*Man made I can understand that as well.*
S2	*In which we cannot interfere.*
F	*No. Sad. It is sad.*
S2	*But man can, if he finds the will.*
F	*Yes, to change it.*
S2	*To prevent it.*
F	*Yes, to change it, yes. What do you think about all this, I would say chemicals that people are using to alter the brain? You know, I know that in witchcraft they use a lot of good herbs but some of these people are becoming really evil because of the chemicals that they are putting into their body, you know, it's awful, isn't it?*
S2	*Hold my hand, Freeda. Now, remember this.*
F	*Thank you.*
S2	*It is man's choice.*
F	*Thank you.*

S2	*It is man's choice what he does with his body.*
F	*Thank you very much for that advice. It is good advice.*
S2	*It is man's choice.*
F	*Yes, thank you.*
S2	*If they want to taint themselves with whatever.*
F	*Yes.*
S2	*They desire in their base, then, it must be so.*
F	*Thank you. Thank you for giving me this information.*
S2	*But we must try, and tell them, and show them.*
F	*Yes.*
S2	*There is a better way.*
F	*Yes.*
S2	*And that better way is through Spirit.*
F	*Yes.*
S2	*This is what we, and you, must do.*
F	*Thank you. I try. I try.*
S2	*You try very well, Freeda.*
F	*Thank you.*
S2	*But there is greater.*
F	*Thank you.*
S2	*Things to come.*
F	*Thank you.*
S2	*In this life, as well as the next.*
F	*Thank you.*
S2	*But you will be given time, to complete, your work.*
F	*Thank you. I need that.*
S2	*On the earth plane.*
F	*That is what I need to do, complete my.*
S2	*You should not worry, child.*
F	*Right thank you.*
S2	*Do not worry.*
F	*Right.*
S2	*There will be enough time, and more.*
F	*Thank you.*

S2	*But you must follow your guides.*
F	*I do.*
S2	*And they will tell you when.*
F	*Thank you.*
S2	*And how.*
F	*Right.*
S2	*You must, nay, not must. You will be told, child.*
F	*Right, thank you.*
S2	*You will be told. Believe.*
F	*Thank you, oh I do, I do.*
S2	*Believe you will be told, and it will be so.*
F	*Thank you. I really do believe.*
S2	*Right, child. (Hand released.)*
F	*Thank you, thank you. Thank you. Right, Irene has just indicated that it is time for us to come back, right. Right, I am just going to stand up and tell you, Bill, what we are going to do with you. Just keep breathing as you have done right? Just take your time, Bill. Take your time. Take as much time as you need. If you want to come back quickly, that is fine with us, but I would like to say thank you so much for all the wonderful people that have come today and used Bill as an excellent vessel. It is all on tape. Just take your time, Bill. Take your time. When you are ready, could all the people that are standing; there are loads of people, you know, Bill, that want to come through you but I am sorry that today we are going to have to relax. Bill is just new at this and he wants to come back slowly into himself. I want Bill to step forward please and I want him to come back. Now. Come on, Bill, open your eyes up now, you are back into this time and space. Thank you. You are back, Bill. They have stepped back.*

At this point Irene grounded me, as I could not move my legs and my back was stuck to the chair! Freeda gave me a glass of water.

Irene asked me to visualise golden roots going deep into the earth, grounding the energy still present with me. It took a little while for my right leg to loosen up once again and I was then able to sit forward on the chair.

It took some time to return fully to reality, but I had no worries at all. I felt quite calm and relaxed. My eyes were watering but I did not feel at all tearful. There were many tears in my eyes. I felt as if I had just been for a long walk as my legs were a little shaky, but this first experience is something I will never forget.

Four hundred and twenty three years ago, as the peaceful Spirit had said, takes you back to around 1596. Looking through the records of people burned at the stake gave me a potential site of Scotland for trial and despatch. Many people accused of witchcraft were first strangled then put to the torch, at this time in Scottish history; precious few records exist of the people charged for many places in Scotland. Records do exist of more than two hundred people burned as witches during the reign of James VI of Scotland; but many remain nameless.

Perhaps the tears in my eyes were for these people, who were wrongly convicted; and put to death because of fear, superstition and ignorance. Man's inhumanity to man.

This wonderful, peaceful lady came through later in our meetings with the information that I was thinking about writing a book, and that it would be nice if I would mention her.

Her presence had manifested an icy coldness around my legs and slowly up my back as she came close to me.

As she had blended with me, she gave me such a warm, relaxed feeling of calmness when she channelled through that I felt a tremendous sense of peace, calmness, and love from her. I felt so privileged to have met this marvellous Spirit. She had instilled in me such a wonderful love and contentment that is impossible to describe. To experience this feeling is to know unconditional love and peace.

This first experience of channelling was a weird feeling of not being fully in control. The feelings I experienced was of my legs gradually lowering into a bath of iced water that you could not stop. The icy coldness remorselessly creeping up from my feet, yet allowing it to happen. A feeling of expectancy for something greater, yet no awareness of what that something would be. The words slowly filling my mind like a car engine spluttering, hesitantly trying to run for the very first time. My own voice box and mouth acting as the exhaust. Signs of life when the words came out; misfires of hesitation that chopped the rhythm of fluid speech. That first few minutes of awkwardness transitioned into the smooth steady flow of conversation as the energy changed to an inner warmth of peace and pure love. I found that the experience of pure love and absolute sadness is the same. You cry tears of joy and tears of sadness. This experience was my first spiritual communication but where would it lead me was the question.

Chapter Four
– Out of Control

The new day dawned, Saturday 21st September 2019, and the development circle to attend at Horden Spiritualist Centre. Yesterday had opened a new pathway to Spirit at Irene Harthill's house in Shotton.

The experience of blending or channelling encouraged me to find out more about this phenomenon on the internet. I was encouraged in my thoughts to write about a woman called Emma Hardinge Britten for my next philosophy. Due to time constraints and the growing size of our development group at this time, and after our meditation and feedback to the group, it was necessary to restrict our philosophies to around 500 words. After our philosophies, we returned to the rostrum a second time to try to link in with Spirit. The philosophy below is from 21st September 2019.

Philosophy

Emma Hardinge Britten was an English advocate for the early Spiritualist Movement. Her mediumistic gifts embraced automatic and inspirational writing, psychometry, healing, prophecy, and inspirational speaking. She was perhaps, best known for her inspirational addresses, which were very eloquent, inspiring, and informative: These given extempore. A committee from the audience generally chose the subject in the auditorium.

Most historians agree that, as a propagandist for Spiritualism, she was unequalled in her zeal, commitment, and enthusiasm. For years, she travelled all over the United States, Canada, England, Australia, and New Zealand, expounding the truths of Spiritualism and related areas of thought. She was one of the foremost missionaries of new age Spiritualism of the 19th Century. She was a friend of the Fox sisters, especially Leah, the eldest, and spent a number of years in America and Canada travelling and spreading the word, that life is everlasting. She also visited many other countries in her life's quest of promoting Spiritualistic awareness, proof of life after death and that life of the Spirit is everlasting. From 1878 to 1879, Emma and her husband worked as Spiritualist missionaries in Australia and New Zealand. After returning to New York, she wrote her greatest chronicle of the spiritualist age – Nineteenth Century Miracles (1884).Her definition of her religion and faith in Spiritualism described by the four principles she gave at a lecture in Dunedin, New Zealand.

- *Spiritualism proves by a set of obviously super mundane phenomena, that a world of invisible intelligence is communicating with us.*
- *It demonstrates by an immense array of test facts given all over the world that forbid the possibility of collusion or human*

contrivance that the communicating intelligences are identical with the souls of mortals who once lived on earth.

- *It shows by universal coincidence in the communications that every living soul is in judgement for the deeds done in the body, and reaps the fruits of its good or evil life on earth, in happiness or suffering thereafter.*
- *All the communicating spirits coincide in declaring that the life succeeding mortal dissolution is not a final state, but one, which manifests innumerable conditions of progress.*

Four propositions I emphatically protest are the all of spiritual facts we know, the all that are absolutely proved: or upon which all the immense varieties of persons that make up the ranks of Spiritualism can absolutely agree.

Emma Hardinge died in Manchester, England in 1899 aged 76. She is credited with defining the seven principles of Spiritualism which, with minor changes, are still in use today by the National Spiritualist Association of Churches in the United States and the Spiritualists' National Union in the United Kingdom.

Please note that 2023 will be the 200th Anniversary of her birth and the SNU's best and shortest description of her is "The Mother of Spiritualism".

After delivery of my philosophy and the input from the rest of the group, it was then my turn to step up to the rostrum to try to link with Spirit. My mind was a complete blank. I closed my eyes and concentrated – nothing. I looked around, nothing again. Then, suddenly, drawn to a picture hanging on the back wall. The picture was less than A4 size, to which I had never taken much notice. All I could see was a figure in a long bluish dress: and what appeared to be a crown on her head. I thought she looked like the Queen. A voice in my ear suddenly piped up with a laugh, *"No, I am not the Queen".* I looked again and the figure, appearing to me larger, seeming to be swaying to unheard music. I could vaguely make out a smile on the face. I had never had anything like this happen before. I asked Irene who the figure was. She replied "Emma Hardinge". I was lost for words. I then informed the group that I thought I had this woman with me, not realising that I had just spoken about her life in my philosophy just thirty minutes before!

I looked again and she started to sway once more but the smile was clearer and she nodded her head. A thought immediately came into my head which I realised was Emma communicating with me and I was compelled to repeat what she said.

"Her message was for the group."

Emma swayed again to indicate her pleasure that I had heard her correctly.

"The group is doing very well and I am very pleased with all your progress. I have been listening to you all this afternoon. Please do not let me interrupt you and keep up the good work you are doing."

When I looked up to her, it was almost like a little jig she performed with a broad smile on her face. I thanked her mentally and asked did she want to say anything else? There was no reply, just a little wave. I thanked her again for her lovely message and wished her goodbye. Her picture returned to normal in my vision, just a blue dress on a figure. I was so happy that I had linked with Spirit, even for just a minute or so. I was finally on my path, making progress.

The next evening was Sunday Service, to which I always looked forward. Once the first part of the service is over and the demonstration starts, I try to see the aura of the medium. I half close my eyes as if the sun was shining into them and try to look into the far distance over the right shoulder of the medium. Sometimes, but not always, I catch glimpses of a faint colour outline around the medium. This can be quite close or sometimes a couple of feet above them around the head and shoulders. I found it very interesting as the colours vary and often there is a different colour emanating from points on the head or shoulders. I need to breathe slowly and steadily and over the time of the demonstration I may see it a couple of times or more. Often I see slightly fuzzy faces or scenes on the coloured fabric behind the rostrum, or on the wall. This particular evening I was aware of the figure of a woman standing behind the mauve fabric towards the end of the evening. I realised it was Catherine as she became clearer in my vision. She appeared to be waiting, but never called. At the end of the demonstration, she just faded away. I thought she was not strong enough to make her presence felt and hoped and prayed she would come again.

Friday came round all too quickly and I had not had any inspiration for the Saturday philosophy. I thought I might be able to write something down after another Friday afternoon session with Irene and Freeda where I might find out something to use. At 12:30pm, I arrived and was then introduced to the third member of the group, who I will call Sandra. She is Reiki qualified and training as a medium with the SNU.

We had a chat about Spirit, with a cup of coffee before we started. The tape recorder and camera were duly set up, and we took our places. I was in the centre, with Sandra to my right and Freeda to my left. Irene as ever, facing us all as our witness and helper.

There was some preliminary joking about being on camera and a few laughs before we composed ourselves and Irene entered us into a Yoga style breathing pattern, ensuring we were grounded, before we entered the spirit realm, where we needed to be. After a few minutes, Freeda's guide came through and started the session.

He said, "We wanted to, our friends are coming; we are here again. Thank you for coming, thank you all. Thank you, welcome, welcome, welcome. Welcome, Sandra. You are my friend. You know you are my friend. You like me. You understand my game, my imagination, and you like magic. You like people, you like being here. You will join us today to be better than you think you are. You will join us today, right? (Right, thank you.) *Right, obviously, we understand, sometimes you want to be. When we want you to be here, you can. See, you understand.* (Yes, thank you.) *You want to be here, now. We want you to be here now, welcome, Sandra, welcome, welcome. Be observant. Understand what we are doing. You can use knowledge; you understand you have lots of knowledge. You will enjoy today with us.*

Welcome, Bill, Bill, (Yes) *welcome. Welcome.* (Yes, thank you.) *May I ask you, may I ask you more things today? May I ask you?* (Yes, you can.) *Oh, yes. My friends are here with us today, oh lots and lots and lots, of friends. Come forward to me. Be good; be good; be good. Come on, forward to me. Come on. Do not be shy. Come on. We like you. We like you."*

At this point, he then interrupts the flow by enquiring of one of my relatives who died of cancer. He gave a brief description of the relative's personality (Uncle Bob). He said he was there pushing me on and getting me to stand up before he then made a small joke about owing him a fiver, laughed along with us, then stated he had got it back.

He then turned to Sandra, enquiring about some Catholics in her family. He asked about rosary beads: and did she have them. Sandra replied no; but thought her Nanna (Grandmother) had them. He stated they were with him and she had been feeling Spirit more (agreed) and that sometimes she rocked, as he was (agreed). He stated the rosary beads would help her concentration and that she liked it (agreed).

He then said, *"I am going to go back as I have introduced a spirit for Bill today. I have introduced. I have given.* (I acknowledged I could feel Spirit close to me.) *It is coming through. I can feel the energy blending with yours, Bill. I can feel it, right?* (Yes) *I can feel it. I am going to sit back now. It is coming in very, very, very, strong. Like a big, strong river flowing into you."* (Yes, very strong, very powerful.) *"Yes, very strong, very, very strong."*

After a few steady breaths, I could feel the energy blending with me but it was very confusing. After another three or four breaths, a low, slow, gravelly voice, emanated through me with the words *"Very confusing".* The voice continued after a pause with a short laugh and asked, *"Who is going to ask the first question?"* A pause, then, *"Freeda, (Yes) you have a question."* (Yes, Yes.) *"Please ask."*

Why, why are there so many tormented souls, do you understand, so many tormented souls, tormented souls?

"Yes."

Difficult, difficult, difficult. Yes, tormented souls on their journey.

"You heard last night, and you sent Bill a link which was in his past. It was explained, in that link, about how souls can be left on the earth plane. Sometimes because they have a far greater love for those that are transitioning with them. You could say they missed the boat.

Yes, Yes, Correct.

We can only help at the time of transition. It is the timetable and we know when the transition is to take place. We try to inform, in communication with people like yourself, so we can arrange another time or another opportunity for them to come towards the light.

Yes, I understand, I understand.

"In this sphere, no not sphere, no, no, no, no, no, no, no, no. In this in between dimension." Here he paused for a short time then continued.

"In this dimension, they are in darkness. Their spirit requires that they must eventually come to the light. It may take hundreds, sometimes, thousands of earth years to make this transition. We cannot interfere. We can only help, when we are asked, to provide

the conditions of opening the doorway for them. They carry in this dimension their earthly traits and very often, they get very upset. Mad, that they missed the boat. It is sad to watch their antics, but so is life; and sometimes, we, we, we have a laugh. It is like watching a clown doing cartwheels and they have little bells on their pointy shoes and a pointy hat."

Bill, can you understand me through your spirit guide about the bells because you brought the bells up and it is amusing watching them with the bells on their shoes like little clowns but we have heard bells, yes, bells from Spirit, right? Bells ok? Bells bring us back to being centred. Correct, you understand. When the bell goes, we listen. Yes. At this point, he said:

"There is someone else, Freeda. There is someone else close."

Freeda said, "Yes, thank you. Bill, bring them through otherwise we will ring the bell and make you centred."

He replied, *"A very good day. There is lots of energy. They are very close now. Thank you, thank you all. Goodbye."*

At this point Freeda and Sandra thanked Spirit for coming through and passed on thanks on my behalf for the information passed to us all. They observed that he was leaving and the second Spirit was slowly blending with my energy over a series of quite deep but slow breaths. I was encouraged to keep going. I said it was very powerful in my own barely recognised voice. Freeda welcomed the "friend". Come through, come through, you are welcome. Welcome. Never mind pushing, never mind pushing, we cannot get two in at once.

A voice, sounding female, greeted Freeda with *"Hello Freeda"*. She replied, "One at a time, No. Right, Bill, we have separated them, two wanting to come through the door together. No." A slow, quiet female voice came through me again and said,

"There is two at my knees, Freeda. They are sitting waiting."

After a long pause the voice said,

"Sandra, you have a question?"

Sandra replied she did have, but it had gone. Freeda said to Sandra that she did have a question. The lady said,

"Do not be frightened child. I can only answer one at a time."

Sandra said, "Timelines, when timelines split does one set of energies stay on the earth plane and the other one go elsewhere?"

She replied, *"Timelines. The progress of Spirit once they have transitioned there is no time, no time in our world, but we have many levels that Spirit can reach. The higher we go the more difficult it is, to come back to the earth plane. We are not in the heavens. If you send us there to see, because you are our guides, we may, have permission to tell you, what, we see. It is difficult to explain why. No, no, no, no, no. If you liken our world no, our dimension, to an onion and the centre is the pure energy, of everything, we all, can reach that, central core. You have: you have a miniature likeness, inside. Inside? No. Well, yes. Inside your outer shell, which you call your body. I think yes, I think, I think, yes, that is acceptable, thank you."*

Sandra said, "Thank you."

The guide replied, *"No, I was not saying thank you to you, I was saying thank you to my guide, the likeness of God."*

At this point Irene asked if he thought it a good idea if we wrote our questions that perhaps had puzzled us over time, and that these could be easily answered one at a time. She gave a brief laugh and Irene asked if she would agree with that.

She said, *"Bill did this yesterday and he wrote three questions but before, before he came here, too early because Freeda gets so excited, we gave him the answers. Freeda, you have a question."*

At this point Freeda could not move at all and was only able to speak through a clamped jaw. She repeated, *"Freeda, you have a question."*

Irene moved to help Freeda and with her permission gently touch her to free Freeda's jaw, to settle her down, enable her to speak and reduce the energy that had created the situation. Using some gentle movements Irene was able to "ground" Freeda and after a short while, and some pain, she was able to speak and thank Irene, as she could not come out of it herself. Irene then grounded Freeda's feet and legs as Freeda explained that she was stuck and she could not move.

During this time the guide was quietly repeating, *"Not yet, no, not yet."*

Freeda had become concerned and a little agitated at the length of time it was taking to recover her movement, especially in her legs. After a while, she could gradually move her toes and then her limbs once again, at which point Sandra intervened and asked if she should ask the guide and spirit to move back, to which both Irene and Freeda agreed. The lady guide was quietly repeating every few seconds, *"Not yet, no, not yet; there is someone else, there is someone else".*

Sandra continued to request Spirit to move back, which released Freeda completely, at which point the lady asked, *"Why are you frightened? Why are you frightened, child? No, no, do not touch me, please do not touch me."*

Sandra replied, "No one is touching you. We are asking to send the energy back because we need to be grounded. We need to come back."

The lady then requested, *"We need an answer. Why are you frightened, why are you frightened?"*

Sandra replied that an experience as a teenager and something she had seen in a cabinet once. She knew that she was more scared of the living than of Spirit. At this point, Irene tried to intervene and assist Freeda to be fully mobile to finish the session but the guide was determined to have answers.

The guide replied, *"We do not harm you."* What Sandra had said about the living was, the lady stated, *"A profound truth. When you take your first steps is entirely up to you, child. Irene is telling me it is time to go. The energy we are attracting; you are attracting, is very, very powerful. So thank you all for listening. I am going, Irene but please, do not touch me. I am leaving now."*

Freeda asked if they could have Bill back and she replied, *"Yes, you can."*

Freeda thanked Spirit, guides and helpers for the evidence and that we all had our part to play.

During the after-session discussion with tea and biscuits, it was determined that the third guide was actually the gentle lady from the week before.

Her slow measured voice was so calming to me and gave me such peace and tranquility within. I felt truly privileged to be the vessel she could so easily use to give us information and encouragement during our session.

I was fully aware of the words forming and at times, when Spirit struggled a little to get words out, I asked if I could speak them. The help politely refused, they made me aware of their appreciation of my help by being very careful that I had a lung full of air each time they spoke to make it easier for them to converse, without any stress on myself.

A truly uplifting session and the care and gentleness of the spirit voices was wonderful. The love they gave to me during the session was a magical experience. I am truly blessed and privileged to channel these higher energies through.

That evening as I tried to think of my philosophy for the next day's development circle my thoughts were a complete blank. Searching sites on the internet did not attract me to anything I was reading. I sat back and closed my eyes, mentally asking for some inspiration.

After some few minutes, a thought suddenly entered my head. Some say the first thought is Spirit and the second is the human ego taking over and skewing the message. The first thought was:

"Just wing it. It is time to use us (Spirit) to give you the words. You do not need to write it down anymore."

I was still unsure and thinking about it actually filled my mind with doubt. Was I ready for this and would Spirit actually help me? I sat for some time turning this thought over in my mind. I went with the first thought and decided to try to "wing it" the following day with my philosophy.

Saturday afternoon arrived with me at the development class with a sense of doubt in my mind. Will Spirit help me? Meditation went smoothly but with little to give to the circle or to any of the people present. A bit of a blank really. I hung back from going to the rostrum, letting others go before me. When Margaret and Paul went to the rostrum, Paul had no notes. He explained that he had been asking Spirit for help all week and he had decided that today was the last day for Spirit to give him an answer to his prayers.

You must at this point understand that Paul has a very difficult job caring for people who are approaching the end of life. For such a caring person as Paul, as he said, sometimes you must take on the persona of a clown to hide your inner feeling of tremendous sadness, especially when young people are about to pass away. No one wants to see a sad nurse, as you are not only looking after the patient; you are also involved with the relatives of that patient under your care. You must be the rock that people turn to in their hour of need and it was eminently clear to me, and my guide, that the rock was about to crumble.

As I listened to Paul, I felt a wave of sadness wash over me. I became quite shaky with the feelings that, I felt was a cry from the heart and soul of this man. This incredible person, who for so long had given his life to people in the greatest need, was now drained and empty. He had nothing left to give. I suddenly realised that my guide was desperate to go to him, to force me to go to Paul.

Margaret, quietly sitting on the rostrum, noticed my plight. I indicated it was in my head and I was not sure of what was going on. I tried to suppress the feelings with thoughts of wait. Wait until it is my turn on the rostrum. I will go up next. As Paul continued, I became increasingly agitated, Margaret observing me closely, wondering what was happening and I was trying to indicate to Margaret that I had no real idea myself what was actually happening with me.

Paul finished his address to the class. He was starting one week's holiday. Various suggestions came from the class: meditation, you have a dog, take it for a walk in the countryside and chill out. Some suggestions raised a few laughs with my inner feelings rising and rising, ready to burst out and make the class realise this was not funny. They needed to realise the depth of feeling inside this man, the absolute turmoil he was experiencing, a challenge to Spirit to help him. I struggled to keep down feelings I had inside me. Please wait, I kept saying to myself, and I could see that Margaret was becoming increasing worried at my agitation and appearance. As I looked at Margaret a third time, I saw prison bars above her head. I felt I was in a prison, bursting to get out. The bars disappeared, replaced by a rabbit. Fear or flight? I took the easy option, quickly gathered up my folder and marched to the door, desperate to get away before the feelings I had, gained control. I got to the door and the talking stopped. Irene asked what was wrong. I said, "I am going and I will not be back." She said, "Sit here and we can talk about it," indicating the empty seat next to her. At this brief exchange, the dam of (my?) pent up emotion burst like a thunderclap. I was shaking; inside and out.

I can vaguely remember putting my folder down and approaching the corner of the rostrum. A blurred memory of words coming out of me thick and fast; banging my fist on the corner post of the rostrum. The next memory is being at home making a cup of coffee with tears streaming down my face, still shaking from this unremembered experience.

People sometimes mention a red mist coming down when they are angry: I would prefer, with this incident, the veil of forgetfulness descended and Spirit had taken over at a critical point for the benefit of the class, but most of all for Paul, who had asked for help. In many ways, it also demonstrated to me the power of Spirit and trance mediumship. How much I had to learn.

How can you possibly control energies that you cannot fully understand? You cannot comprehend how powerless you feel, unless you experience it for yourself. Spirit somehow had gotten me into my car, drove home, and even parked up correctly: all without mishap.

They had protected me. Thank you, Spirit for your help and guidance.

Over the next few days, I had meetings with Irene and finally played the CD of my first trance experience to her.

She told me that I had broken the Principle of Personal Responsibility by allowing what had happened to happen. Irene did not have the time to help me as an individual. I asked about when Medium's work, the rostrum and how do they bring Spirit through.

She told me that they only bring Spirits through that are there. I mentioned the appearance of Catherine (so clear to my vision, quietly waiting) into the conversation. The night she did not receive the call to step forward from the medium who was on the rostrum. There was no answer to this question. Irene then informed me that I needed to make a decision between returning to the class or continue going to Freeda Robson, as you cannot do both.

I said I would choose going with Freeda, as in my mind, I would get the answers I needed. I would still support the church by attending Sunday service.

With my thoughts still in turmoil, I wondered, is it time to give up? Should I keep going after these upsetting experiences and inner turmoil they were putting me through? Was I too weak? Was I actually mentally ill through the grief of Catherine passing? Was it part of the grieving process? All these thoughts were preying on my mind. Rather than beating myself up, I left all these questions to Spirit to answer in the next session with Freeda. I had finished with the class. It was time to move out and on, regardless of the outcome. I had tried my best but apparently, I had failed to make the grade. I was definitely at a crossroads in my life, very unsure of which way to go.

During my first few visits to church after this episode, I felt a distinct cooling towards me from most members of the circle. They did not mention anything about the episode and appeared a little embarrassed talking to me, eager to move away as quickly as possible. They must have thought I was deranged. I sensed the raising of barricades against me. I felt that I was not wanted. I felt like a criminal. I had broken the rules. I had lost their trust. Cast out, and abandoned.

I had let Irene down. The one who had welcomed me, mentored me, and advised me. Guiding my path to who knew where.

I had also let down my friends, the other members of the circle and especially Paul. A caring person I deeply admired for his dedication and compassion.

I was like the lost sheep. I desperately needed answers from Spirit. I needed guidance. I needed the love and light that they always said was there. Most of all, I needed the truth.

I now knew that only Spirit could provide it. If Spirit did not provide it then there was no point in continuing with Spiritualism.

I needed a good shepherd to bring me back to the fold. I was now in the same position as Paul had been a few days before, but at least he had the circle.

Chapter Five
– Questions and Answers
and "Wa-Nee-Tah"

The following Friday, 4th October 2019, I went to my third session with Freeda at Irene Harthill's house. I was looking for Spirit to answer the questions that had been on my mind all week. Would Spirit come through for me? What would they tell me? Little did I know that I was about to find out.

After a cup of coffee and a chat about various things, including Spirit, we sat in our usual seats around the dining room table. Later than normal, it was almost two-fifteen and Freeda must go by two forty-five to pick up her grandchildren from school. We had barely half an hour to get any answers to my questions!

We started with the Lord's Prayer and Freeda spoke about our time constraint informing any Spirits listening that we had around twenty-five minutes before we must close our session. After a short time, Freeda's guide (Guy) came through, a little slow at first then building up to his usual strength of voice and clarity of speech. After a little warm up of his link through Freeda, and establishing that we could hear him clearly, he started the proceedings with the following dialogue.

"Welcome, welcome, welcome. I want many things today. I want to be aware of you. You are like a, oh, like aware of you, like a, no, no, not healings, energy, around you. I am feeling much, ah, like, like milk." He laughed and continued.

"No, not like milk, like err, liquid, like liquid. I am feeling that now. Honestly, you are growing in strength every day. You sometimes, errm, behave way too, way too strong. Oohh, you behave like monster." At this point, he laughs again as if he found it quite funny. He continued, *"Monster, but, it is only you, Bill, only you. You like to be aware, aware, and you feel, your liquid, around you, and, you feel it strong. Sometimes you honestly, cannot cope with it, but we are tuning you, finer: less mmm, less, mmm, area, more quantity. More quantity for you. You be ok, oh, wait, wait."*

At this point, it appeared that another Spirit Guide had interrupted him, and a conversation between them in a different language took place. It then appeared that the new Spirit Guide took over the session and said very clearly and in a much more authoritative voice:

"I will talk today on a mountain. A mountain is high to climb. Sometimes we try. Sometimes we fall. Climbing is learning, learning, learning about the cracks, about the invasive trouble; ah, the falls, the strength, the gifts we have of knowledge. When we get to half way up the mountain, we want to go to the top of the mountain, but sometimes the top part of the mountain is harder, harder. Right? You, you feel like you are climbing a mountain but you are at least trying, at least trying to climb the mountain. You want to, test yourself. You want to try so I am talking today for you. No, you need; you, you will be beaten with a stick, right? If you do not listen, I will prompt you and help you, right? My goodness, my goodness, this man. Oh this man. Welcome, welcome, welcome. Also. We want to talk about diving into the depths of emotion,

emotion. When you dive into the depths of emotion, sometimes you cannot swim and drown. You drown yourself, right? Remember, you drown yourself, right. You drown yourself, but when you go in slowly, and like it, you enjoy it. You like to bathe in it. You like to feel it. It is lovely all around you. Like the mountain, it takes time, time. Right? So today, Bill, Spirit is here because they are; making sure you understand that once you dive into this water you like it, you like it and you want to feel; the energy: of pure love around you. I have a small gentleman who is knocking on the door at the other side. Oh dear me."

At this point, Freeda starts to slap her left leg quite firmly, simulating a knocking sound in three distinct periods of around a dozen or so slaps at a time.

Spirit then said:

"Listen. Listen. (Long pause.) I am going to sit back... and let you feel... I am aware... there is lots of energy around you. Please, if you would like to use this energy, please think... I am privileged. Privileged, to use this energy. Remember; you are privileged. I would like to ask Spirit to come and work with Bill a little bit. Now! Thank you."

Firstly, we must look at what these two Spirit guides had touched on talking about me. I had a number of questions I wanted answers to. It looked like they had given me some answers or at least some explanation and a little comfort as to what was happening to me.

I had behaved like a monster, far too strong. I had lots of energy around me getting stronger by the day that I could not cope with it. Well, I had to agree without really knowing exactly what I had actually said the Saturday before in the class. It was down to me and only me.

It seemed that Spirit had allowed me this energy, but it was too strong for me to cope with as a novice, and I was unable to control it, as I should have. I had fallen from the mountain climb:

but I had picked myself up and was again, trying hard to climb the mountain.

They were reducing the area and giving me more quantity, which seemed a little strange to me. He had also referred to my "invasive trouble" which I understood to be the unconscious state I was put in a few classes prior to the outburst. This qualified by it being part of the learning process of climbing the mountain. It appeared that I was half way up the mountain and fell, twice, without even being aware of climbing in the first place! I did not feel too happy about being beaten with a stick either, because at this point in the dialogue, I had felt a sharp blow just under my ribcage and it had hurt!

I also knew about emotion as I had often had tears when giving little messages out, especially when Spirit made me aware of their sadness. I really felt the emotion and could not stop the tears, even when I asked them to take the emotion away. Thinking about the loss of Catherine usually brought tears to my eyes and it was something I had little or no control over, but it was improving, very slightly. It was heavy, heavy going at times, and the thought often occurred to me, this pain would never end. It is so raw and uncontrollable. It sneaks up on you then smacks you in the face at the most inopportune and most embarrassing times.

The energy I feel around me at times is very, very, cold. It creeps up my legs, like standing in the sea and the water gently lapping around my ankles, gradually getting deeper. My feet turn to what feels like blocks of ice, but it is a gentle feeling, more like a thick mist than liquid. It has no weight, just a creeping, gently moving, slow swirl of abject coldness. The energy of Spirit.

In just a few weeks, I had learned from Spirit. We have bad times as well as good. They will guide you, but not lead you. They will tell you, but not force you. They will show you, but sometimes not clearly. They can hurt you if you do not listen. They will laugh at you, with you, and they do have a sense of humour, and of time. If you allow them, they will talk to you as long as the energy is there. They will take care of you. They will ensure that the energies they bring to you are not too strong to damage you. They will lock you rigidly to a chair to ensure you do not fall off and they keep your eyes firmly closed to ensure total concentration. This is all part of the trials and tribulations of working with Spirit. It is not easy. It is not a right and neither is it a gift. We all have the tiny spark of Spirit within us.

People become aware of Spirit at different times in their lives, some as a child when their minds are new and open to everything.

To others, it comes later in life when circumstances change, usually through one of life's low points when nothing you do goes right. You start questioning the meaning of life. What is life? Why are we here? What is our purpose? Is there something else? Why was I not born rich? Why do I live where I do?

Spirit can answer all your questions except perhaps what lies in the future. They will hint at possibilities in the future but the truth is that your decisions will probably affect the outcome. We have free will and actions. Even thoughts have consequences. Your actions will reflect on your future. It is entirely up to you.

It is your choice, but in this short time of a few months, I have become aware of Spirit, I do believe we have a purpose in life. We take this life experience with us as memory into the next world; dimension, sphere, heaven; or whichever word you use to refer to the place your energy is after your body dies. The inescapable fact is that energy cannot be created or destroyed. It is a scientific fact, proven beyond doubt. Energy can only be transformed. It can be concentrated or expanded. It can have higher or lower vibration. It can be stationary or moving. Above all, it can be discovered within you but it is your choice how you use your energy. It is always your choice.

I was now aware of the energy available to work with. It was now up to me. It was my choice. I decided yes, I did want to work with this energy and yes, I felt privileged, very privileged. I hoped that I might receive further guidance and information or visions that would mean something. Anything that would make matters clearer in my own mind or allowed some respite or help with controlling my emotions.

I now felt the energy getting stronger, slowly building closer and closer to me. I felt slowly surrounded in a cocoon of coldness, although feeling warm on the inside. The energy felt different this time.

Rather than blending within me, this energy wanted me to describe what I was feeling, sensing, and seeing. I felt urged by an unknown force that I must describe what I saw for the benefit of Freeda, Irene, and our recordings. They would know what I was experiencing and Freeda would be able to ask questions, or sense the presence of other energies who may join in listening.

I could feel the energy swirling around like the bottom of a waterfall. In my mind, I could see the boiling, swirling water at the bottom of this waterfall.

I was standing at the edge of the pool looking at the waterfall. I could see, no, I had the impression of indistinct faces in the waterfall. As the water cascaded down into the pool, so did the faces, many different faces slowly descended, slower than the water itself. The waterfall was not large, perhaps twenty to thirty feet high with a good flow. As the faces became clearer, some of the faces looked like Indian Braves. I felt the pool was getting deeper, although I had no impression of actually walking into the pool. I was standing on the bottom with the water over my shoulders. There were pine trees on either side of the waterfall and my surroundings. At the back edges of the pool, there were dead trees that appeared to have fallen from either side of the waterfall in small landslips. On the sides of the pool there appeared to be an area devoid of trees where the pool had once been larger. These areas partially covered in ground plants and small bushes. The left side gave me the impression of wild berry bushes although too far away to see clearly.

During the next few minutes, Freeda sensed what I was seeing and shared my impressions. She also sensed that other energies were coming close to us and observing what was happening to me. Each time she felt these energies, she welcomed them as friends.

I asked myself should I swim or just stay here with this view. It was a wide pool. I could feel the water gently passing over my body. It was cold but I felt used to the cold. I can, I am not cold inside. Nature is a marvellous thing. There is blue sky and fluffy white clouds and the silence. There are no birds singing, only the sound of the waterfall. I felt quite safe standing there. I washed my hair. I was under the water, rinsed my hair and shook it. I come up for a breath. It was good to be alive. We have a lot to be thankful for. There was someone on the other; there was someone on the other side of the bank.

Freeda asked if it was "someone waiting for you, Bill".

I replied, "They have waved. I am not sure which child, this, of mine? It was too far to see clearly. Two hands waved. About fourteen, fourteen years, many moons. I must swim across the pool."

There is no mention or recollection of me actually swimming.

The energy made me aware that it was his oldest daughter on the other side. Therefore, I must have swam across the pool to actually recognise that it was the daughter of the Spirit energy that I was so privileged to use. She greeted me, she hugged me, but I was not made aware of why she had come this far. She did not usually go there when I was there on my own. The pool was turning purple.

Freeda remarked that she could see this in her mind.

I continued.

"The first shadows of evening, no, not yet. I am very fond of my daughter. It was time to go back. My clothes were wet and the

summer was over. We must prepare for the winter. She had not brought my buffalo hide for me. It would be heavy for her, too heavy for her to come this far but I am, I am glad of the company."

At a pause in the monologue, Freeda asked if this energy had a name. Could he give us his name please? Could he give her an idea of his name?

He said, *"Wah-nee-tah."* Freeda repeated this but said it like a single name, Wanita. He repeated again, *Wah-nee-tah giving emphasis to the gaps in his name. He then said he was Pawnee, Pawnee, affirming to Freeda once again the correct pronunciation.* Freeda asked if he had been to our group before to which he replied *"No".* Freeda said, welcome friend, welcome friend to which he replied, *"Thank you, I think, I think you come here often".* Yes, Freeda replied, we will come each week.

He continued.

"But this is the first time I have seen you. We are friends but I do not know why. I know you. I know of you. I feel comfortable. Comfortable? Happy, no, no, no. It is like meeting family friends who I have not seen in many, many moons. Twenty, twenty-seven, twenty-eight moons ago, my son left, with his family and his trav, travi, travi, travios (Travois) to follow, no, to find, the buffalo, down on the plains."

At this pause, Freeda asked him if it was nice for him to come to us today.

He replied, *"Yes, because you have, told me, my family is returning."*

Freeda said that she felt that there were a lot of his family, your tribe; your relations would have been there as well. It would have been good for him to use Bill to come through today. I would like to say thank you. He replied:

"When they went away, perhaps forty, perhaps fifty, we came to the mountains because of the soldiers. They chase us, they kill our

buffalo, and it is very hard in the mountains in the wintertime. There is not enough game and it is not very often that our bellies are full. I am getting too old for this."

Irene indicated to Freeda that our time was up and Freeda asked him to step back please and thanked him very much for coming.

We have your name, we have a bit of understanding of you and that she thought he must have been a very learned man. "Could we have Bill step forward please? Could you step back and go through the doorway you came in from and we will bring Bill back now please. Thank you so much, thank you. Please take your time. Please take your time. Please just take your time. Until we meet again, thank you for coming." He replied:

"I am back in my tent, my teepee now, beside the fire."

Freeda continued and told him to rest peacefully and asked that I return. She was trying to bring me back from that place this energy had taken me. She said for me to take my time but please return. It was taking some time for me to return to reality. Freeda thanked all the Spirits that had come today and asked that they return to a place suitable for them but taking their time as there was no rush. We were going to open the little hatch in our ceiling and allow them to go back to where was most suitable for them as they knew where they had come from. She thanked them once again for coming today and joining us, but time goes so quickly when you are working with Spirit, but thank you. "We are going to close the hatch now and bring Bill back in so thank you, until we meet again."

He replied, *"Thank you, goodbye friends."*

Freeda replied, "Thank you. Just take your time, Bill, take your time."

His last words were:

"Let me, come back please. It is so cold in the winter."

I was vaguely aware in my mind of the freezing cold but my body was actually showing it. I was trying to come back but I was experiencing a mind numbing cold that I felt was dragging me back to that time and place. I tried to open my eyes but failed; even though my eyebrows had lifted to the maximum, the eyelids remained firmly closed. Both Freeda and Irene had felt the power of the energy and some of the coldness around me. With gentle coaxing from both, I slowly returned to myself, while stating it was freezing in the winter and asked them to put another log on the fire! My face had turned blotchy as if I was freezing cold and I had my arms wrapped around my body.

Irene placed her hands on my shoulders to warm me up a little. I had felt that there was a stream on the left side of my vision and that I was a young man. As I crossed to the other side of the pool, I had felt like an old man and that Wah-nee-tah was suffering with his chest from the numbing cold of the winter. He had shown me his spiritual place, where he communicated with the ancestors of his tribe in peace and solitude. I had felt that stillness. The peace and solitude he had shown me, given to me with his energy was with me. I was truly privileged and humbled to use the energy he had so graciously given to me.

The strange thing about these sessions is that sometimes I have a clear memory of what was being said. I am very aware as the words form in my mind but helpless to prevent myself from saying them. When my voice box stumbles on certain words, I mentally ask them to allow me to pronounce the word, as I know I can. Spirit always politely refuses this solution and they continue in their own unique way. Other times I have a vague or almost total lack of memory of the events unfolding and it is not until I have listened or watched the session a few times that I begin to understand what they are telling me.

I am extremely grateful to Spirit for allowing us to record and video our sessions as it is easy to miss or forget what has been given, more especially in working as a channel or physical medium. I would suggest that while "channelling", I usually work in a light to medium trance state most times, as it normally takes me quite a few minutes to "come back" to the present time and place.

In addition, quite often, it appears that when I am coming back, "The Veil of Forgetfulness" draws over my mind: and my memory of the proceedings are missing, or very indistinct. Only odd words or short phrases remembered.

It is clear from the video evidence that on opening my eyes, I am looking around with a vagueness on my face. My eyes are darting around as if the present is unfamiliar to me.

I appear to require further time to reacquaint myself with my surroundings and take little notice of Freeda and Irene talking to me. Although the body appears fine, the mind appears as if the consciousness is still a little behind. I do look a bit lost for a short time before I become fully aware of my surroundings. I am then back in my time and space and back to normal. Whatever that is!

Chapter Six
– The Watchers and the Plane of Understanding

Friday, 11th October 2019 was session four at Irene Harthill's house in Shotton. Sandra was once again with us. Her work pattern was changing and after this time, it would not be possible for her to be with us for a while. This news did not dampen our spirits and we had a few laughs and a chorus of "Somewhere over the rainbow" from Freeda which helped to lift the atmosphere. We settled ourselves down and started in our usual way of the Lord's Prayer and asking Spirit to come through and use us as guides and channels for answers to our questions. Freeda quickly linked in with her guide who took little time to blend with Freeda. After settling in his opening words to us all were:

"Yes, come now, yes, and join us. You are particularly understanding. Thank you for making promise of need and hope and kindness. You are good people. We want to bring our friends through today. You understand we are ready. You observe us because we are becoming stronger. Each week we are ready. We are preparing you for more evidence each week. You will see our eyes change; you will see our no, no, sound change. Me, I am a hard working guide if you want to say Guy. I am here to help organise all you: you who are here.

We have about fifteen people here today but they are observing you from our side. Understand you are not the only ones who are watching us. Do you know there maybe, mmm, nearly ten thousand people who are watching you tonight like on a big screen so we will try to do our best for you.

Colours, mostly colours will come to you when we want you to find us. Tunnel us. Tunnel us. You understand it like looking; view, view, view us. Wanting to share with us. Well we are ready. We have been working a long, long time for you to come. Today we will inspect you and hopefully, we will find out what you can do and what…This is a test. Right? You are being tested today so do not worry we are not here today because we want to understand you; it is because we want to help you. Please be open. Give what we want you to tell us. Open your mind, concentrate on thinking, well, I will give. That is all we want from you. Just giving and giving and giving and giving. Remember I am here as an organiser to help you. I will step back for a minute. Right, thank you."

After a long pause in the proceedings, Sandra said that she would give the little bit she had. Guy replied, *"Thank you."* Sandra said she had seen almost like a scarab beetle. A red insect of some sort. Guy said, *"Thank you."*

I said I could see purple with white snowflakes, floating snowflakes. Faces. It was getting whiter, the colours changing. Orange. Oranges, purples, yellows, purples again with white, like clouds. Like the mist rising off the marshes in the morning when the summer sun is wanting to come up. The sky takes on a purple. It changes all the time.

Sandra said she also saw a motorbike. Like a trail bike. Which she thought was symbolic of something.

I saw green. It was going pale green, yes, pale green then a yellowy type of green with some indistinct faces appearing then disappearing. Energy, a lion.

Sandra said she had been getting a lion for a few days.

I saw snowflakes again. Yes, like a snowflake.

Sandra said there was importance in the lion.

Guy said to me, *"Bill, can you make out what you see in the distance?"* I replied, a doorway. Guy said, *"Thank you. Would you like to go through that doorway?"*

I replied, "Yes, I would, thank you."

Guy replied, *"Thank you. Right, you walk with me, just you walk with me; I will help you go through the door. Right, walk with me to this door, Bill. Are you ok?"* I replied yes, I am thank you. He said. *"Right, come, come."*

The light was getting brighter, white, white, yellowy white. *"Good, right, yes."* Like white clouds on a sunlit day (*"Lovely."*) very white, very, very strong. Intense.

Guy said, *"This door is opening the visions for you, it is opening up your mind. You are on an understanding plane. Understanding plane now. Ok?"*

"Yes," I replied. Sandra said she saw a white triangle flag as well.

Guy said, *"Right, Sandra. This means that it is time to start, start. Very good, very good. It means we are ready to start the journey, to begin. Thank you for that white flag. Thank you. You are very kind but Sandra, you organise your mind every day with different things that do not matter. You know you should generally just wait. Do not make things happen. Wait and it will happen for you. The beetle you saw is really something to do with you. You will find that this beetle might be a one that buries under the ground and I do not understand that bit, but you can find it out. Right, ok, you have a rabbit with you, a rabbit going down the hole, hiding; hiding. You know that is you when the bright lights come; you run, right; but remember the bright lights are good for you, right? Step forward into the light, Ok, and climb those steps one by one by one by one, and then you will do it, you will get there. Thank you for listening to me today. Sometimes I want to put a big chest on you and make you smile, open your heart up and smile and say thank you, thank you. I am getting 100% proof of spirit. You will start to understand, you will start to talk. You will find it fascinating because you are remaining a good channel for us, thank you."*

I described what I was seeing in my mind. I could see the shadow of a man, purple, very much purple. Changing to yellow purple, like a mist. Did I see myself there? I am looking at myself. *"Good."* I saw my face. *"Thank you."* It is gone again and the clouds are gold, white.

Guy said, *"I feel very emotional, Bill: I feel you have been, maybe, feeling in this session very emotional, right? Could you please speak up please?"*

Yes, I can, I replied. *"Thank you, thank you,"* Guy replied. I had two tears coming from my right eye but I did not know why. Guy said, *"Thank you."* I was feeling very peaceful and had not realised that my voice was getting quieter and quieter as I was describing what I was seeing in my mind. On this understanding plane, I was aware of a "ground" of limitless area with the "sky" around me gradually changing in colour, slowly shifting through the rainbow colours. Small mist-like clouds would appear and disappear of different colours, mainly white or yellow white and some were a shade of purple from a pale mauve to a dark, rich, regal purple, white… and I was aware of two small tears from my right eye.

Guy continued, *"Because there is someone who is trying to bring. Right, is your mother in spirit, Bill? (Yes.) Yes, she. Understand that a tear came from her eye when she passed please. (Yes.) Right, she is bringing her energy into you and giving you a big, motherly hug, right?"* I could feel the energy of my mother envelop me with a wonderful feeling of a small child once again and feeling that warm, loving hug that only a devoted mother can give. A sense of unconditional love and attachment to this energy that was my mother washed over me for a few seconds and it was wonderful.

I felt like a small child once again, sitting on her knee, loved and protected in my mother's arms.

Guy continued: "*We are seeing lots of good things around you. Amazing future, good times, intelligent, and we wanted you to come. Please understand I am observing people who are coming around you. That is why I said you were very tearful so you can understand you are getting things, feeling things, seeing things, hearing things. This is good. This is good, right.*"

At this point, I was trembling. My knees were trembling, shaking with the energy, I was feeling coursing through my body and I said so aloud.

He continued, "*Let it happen, let it happen. Take your time. I am seeing lots of people coming towards you, perhaps too quickly. Too quickly. They are coming in and out too quickly.*"

I could see faces that changed before I had any sense of who these faces were. They were appearing then disappearing and changing too quickly for me to determine whether I knew the faces or not. I was getting confused.

Guy, reading my mind said, "*Yes, too quickly, too quickly.*"

I saw a face, a golden face then it was indistinct but I was aware of the golden head and shoulders of someone being there.

Guy asked the person, "*Please step forward, please step forward for Bill. Thank you, we are inviting you. Invitations for you to come forward. My goodness, oh dear.*"

I could see a yellow something. It was difficult to describe. (*Guy said, "thank you".*) It was like a pulsating orb. "*Lovely,*" *Guy said.* Golden yellow. "*Angelic, Angelic,*" *he remarked.* "*Angelic. The seed of Angelic information.*" It is wonderful I said.

"*You feel the sun off it and the heat of it, correct?*" I do, I replied.

Guy said, "*Feel it, Keep it, hold it. Let it vibrate within your soul.*"

It was making me shake. My stomach was fluttering like a million butterflies inside me, all taking to the wing at the same time and shaking me to the core of my being. A truly strange yet wonderful, wonderful feeling.

Guy said, *"It is ok. It is because there is so much energy, Bill. There is so much, energy."*

I could see the doorway. I said I was standing at the doorway.

Guy said, *"You will go through that doorway."*

It looked like a tunnel cut through the rock. It was lit but without light. There was no light bulbs but it was really, really, bright. Bright yellow and light green; now grey, then purple. It was like being in the clouds.

Guy remarked, *"It is like Heaven."*

It felt so peaceful. The light was changing all the time. It started to get bright, really, bright. Then, it started to get dark but there was a light in the darkness, an energy.

Guy commented, *"The energy is pulsating."*

Yes, I was aware of the energy pulsating. It was green, yellow green. It was like being under water, watching the seaweed and the plant life on the rocks gently waving.

Guy said, *"Beautiful. Can you see anybody around you?"*

I could see, yes, I could see a face.

"Thank you.".

I do not recognise the face. A beard, a long beard, big beard. The images go too quickly. *"Yes."* Purple, purple again with large eyes.

"Right."

Then it changed, it was like a wig then it changed. Someone from a long time back.

"Right. Time when they wear wigs."

Perhaps 1600s.

"Sixteen hundreds. Right, ok."

A bit like, no, further back.

"Right." Ancient Greece.

"Right."

The beards of ancient Greece.

"Right, the scholars."

The scholars, yes.

"Yes, we are getting somewhere now."

Purple colours again.

Freeda said, "I am sharing this, Bill. This is me; not my guide. I am sharing this. There are some scrolls."

I could see the tunnel again. I am going backwards. Why am I going backwards? Purple then going yellow again.

Freeda said, "Wonderful. It seems like when you are travelling backwards you are doing the purple and the yellow, the purple then the yellow."

"Yes," I said. "It does, it does. I can see this myself. A bright purple and then it fades and the yellow comes in really bright."

Freeda had described exactly what I was seeing. We were sharing this vision, this experience, together. It was if we were rolling, the colours getting brighter. It was like the, like the space shuttle travelling, over the top of the world. The skies change as the sun comes round. It then goes purple and then dark again.

Then it comes light again, the first rays of the sun in the morning, pre-dawn.

Freeda remarked, "It is funny how you are going beyond time, the beginning of time."

I said, "Yes, it is just nice being here. It was like a starburst. High cloud on a summer's day but the sky was a light green."

Freeda remarked, "Interesting, very interesting, very, very interesting."

I was seeing lots of bright light then I could see stars, pinpoints of light in the distance.

Freeda asked if I was happy being there.

I could see a horizon. The sky was orange with clouds, big clouds.

Freeda asked if there was only me there.

I could sense that Freeda was standing beside me. I thought I saw an angel.

We were looking out from a cave to the world beyond.

Freeda said, "The beginning of Time."

There was nothing there. It was not black, but it was dark. The colour started changing. There was something in the distance, floating in the sky. With the colour changing, it was like looking up from the bottom of a well. There were no bricks; it was just natural stone. I seemed to float to the top of the well with just an awareness of surroundings that were purple but not a rich purple.

Freeda said, "Bill, Spirit is there to help you come out of that well. Spirit is all around you."

I was out. I had a sensation of fir trees at the bottom of my vision. Now I was above the fir trees, the fir trees were below me. I was floating among the trees. It was evening time and so peaceful and quiet.

Freeda said she thought that they had taken me back to the beginning of time.

I sensed people around me. I could not see them but I could feel the presence close to me. Aware but not aware. No names, no pack drill, as the saying goes.

Freeda remarked it was because I was an observer.

I replied no, because they were observing me. They were listening to my description of what I was seeing. It was shaking me, so many people watching. I took a deep breath and shuddered from within.

Freeda said, "Bill, would you like to come back now?"

I replied that I could come back but it was nice being there. It was wonderful being there just floating, weightless, but aware. I could see reds, but yes, it was time to come back. It is time to come back. I said goodbye to my friends and I would see them again soon, thank you.

Freeda thanked them herself for the wonderful colours and sensations she and I had experienced in travelling through time, this wonderful gem, this gem of knowledge, the crystal of light and the joy it has brought with us. Thank you, Spirit guides and helpers, thank you very much but it is time for us to come back into the physical manifest person and let all these lovely Spirit people go back through the door and travel back to their home. Thank you very much for coming, Amen. I sensed the door was closing.

Sandra had seen and felt that there was a beauty about the dawn of time, before man came and began to destroy that beauty. There were voices in the wind that was bringing times of change. An Indian headdress, Geronimo and Leonidas were both there as well.

Freeda said to Sandra, "I do not know why but they have just given me a bucket of sand for you. Sounds stupid, but it is like the sands of time running through like an egg timer."

Sandra replied that there were also many orbs but there were also strands as well coming down. She did get many colour changes through that experience.

Sandra had seen many other things but had been unable to break in while I was speaking. Freeda thought that Sandra was a "closing guide" who observed and remembered things to add to our recollection of the experiences as we discussed the session.

Freeda sensed there was a lot of energy coming off Sandra. Freeda's own guide was the "introduction guide" who starts the session and this time, I was the channel to give out the description of the journey.

While they were discussing their thoughts and visions, I felt that I was not fully back to normal. My last vision was a small log cabin with a roofed veranda and the door was open with a purple light coming from within. I knew immediately that this was Freeda's guide, Running Water, and this was his cabin. The open door was an invitation for me to step in.

Interrupted by Freeda asking, "Are you back yet, Bill"? I then related to Freeda about the last few seconds of my vision at which she felt quite emotional. What I had not known or understood was that Freeda had once had a dream when she felt she was on a different level, but the sky was green, the grass was blue and the sea was yellow. She had felt that she was in a different dimension where the grass is blue unlike ours where the grass is green. Sandra had seen similar colours during the session that represented Angelic colours, as told during her Reiki training.

Without really thinking, I said "Blue Grass Music". As I turned to face Freeda, I knew instantly I was not back, as Freeda looked so different. I told her she looked different. "Do you think so?" she said. As I placed my hand on her forearm, I said, "Freeda, I do not know you, I do not know that face, flower."

"Right," said Freeda.

Sandra said, "Are you not back yet, Bill?"

Freeda said, "He is trying to see who I am, welcome friend."

I studied the face a few more seconds before the sudden realisation hit me like a brick in the face.

Waves of emotion washed over me, shock first, time stood still, hand up to my mouth, a living, breathing ghost of a face right next to me, looking intently at me. Mesmerised, I looked back at the face of a woman I did not know. It was not Freeda, who I had sat beside for the last hour and a half. This woman looked different, was different. She held my gaze, staring intently at me. I felt powerless, helpless, locked in, held tight to the unblinking eyes of this stranger. A sudden surge of energy from those eyes, another psychic brick in the face as it registered who was in my sight and who she actually was.

I could barely whisper, "Freeda, it is your mother, she looks like you. We instantly changed places. I was now her mother, reunited with my child once more.

The dam burst. Uncontrollable emotion flooded out; I felt the emotion of forty years of waiting to hold my precious daughter. I reached out to hug my child once again. A mother reunited after years of waiting. I sobbed as only a mother can over her child. Heart-rending sobs, words of comfort, apology, encouragement, and a worry about getting her jumper wet from the tears. All these emotions, like a mighty river of tears, flooded out at the same time that only a loving Mother and a loving child can experience after so long apart. Wrapped in this unfathomable love, reunited as one, tightly holding each other, and never, ever, ever, wanting to let go.

Eventually, we eased apart, the flood reduced to a trickle. Freeda had certainly felt the emotion. After so long apart she knew that if there was no emotion it was not real.

We reached for the handkerchiefs, like two friends who had just watched one of those old heart-wrenching black and white films. It was strange, but I did not feel sad within myself. Freeda's mother had been a very powerful woman, and she had wanted to get all that emotion out: big time. She had known that it was her time and that I was the channel she had been waiting for all those years. For Freeda's mother it had been the right time and the right place.

For Freeda it had been a long time in coming. She had waited over forty years for just this time, this reunion with the lost soul of her mother. We discussed the session for some time and I owe Spirit so many thanks for this experience. We had so much colour in our visions of the places they took us and showed us both.

The grand finale from Spirit, given to me by the Council, repaid the debt of gratitude I have to Freeda and Spirit for the wonderful journey I am travelling in the winter of my life. Believe me; I feel humbled by this experience, and extremely grateful for the time Spirit is taking to help us on our journey, both as individuals and as a small group.

The experiences we are having are not for the faint hearted. We feel that you could not give this type of evidence from a rostrum at a spiritualist church. We have given, and will continue to give, our Spirit to Spirit, without fear, and in pursuit of the answers to questions that arise each week. Spirit knows when we meet, and appear to know what questions we are going to ask. They arrange suitable Guides and helpers to give us the answers by direct vision, channelling or trance of varying degrees. We, for our part, must in turn speak, to give our explanation of what we are hearing and seeing in our thoughts and vision. Spirit has graciously showed us they are with us, and allowed us to record our sessions. We will be forever grateful for their interaction with us.

Chapter Seven
– The Test and the Council
of the Ancestors

A few days passed and once again, a visit to Irene Harthill's house in Shotton loomed closer. What would Spirit have in store I wondered?

Thursday 17th October 2019 quickly came round. My fifth session with Freeda and Irene. We had our customary cup of tea or coffee and a discussion of spirit happenings or articles we had seen over the last week. We knew that Spirit listens in to the chats we have, as they often remind us about certain topics that we discuss and give us a truth about it, if they are able to tell us. It is strange how just an odd word out of place generates an entirely different response from them and quite often turns the tables on what we believe to be true.

A brief period of camera angles and best photographic side discussion had us all laughing, which tends to lift the energy. Negativity suppresses the energy. With eyes closed, and bowed heads, the Lord's Prayer was said which is how we start all our sessions.

We had discussed the procedure we would use to return Spirit home when our session was closing and we decided to think about a hatch in the ceiling and Spirit going through the hatch and the door closing behind them. As we finished the Lord's Prayer, I had the sudden vision of a hatch and a head appearing over the edge as if checking we were ready to communicate with them. My legs were starting to feel freezing cold, a sign for me that Spirit was around me.

Irene settled us down to our breathing regime. In for a count of four, hold for four and out for a count of four. Slow, steady breathing to calm our bodies and prepare. The time was set for thirty minutes. Irene asked us to imagine a beam of pure white energy entering through the crown of our heads and on the out breath going through our heart chakra and out through our fingers into our auric field and slowly expanding it. With each in breath, bringing in the pure white light through the heart centre and out through the fingers into our auras, the Auric field, slowly expanding outwards to an egg shape size which feels right for you. Once you have your aura expanded to your satisfaction, you can now go into your zone and then begin your communication.

Within two minutes, I could hear that Freeda's guide was blending with her. I felt sure it was one of her First Nation Indian guides. The strange language being spoken seemed vaguely familiar to me, although I had no understanding of what he was saying.

Freeda, in her own voice, welcomed his spirit and others she felt were around us. She was performing hand signs and felt that he was part of what we were doing that day. She had invited him to come and he was asking her why she wanted him to come today. She said her reply to his question was that she wanted him to come to tell us what he might have had to say today, whatever was in his knowledge or his understanding. She was now going to step back until he came through again. He was making her laugh as he was telling Freeda that this would interest Bill.

He was standing up and showing Freeda his belt and it was not for holding up his trousers! There were different designs on the belt and Bill would understand and look at what was on the belt. It was very symbolic for him. I spoke the words, "Medicine Belt". Wise men had done this and Bill would understand, he said. They were not inferior. They were not stupid as people think. The symbols had symbolic meanings as they induced a number of their Spiritual Rites, their keys, their knowledge, to the next level. They were used to open the next door, the next timeline. They were used to open doors as the medicine men knew lots about the ancestors and they could bring them forward with these symbolic rites. You think men of my time wise men but they were children, children compared to what their ancestors were. They (the elders; ancestors) used to put us through strict rules, rites, to get anywhere. You did not get an easy passage, an easy ticket to anywhere. You must put the work in to get anywhere, just as we were doing.

Work to get your key before you can get anywhere, your initiation, their acceptance of you. It was not a right: it was a privilege and I, as Bill: was being judged! Whether I liked it or not, they were testing me!

If they said there was a fire there and you walk across it, then it was a test to see how genuinely you are connecting. Ok, they are testing you now.

Freeda's spirit guide said, *"It is not me who is testing you, it is the elders, right? Ok."*

Yes, they were showing me faces that appeared and disappeared in quick succession, all native Indians with various headdresses on.

Freeda was translating to me what her guide was saying.

"Please look hard and recognise them all, ok? Because they will come and help you."

Freeda was smiling, as one of them was quite small in stature when the guide stated:

"Remember you did not have to be the tallest to be the strongest. There was sometimes a lot more power in the small bundle."

He then showed Freeda magnificent views of the mountains and the surroundings. A thought sprung into my mind and I remarked, "The Sierra Nevadas". Freeda said yes it is so beautiful, wonderful views. Another thought in my head: Snow on the peaks. I was now sure that Spirit was very close to me, pushing these thoughts through my head as I shared the views with Freeda. She said this was why her Spirit guide wanted to come today to tell me about the belt. I would understand but she did not.

He said, *"Bill would know."*

I could see a storm in the mountains, clouds. Heavy dark clouds were coming into my vision. As I looked towards the tops of the mountains, I could see the tree line. It was cold again. I could feel the cold. It was like a winter storm. I could see a face. They were showing me faces, native faces, young and old. They were stepping closer. I could feel them stepping closer to me. They were walking round me looking closely as each face changed. There were many feathers in his headdress. This vision replaced by a yellowy pale green.

Freeda said her guide has asked if he could use my body to talk.

I replied, *"Yes, he could. He is welcome."*

"Thank you" was his reply. He stepped very close. I saw a purple aura. I was ready.

Freeda asked me about a question from Irene. Was there anything significant about the storm clouds?

I replied that, *"he did not make me aware of any significance but that it was the first storm of winter approaching. There is a chill in the air that makes me shiver but I know that it is also Spirit shaking me".* I was coming down from the mountain through the trees, backwards!

Freeda prompted "First recognition".

I replied, *"The faces were faint, a yellowy sky with yellow clouds."*

Irene asked if the yellow cloud was significant.

I told her, *"They asked me to look at the clouds and I could see faces in the clouds, indistinct, not clear but, an awareness, of the ancestors. I saw a figure but I was not sure whether it was a man or a woman. Not on the reservation. Not free to roam, with a white woman's dress. Then the vision changed. I saw her sitting on the porch of a cabin. I could see trees but not fir trees. Deciduous trees with very few leaves left on the branches."*

Freeda said, "I can see", when I interrupted her with *"I can see an eye, closely looking at me"*.

Freeda continued that the Yellow cloud that Irene had asked about was significant and that I must look up "Yellow Cloud" please. Freeda could also see heads peering down with all their Chiefs' headdresses on as if they are looking at you in a circle around. It was not the body, just the head of each one of them looking at you.

I could see a hole in the clouds to which Freeda replied yes, that is where I want to be. *It was not yellow, it was a pale mauve colour but it was open to the skies, like looking up from a well but there was no awareness of the well. A pale blue then it changes to yellow. Yes, I could see that there were many heads looking over the edges of the hole in the cloud.*

They were looking deep into my soul. The colour changed to purple with an awareness of shadows. A light appeared in the distance passing through the clouds. Like moonrise but not of the moon. I felt I did not know this place.

Freeda suddenly interrupted that she was getting "the Yankees is coming, the Yankees is coming; the Yankees is coming. They are disturbing us. Also, in the wintertime we burnt a different kind of wood because it gave off a euphoric effect, euphoric effect".

"Sagebrush," I interjected.

There was something darker in the deep purple colour I was seeing. A symbol: an eagle, an eagle. Irene asked if the eagle was significant. I immediately replied, *"It is on the belt."* Freeda said, "Right, ok."

I resumed, *"It is the top of the totem pole."*

"Right," Freeda said.

I continued, *"Have you never seen the top of the totem pole with the beak of an eagle and the wings outspread?"*

"No," replied Freeda, "I have not. It must be significant, very significant."

He showed me a man with a moustache, dressed in a suit, with an old woman sitting in a chair. They were white, yes.

Freeda said that she was aware that in the wintertime they used to hum, not sing, hum songs to which she gave a short demonstration of this humming of a song. Her guide explained that in the long summer days, they would sing these songs aloud but in the wintertime, they would hum the songs but not aloud. They were just remembering the songs and the power of them so to keep the energies going they would sometimes hum (another demonstration) and they would sing them in the teepees, and it would take them into a deeper trance until they were visualising, visualising.

He showed me yellow green. He showed me the bushes.

At this point, Irene asked if he was able to channel through any words of wisdom for the human race.

After a pause he said, *"What would you like to ask?"*

Freeda's spirit guide said, "Knowledge."

I replied, *"Why did you bring me?"*

Freeda repeated his question and said we are using you (me) as a channel to higher understanding. We are grateful.

He replied, *"Of what?"*

Of a lot of things, a lot of things, Freeda replied. She said she was getting "My dear friend" and he is not saying it nastily. He is saying, "We have brought you for understanding of a lot of things, my dear friend. We used to discuss things and understand them. So yes, my dear friend, we have brought you here to understand you and you to understand."

He said, *"I feel, I feel I have been disturbed."*

Freeda asked if he used to practise things on his own.

"Yes," he said.

Solitary, Freeda asked.

"Yes," he replied. "Yes, solitary." Freeda stated.

He interrupted. *"I do not know why you have come for me. I do not know who you are."*

Freeda replied, "Yes I know that but I know you."

"But I don't know you," he replied. *"I cannot see you but I can feel you. I am looking in the skies and cannot see you."*

Freeda interrupted him and stated, "Father, I am looking for further knowledge, Father. Not as a Father of mine, but a Father of a lot, more people.

"We want to ask questions of you on higher energies, higher ceremonies. That what you used to do that was so powerful to help humanity as it is now. What can we do or prepare for, Father?"

I felt his energy becoming more intense, more focused and becoming angry. He said, *"I see purple. What can man do? Man is destroying the planet. He is destroying our Mother Earth."*

Freeda replied, "Some are. Some are, Father. Some are, some."

He went on, *"Most of them are."*

Irene asked for any pearls of wisdom.

He ignored her and continued, *"There are stupid demonstrations. Why cannot they not plant trees, and corn instead of leaving their filth in the streets. They are totally misguided these people."*

Freeda said that she had been told, "Arrogance, arrogance, arrogant, arrogant."

He stated, *"I would not have patience with them: but here, we cannot interfere. We have to just sit and watch them destroy themselves."*

Irene said to him that, "he could give words of advice on how to raise the consciousness of the masses".

Freeda said she was being told that this is what we are doing now, this is what we are doing now. This is what we are preparing for, helping this.

The guide then coughed and thumped my chest moaning slightly, *"Oh the atmosphere. You have already been told. People of my age, we had more, no, not more. We were, part of, Mother Earth; we understood her; we looked after her, and so, she looked after us. The more modern the generations become, the less; the less, like a grain of sand is their understanding of Spirit, and of Mother Nature. They, are they worth saving?"*

Irene broke in saying we were just attempting to get words of wisdom, pearls of wisdom, from you, great Masters, as to how to help the planet.

He replied, *"You fight among yourselves. Your ego is guiding you, not here, but around the world. They all want more than their neighbour. They want more material things."* He coughed and retched at this point and remarked, *"Oh, the air is terrible"* and coughed again.

Freeda said, "So please can I ask, Father if that is why you decided to do solitary stuff?"

He sighed deeply, then continued,

"I must do penance to Mother Earth. I must try."

Freeda broke in saying, "Yes, I can, yes. I keep getting told "young man, young man, you know nothing". But yes. I think seeing that we are grateful for everything that is good, is perhaps, done in a solitary way; is appreciation. Learning to appreciate, appreciate." *"Yes,"* he replied. Freeda continued, "And I definitely feel as though, Father you did a lot of solitary, solitary working as my friend here is working on herself."

He broke in stating, *"You don't know what you have got till it is gone; and when it is gone, it is too late."* Quite sharply, he continued over the top of Irene speaking, saying, *"Wake up and smell the coffee!"*

Irene continued by saying, "A lot of people on this planet are now awakening and are trying hard. What we need is help as to how to go forward.

He took a deep breath and sighed deeply saying, *"You have the solutions. You all have the solutions. Just got to believe. Hot air is no good. If you have hot air, you cannot smell the cool breezes of winter in the mountains. You must control, control the emissions. Not from cars. Factories, power stations, pumping out vile filth into the air that we breathe; you breathe. We do not breathe but we feel it. Makes our lungs heavy, heavy with sadness. It interrupts our concentration."*

Freeda remarked, "But surely, Father, if we believe in your help and the power that you have and more of us start and believe in the power of Spirit, the power of delaying an accident or getting the synchronicity right, there will be changes. Do you think this synchronicity is right at this time?"

"No," he said, *"It is accelerating, it is accelerating for change but it may be too slow. So many of the people of the earth have lost their link, their spirituality. They feed their base ideas and live for today and not for tomorrow. We up here have no tomorrow."*

Freeda said that she was being told, "The biggest thing is that the sound, the deafening noise all the time. We do not have enough silence to listen to Spirit and our inner voice. If people could understand that, the sound is just so deafening all the time that there is no peace. You know, no peace within the body for their soul or their (Here, the guide gave a small laugh) intuition."

He asked, *"How do you think we feel like up here? The noise and the vibrations, the radio telescopes, everything is going absolutely haywire. We have to move higher and higher in frequency to get rid of them. The rubbish and the noise, but it is man. Man must find his own destination. Why does he look out and not in? What is the point of going to the moon? There is no cheese there. Laughingly, no the moon is not made of cheese. They have a planet. I just, thank God the oceans are so deep."*

Freeda remarked, "Well the oceans will cleanse this, won't it. The oceans will cleanse the Earth."

He replied, *"Well, when they meet, meet, meet, Meet? Melt! They melt all the glaciers they will have less land to live on. There is too many of them. They breed like rabbits. They expect others to provide for them instead of providing for themselves. They rely too much on others. They need to look inside themselves. They need to find Spirit: And when they find Spirit. When they find Spirit, if they find Spirit; then they will know what needs to be done. The light will come on. But, I do, not. No. I do not. Can I say this? I do not hold out much hope."*

Freeda replied, "Well, perhaps if we are going to move on to higher vibrations, some of these negative, vibrations, will have to be, changed."

A low growl was rumbling from me. At this point, the guide raised my hand to touch Freeda's forearm with mine as if to stop her and to carefully listen to what he was about to say.

He spoke with authority saying, *"It is not a negative vibration, child. It is what is happening. When you start, from the age of machinery, pouring the filth into the air. Then you started on the downward slide. But man is fueling their want, without, without looking after the planet, without looking after the trees, the open spaces, the grasslands that fed the game. The Sahara desert, it was not a desert in my time. It was the basket of Africa. Plains, plains of grain, oasis, with palms and dates."*

Irene broke in by saying: "But that was before, before the days of machinery. It was a long, long, time when that changed so is that not part of the natural cycle?"

His voice became very tight with exasperation as he asked Irene, *"Have you been there? Were you there at that time?"*

Irene replied, "Very likely. I have had an Egyptian life, I know that."

He said in a dismissive voice, *"It was before the Egyptians."*

Defensively, Irene replied, "Right, well no, well maybe I was, I do not know."

He mused as he said *"The Egyptians"* with a low growl.

Irene continued on her track saying, "I think this is why we are trying to come to you."

I could sense that the guide was upset with Irene. He was starting to shake my insides as he quickly interrupted her by saying, *"It started to change and the peoples of the plains of Africa, some moved north and others went south. The ones that went south got darker because of the heat of the sun. The ones that went north became a little bit whiter, not so much sunshine. There was greater, greater lands in."*

Irene interrupted again asking, "Can you tell us about Atlantis, did Atlantis actually exist if we are going back so far in time?"

He said, *"There was maps made."*

Freeda said, "Crystals. Crystals did."

He continued, *"There was maps made which very few people are aware of. They were made, many, many, many, many, many, many, many lifetimes ago. The earth was not like it is now. The landmasses, it is evolution. Things change, all the time, all the time. You talk about ice ages, carboniferous periods. There was a greater pollution in the early years with the volcanoes, spewing ash, but it created life. It levelled things out a little bit, with the ash, building up, and the winds blowing and eventually creating seeds of life. Tiny grasses and mosses, and so it fertilised the ash and then, you got bigger grasses. You got bushes, you got trees, and the trees breathed and the grasses breathed, and the sunlight changed: and then you* had a rich, a rich, verdant planet given to you. There are few places on your planet now, left for Spirit."

Irene quietly interrupted to say, "Well, Father, I need to say that in a few minutes you will have to bring this to a close."

He went on, "Very few places on that planet, even the Himalayas. That yellow race."

Freeda broke in and said, "Thank you, Father, for coming. Thank you for the information that you have given us today. We will take it with us and listen to your words of wisdom; and what you have had to say. There will be quite–"

He broke in by saying, "It is not wisdom, child. It is what is the truth. It is a positive message and I think, in earth years, you are old enough for the brutal truth of life. You are all concerned with Mother Earth and I thank you for that. You almost make me cry, but you are so few."

Freeda said thank you once again for coming and we would like to meet you again.

"I like to be on my own," he replied.

Freeda said that she knew he did and that he had worked solitary but she must say thank you to him for coming today. Freeda then asked Irene to ask us to come back please, as she was unable to return without being asked.

The guide said, "You can, child, I am going now. I am sorry if I have upset you. I must return to my meditation."

Freeda thanked him once again for coming and said that we would have to meet again.

He replied, "Good afternoon, friends but it will be a while."

Freeda replied, "We will see."

Both together they said, "Yes, we will see."

"Goodbye," he said.

Both Irene and Freeda wished him goodbye.

Freeda was coming back slowly but had the impression of a void going down beneath me. It seemed to Freeda that I was going through time. I said I was back to which Freeda replied that she was not back yet and we would have to wait a bit. Freeda said that if she were not careful she would go back in. As I was fully back, I said thank you to Spirit and that our time we could give today was now ended. I asked them to step back from Freeda and to give her peace.

Freeda then came back. She gave our thanks once again to Spirit Guides and helpers and asked them if they would please return to their proper place.

The following week I did follow up the request by Spirit to look up "Yellow Cloud". After considerable time spent trawling various websites, I eventually found the following information. In the National Anthropological Archives of the Smithsonian Institute in Maryland, USA, there is a collection of eight-inch by ten-inch glass plate negatives taken by a Dr Paul Vanderbilt, taken in the early 1920s. The location of a photograph of Chief Yellow Cloud of the Lakota Sioux is opposite Negative 57384.

Yellow Cloud lived on the Rosebud Reservation and the negative was one of a number taken at the White River Fair. Yellow Cloud joined the ancestors in about 1925. The Rosebud Indian Reservation (RIR) is an Indian reservation in South Dakota, USA. It is the home of the federally recognized Sicangu Oyate (the Upper Brulé Sioux Nation) – also known as Sicangu Lakota, and the Rosebud Sioux Tribe, a branch of the Lakote People. The Lakota name *Sicangu Oyate* translates into English as "Burnt Thigh Nation"; the French term "Brule Sioux" is also used.

The Rosebud Indian Reservation was established in 1889 after the United States' partition of the Great Sioux Reservation. Created in 1868 by the Treaty Of Fort Laramie, the Great Sioux Reservation originally covered all of West River, South Dakota (the area west of the Missouri River), as well as part of northern Nebraska and eastern Montana. The reservation includes all of Todd County, South Dakota, and communities and lands in the four adjacent counties.

I would ask that readers who are interested in The First Nation of North America, the indigenous peoples who lived in Canada to the Gulf of Mexico, do a little research and realise that the times between 1750 and the present day (2020) cover the greatest "ethnic cleansing" of a country in the history of the world. Conservative figures put the death toll between 80 and 150 million, yes, million. Men, women, and children killed or starved by European migrants and the Government forces. Their tribal lands taken without recompense. Their culture, religion, and languages suppressed and their treatment at the hands of the white invader beyond belief. To say that North America is one, if not the richest country in the land of the free, is an insult to intelligence. The tribes moved countless times to poorer and poorer land. The original treaties amended and reservation land grants overturned. The average life span of the indigenous peoples in 2018 was 43 years old for a man and 52 for a woman. Some ninety percent are unemployed and teenage suicide is five times the national average.

Infant deaths are also four times the national average. Most of the reservations have no running water, sanitation, electricity, health care or shopping centres. Over half of the indigenous people cannot even vote!

The United Nations have upheld their action against the Government of the USA who have done nothing to alleviate the abject poverty of the majority of the reservations.

The American Native Spirits that I have had the privilege to channel have always treated me with the utmost care and respect, as I give them.

They have shown me their respect for Mother Earth and our planet, which the so-called civilized world has raped and pillaged for self-gratification, the base desires of the human species. These "Rainbow Warriors" were the first true conservationists who actioned conservation rather than just generating "hot air".

When you look back through history, man has always made war. He has always tried and most times succeeded in invading other countries to make his country larger and better and to strip the invaded land of food and cherished objects, some of great value, like gold, silver and precious stones. He took livestock and prisoners.

In the early history, the prisoners were enslaved, women and children abused, some sacrificed to the gods of the invaders. The religion of the conquered either suppressed or banned; temples and holy buildings destroyed, with no freedom to do anything except follow the orders of the new rulers.

It has not changed at all. If we just look at the recent past we can list man's atrocities to man. No one, but no one is exempt.

The holy land, Christian, Jew and Islam, Shi'ite and Sufi. South American Maya, Aztec and others by Spanish invaders. North American tribes of every type by "migrants", still going on now. Yugoslavia, Serbians and Croatians, Germany and the holocaust of the Jews. Iran and Iraq, Syria, Egypt, all sectarian violence. England and Ireland, Catholic and Protestant. Russia, Japan, China and Tibet. North and South Korea, North and South Vietnam. Tribal genocide in Africa, the Somalian internal war, still going on since 1991. The list is endless. Every nation has attacked another at some time.

This self-destruct mechanism driven by the greed, jealousy, ego, and want, of both the ruling classes and the terrorists; is not limited by colour or creed. It has filtered down to the masses by a gang type culture, but propounded the disrespect for life itself.

Regardless of colour or creed, we are all collectively responsible for our actions. Unless we can all forgive and become a fellowship of all humanity, without prejudice against colour and creed and all work together for peace and conservation, we have the supreme capability to destroy, not only ourselves, but also the entire life on this planet. It is our choice.

Chapter Eight
– The Power of
Prayer and Love

Freda Robson is my teacher and mentor. She has been in touch with the world beyond from her early years. Her mother was also a spiritualist but neither encouraged nor discouraged Freda in the early years. She has lived in Easington Colliery all her life.

Situated less than a mile from the North Sea it is one mile north of Horden and adjoins Easington Village to the west. Easington or Essingtun; to give it the Saxon name was a parish of Durham and the major settlement in the east of Durham. The local Church stands on a hilltop and parts of the building date back to those Saxon times. One of the priests from Easington became a Pope in the Middle Ages. Easington Colliery and the associated settlement is further to the east of Easington village towards the North Sea and built on Church land of the Durham Bishopric. Tourism call the County of Durham "The Land of the Prince Bishops". The Crowned rulers allowed the Prince Bishops to raise their own army and mint their own coinage as protectors of the Northern border of England against the marauding Scottish clans who were defeated at the Battle of Neville's Cross, situated one mile west of Durham City, on the 17th October 1346. Scottish prisoners held in the Cathedral were responsible for the damage to tombs and edifices within the building. Durham Cathedral is a World heritage site.

Freda is a Mother and Grandmother who adores her family. A bubbly woman of average height and pleasing appearance with light, straw-coloured hair verging on the angelic. Her sharp mind and quick wit puts you at your ease in a few short minutes. She has a tremendous curiosity and is experienced in all things spiritual, yet at the same time, is unassuming and kind and would help anyone, without thought or acceptance of any reward. Freda had worked in the local chemist at Easington Colliery for many years and knows many people in the area. She does make appearances at local spiritualist services but these have been few and rare over the last twelve years. When you first meet, some people sense there is something indefinable about her, a latent energy bursting to get out. Freda is divorced, both a complex character, yet open and honest. She looks after two of her son's children full time and her daughter and family live next door to her. In my short time working with Freda, we have both developed a closer affinity with Spirit, guided by a far greater power. Spirit had told her to use "Freeda" in her spiritual work probably because when she is excited, she often says "eeh" before passing information. I am so proud and privileged to call her my friend. We both look forward to our weekly meetings at Irene Harthill's house.

Our sixth session with Spirit was on October 25th, 2019 starting at 2:20pm. We took up our usual positions with Freeda to my left and Irene facing us, at the opposite end of the dining room table. Freeda remarked aloud that she should settle down. She gave me the sense of being a little excited inside her mind as to who or what information we might bring through today.

We thought we would try a slightly different introduction this time. Irene had brought down a brass bowl she had from India with a stick to strike it. This action produced the most nerve tingling vibrational sound I had ever heard. It just went on and on for quite a while, slowly settling to a background of a felt slowing rhythmic pulsing before eventually fading out. The vibrations brought my nerve endings into sharp focus, as well as the ears ringing! We followed with the Lord's Prayer and Freeda said, "Welcome, friends and to those who are joining us today, thank you."

After a few minutes of quiet, steady breathing to calm the body and mind, it was soon obvious to me that Freeda had a guide coming through.

Starting at first with a few low oohs and aahs, then a little lip smacking, a small faint voice saying, *"Keep me here, to me here. I am finding it hard today to talk. Yes, sometimes it is me, sometimes I find it is Freeda who is (a little laugh) uncomfortable, yes, oh yes, oh, yes, we come, yes. Yes, today, I am now settling down into Freeda. Yes, I can how you say, welcome to you all today. Yes, my name is Kan-a-Kuah, Kan-a-Kuah, Kan-a-Kuah. Yes, I am giving you my name, Kan-a-Kuah. Yes, my name is Kan-a-Kuah. Obviously, I am sometimes finding it funny. Yes, right. To get into your discussions today I have been listening to you talking, very good, very nice, but obviously, it is not right. You do not understand that all you have to do is listen; listen and we will direct you. Honestly, we laugh at you sometimes because obviously you are discussing irrelevant things. My wish is to come in to this group and help you understand, just listen. We will send thoughts your way. Obviously err, sometimes difficult for us, difficult for you, but we want to talk to you today about electricity. Electricity is honestly your way forward."*

He gave a small laugh and continued, *"Freeda is making me laugh. She is saying should you electrocute us"* as he laughed again. *"No, (laugh) you do not need to electrocute us. We just–"* Here he broke into an unknown language as if telling someone off quite sharply.

He continued by saying, "*Get the energy moving. We are surrounding you, coaxing you, building up the energies. You do not know, but we are working very hard behind the scenes. Now we will come to our place within the World. We are knowledge seekers, knowledge seekers: universal knowledge seekers. Maybe, ok, maybe you will join our circle of the masses; yes, because we not only come to you, we come to many masses. Sometimes we work on a very small island, not Ireland, not Ireland, a very small island. Information builds up in this island. You understand where the turtles go. Where the turtles go. Where the turtles go swimming. That is where we are about. You might say why we have to have somewhere physical. We have somewhere physical because the energy is right there. The energy builds up there. Yes, we like it. We like it. It builds up better. You know, you are building up electricity with this group. Your thoughts, your mind. Irene, why don't you ask me a question?*"

Irene asked, "When do you think the human race will be ready to hear things about the Planet and how to save it?"

He replied immediately with, "*Well, people are listening now, perhaps more than we think they are listening, right. I am trying to show you the Milky Way, right. I can see the Milky Way and I can see several planets near or stars near because I am maybe making you not understand properly. But, there is the Milky Way and there is two energies coming from those directions of the Milky Way, around that area that–*"

Suddenly he broke again into an unknown language in which he appeared to be remonstrating with another energy.

He continued by saying, "*In a very high energy force changing everybody's mind-sets, mind-sets, right? Transmitters. These energies are coming from; yes, the Milky Way area. Right. Ok. Yes. Divinity is not part of it. Right? The divine is not part of it. It is not that way, at all. It is not divinity at all; it is part, participation, participation. Shuck, participation. Not divinity, no, no, no.*"

The word "Shuck" spat out as a forceful expletive due to him mispronouncing "participation" three times. Spirit can get it wrong sometimes. Bless them. He continued.

"It is coming in and we are participating in the energies on this energy field, right? This is coming in very, very quickly now. Whirling round your world hitting places one, two, three, four, five, hundreds of places but it is this energy that is hitting the places. This is where we will start. You will see it. You will see it. In your time. Right? You will see it."

Irene interrupted with a question of, are we able to help here with this group?

He thought a moment then said, *"Yeah, ok, right. This group came into being through participation. We want you to participate. We want you to tune in, tune in. You are making progress; you are making progress. Much quicker than what you think. Believe me, Irene; you will see changes within your time. Honour me and I will honour you. That is the key to lots of things. Honour me and I will honour you."*

Irene said that she understood that, but he was not satisfied with her reply. He continued by saying, *"It is no good saying that I understand you if you don't honour me. I am trying to explain this so that you understand it later. Right?"*

Irene replied, yes.

He responded, *"Once, once before when we came here, no honour, no honour. This time, yes, thank you."* He paused and appeared to be waiting for Irene to reply.

Irene stated that she felt certain that she would listen, and she hoped to take in the answers to questions you are giving. To this statement, he replied *"Thank you".*

After another pause, it was Freeda's voice that resumed the dialogue by stating, *"This is stupid this. My Spirit guide is showing me daisies and it sounds stupid. Daisies, like picking the petals off* the daisies like, you know, a little bit more and a little bit more, and a little bit more. Right? Ok. Right, why is he showing me that. Right, he is showing me the daisies and the clocks when you blow them and spreading the seeds. Dandelion ones, yeah but sometimes it comes naturally with the wind. It travels on the wind. You do not have to blow it, it travels on the wind; it travels on the sound; it travels on the vibrations; but it travels from the universe." A long pause.

Irene then said, "Are you saying that from honouring you and listening to what you have to say we are actually seeding the thoughts around the area in an ever increasing circle."

Freeda agreed yes. "Thank you, thank you," Irene said.

After another long pause Freeda remarked, "By he is "gobby" (Very talkative) this one. He is saying that they are looking at us with all the different colours of us you know so he went on what projections what. Then he said, you are lilac and you are lavender, Irene right? Lavender." Irene asked, "So I am lavender, am I?"

Freeda replied, "Yes, you are lavender. Bill is indigo. I feel I am on the same level as you but I am not. I am lavender, right?"

Irene said to Freeda, "So we are both lavender."

"Yes," replied Freeda. A pause, then, "here we go again" from Freeda.

"Bill, this is for you again. Oh God. My Spirit guide is talking about tormented souls again and I think it is because I have thoughts of our Christopher in my head, you know again. He is saying that Bill is going to answer about these tormented souls. So Bill, I would like your Spirit guide, or who is with you today, if they could come forward and contribute to this circle please. You are very welcome to come."

I said that I felt that he was already here. He was shaking me.

Freeda said, "Good, we acknowledge you and honour you."

I said we were very privileged. He was bringing in a lot of energy, making me breathe quite deeply.

Irene, looking at me and seeing what was happening said, "The spirit in me bows down to you."

I was stretching in all directions. This energy was a very big man, much bigger than I was. I knew he was trying to blend with me far too quickly and I could not keep up with him. I was trying, but failing and it was stopping me breathing. I was gasping for air. I wanted it over with but knew I just had to keep myself open for him to blend quickly with me as he was making me shake uncontrollably.

Freeda said, "You can take him, Bill, you can take him."

He was stretching my face, neck, and throat. I was hurting under the tension. It felt like I was choking as it was becoming difficult to breathe.

Irene was quietly panicking and asking if there was anything she could do.

I was trying to breathe in and he was crushing my chest. I was starting to see stars. I was determined to allow him to blend with me.

I needed to get this part over as soon as possible. The sounds I was making were as if I had a very severe attack of trying to throw up, then, I grabbed a breath. I was gasping to replace the air crushed from my body but at last, I felt that the transition, the blending, was almost completed.

Freeda said it was ok as he was in and starting to settle himself in my body. "He is very strong, very strong. Take your time; he is in; he is in. Very powerful. Take your time. Take your time."

I knew he was powerful as I fought to get my breathing back under control.

"Take your time with him, Freeda said. "He is in."

I was out of breath but I managed to gasp out, "I know he is". I felt like I had just run for my life and had nothing left.

Freeda said, "Take your time, it was hard for him to get in, hard."

"Was it not," I replied. I was still gasping for breath, the air taken in with huge gulps to try to calm myself down. I was slowly starting to get my breath back as I remembered to take each breath as slowly and deeply as I could rather than the frantic gasps I had been taking. "It was hard for me, I offered." I took some time to settle into my regular breathing pattern and for him to settle completely within me.

Freeda was encouraging me to calm myself and breathe slowly and steadily and to keep it going. Encouragingly she said, "Let him talk now, let him talk." Remember the breathing she kept reminding me. Adjust to his size, shape, form, and strength. Keep it going nice and steady? Freeda now felt that he had settled into me a lot better and that it would not be so bad the next time. Freeda said that she would ask the question again. "If this guide would like to talk about tortured souls and I would like to say again, thank you. Because this is for me to understand. I think about my son and not only my son, but other people today who are into drugs and alcohol and are poor tortured souls.

"Ask your spirit guide, welcome friend, for any implement on this subject please. We are asking for help and understanding in me, please."

My breathing was very slowly coming back to a normal pattern, but still heavy. I felt that the Spirit within me wanted to speak but that he was having great difficulty in adjusting to my ragged breathing. Each time he wanted to speak, my breathing would stop for a few seconds then start again.

Freeda stepped in and said, "Just take your time. If your spirit cannot give anything today, it is ok: just take your time, thank you. If you do not want to talk on this subject, talk on what is right for this Soul to talk about; it will probably be connected."

In my own voice, very quietly, I said, "It's difficult."

Freeda said, "Take your time. It will be hard for him to use your voice and everything else." A series of grunts and moans emanated from me verging on trying to speak.

"Take your time, take your time," said Freeda. After attempted starts over a few seconds in quite a loud and very deep voice, Irene interceded.

She said, "Sometimes speaking on an in breath, as you breathe in and not in your voice and that may help you to settle in."

Freeda said, "Welcome friend."

Here, I feel an explanation of how the event unfolded is required, to aid the reader in realising the difficulty both I, and the guide, were experiencing. The spirit within was having great difficulty with co-ordinating his words with my breathing and also forming the pronunciation of exactly what he was trying to say through my voice box. He had almost taken full control of my breathing and the interface to my vocal cords. He appeared to be having great difficulty in speaking English and Irene had asked if he could speak in English please after a sudden outburst of unintelligible words. The performance lasted over thirty minutes punctuated by periods of him allowing me to try to regain a reasonable breathing pattern before he once again tried desperately to make himself understood.

During this time both Freeda and Irene encouraged him as best they could while also trying to keep me in some semblance of breathing pattern. Many times, he repeated his words, which were long and drawn out: heavily accentuated syllable by syllable, as they could not understand the information he was so desperately trying to impart to us.

I was unable to break in as I had tried with my thoughts to ask him to allow me to give the information. I knew what he was trying to tell us, but he made me aware that only he must pass the information to Freeda and Irene and it had to be through me, regardless of how difficult this was going to be, for both of us!

The following message is the information that he passed to us without all the stops, stammers, and restarts plus most of the long pauses for breath.

"Thank you. I am trying to speak in English. Christopher is not a tortured, not a tortured soul."

This brief sentence took all of four minutes to get out and Freeda thought he had said tormented soul! Almost every word took at least two deep breaths to get out with pauses in between to try to let me recover.

He replied, *"No. Tortured soul, not. Not."*

Freeda said she would wait to let him get it out totally. They understood tortured souls and told him they thought he was doing very well. "Welcome Friend".

He replied, *"Thank you all. Christopher is not a tortured soul."*

Freeda said, "Ok. Thank you, you are doing very well. Bill, you are doing very well handling this energy. He is very strong."

He started his reply almost immediately.

"He is feeding his base desires: because he has lost his self-respect."

The last sentence was split into two parts due to the pause for breath and the allowance he made for me to regain valuable breathing time. Freeda and Irene had offered words of encouragement and praise to both him and me. This further pause at the end of the sentence allowed me to recover, as it had taken a lot of energy out of me and my face was showing signs of distress.

Freeda said, "If that is all you have to say."

He interrupted by starting again, saying, *"He, he, he must be reminded, (Long pause) reminded of this. Until he realises this, then he will not make progress."*

Both Freeda and Irene thought this was marvellous as it was eminently clear to them that it was taking a lot of energy out of both of us, just to get a few words of information across. They were both very encouraging at every pause for breath, praising both Spirit and me for our efforts. They asked if he would please give them his name. They said he was very powerful and they were very privileged to have him.

Freeda said, "Thank you, friend. Thank you very much for what you have given. I know you are tiring Bill but it is worth it. It is what he wants to do for you. Please could you give us your name? Take your time please. Do you want to give us your name?"

He paused, took another deep breath: then resumed.

"I do not have a name. I have come because Freeda asked for help. It is a long time since I, my last: my last visit. My last visit to the Earth Plane."

He had repeated his words towards the end, as both Irene and Freeda were not sure that they had understood the full sentence he was trying to say. He had used a huge amount of his energy, and mine, to undertake a repeat of these few words.

At this point, I was exhausted. I started coughing and growling deep inside my throat. I was breathing heavily and it took a while to recover. Irene said she believed it was time, as they did not want to exhaust me too much in working with this very powerful energy. There was always another time.

Freeda said, "Welcome, friend. Thank you."

I was coughing and spluttering and Freeda said, "Bill, I just want to bring you back." He tried to speak again as Freeda said that she would like to thank him again. He resumed speaking.

"I do not come here but I was asked to come by the Council."

Both Irene and Freeda were absolutely amazed at this remark and said they were very, very privileged to have him with them. They both thanked him. Extremely privileged were Irene's words.

Freeda said, "Take your time. Thank you very much for coming. Thank you very much. Your words were of real wisdom to us today and I am sure we will get more wisdom as we go on."

Irene agreed and said, "If the Council has asked you to come then maybe you are going to be our link to the Council, which would be wonderful for us to set our seeds."

"Thank you," said Freeda.

I was aware of a powerful sense of peace and love as my voice changed to a quiet calming tone of a woman saying, *"He is going, Freeda."*

I knew in my heart that it was that wonderful lady guide. She was so skilled in blending with me that I had not felt a thing. I felt a wave of love and warmth flood through my body. She was reviving me. I was so, so grateful to her for coming.

Freeda said, "Thank you. He has been very, very strong."

With her soft and calming voice, she spoke, saying:

"It has taken a lot of energy to come down this far. You are blessed, child. Yes, we the Council of the Elders, although I am not a member. The Council of the Elders were requested by your Guide: and we asked him, they asked him, if he could intercede. We, we never. Well, it is very, very rare for this to take place. Bill has done exceptional to accept this spirit. We have stressed him really beyond what we would normally. Normally? No, usually do, but the request was so powerfully from love that we, no, not we; that they could not deny this request."

Freeda said, "I am very grateful and it must have took a lot of energy out of Bill, also yourself because I know that you found it very hard to fit into Bill's shape and form because you are so very strong; but Bill managed to take you so that's good. That is good. Thank you and we honour you."

The lady replied, *"Yes, I am helping, me, help, helping him to recover. He will be ok but–"*

Freeda broke in saying, "This is funny, so funny as I see you not a really old man you know, not a really old man. You are quite a man in his prime and this is where you found it so difficult as the strength of you, which was very, very powerful came into: I am not saying you are old, Bill, but an older body and he was very, very strong. He was coming in like a boxer there."

The guide remarked, *"A very powerful spirit. There is many about, Freeda. There are many Spirits here with you today."*

Freeda remarked that she felt that we had a room full today.

She replied, *"You have. They are all withdrawing now. Through the hole in the purple cloud."*

Freeda said, "What we will do is, Bill, just think of it, coming back."

The lady interrupted by saying, *"Goodbye friends."*

Freeda continued, "And what I would like to say is you do not have a name because you are a part of a Council that requested you to come whether you are a soul solely on your own but they brought you through today and it must have been very, very hard but you are blessed. Just think of the hatch in the roof opening up: and I would like to say thanks to all our Spirit guides, friends, and helpers that have come and joined us today. We know we are on a very powerful journey. Each time we are getting more and more information. What I would like is all these Spirit guides and helpers to do, is to show us how to work correctly with Spirit: in the name of our Father, Son, and Holy Ghost, Amen. Till the next time we meet. Amen."

A phone ringing and Freeda striking the bowl twice instantly brought me back, eyes opening.

Both Irene and Freeda were very happy with what had happened. Freeda placed her hands on my shoulders as she said I was a star.

Her hands were lovely and warm on my cold shoulders but I felt anything like a star. Freeda said that I had some good information for her today. I felt like I had run a marathon and was drained of energy. I told Freeda he had squeezed tears out of me. In fact, he had squeezed everything out of me. I knew there was Spirit present earlier on, before Freeda's guide had made his presence known. I could feel the energy building and I was getting the "shakes".

Freeda admitted that she and Irene were worried about me.

I told Freeda that the last spirit with me was "the Witch" but she was not a witch: God love her. She was so warm, loving and peaceful. Perhaps she would visit me again and tell me her name. I felt that I had known her a long, long time ago. Perhaps in another lifetime. Bonded to her. Forever joined in spirit. I thanked her sincerely for her help and assistance.

Time for a cup of coffee and a nice biscuit!

It is now 31st January 2020 and I thought I had finished writing this chapter last night, on Thursday 30th January 2020. I had felt the presence of Spirit with me all day. I could not keep warm and it felt like I was pushed to keep writing. I could feel pushes on my back after our evening meal and Spirit coming closer to remind me to get up and just do it!

Early this morning, 4:00am to be exact, I was wide-awake and did not know why. I lay for an hour or so then decided to get up. Sitting downstairs on the settee and I suppose I was daydreaming, I suddenly received a physic brick in the face.

Pieces of the jigsaw started falling together: My mind was in total chaos but at the same time making lots of sense. I felt the power and serenity of a Spirit and knew exactly who it was. She took me back in my memory to my first trance session with Freeda and said, *"Yes, this was me. It was also me, whom you call, the witch. I am the one who came to you in this session also: and yes, I am Bella and I am Catherine.*

"We showed you the plane of understanding and understanding is awareness. It is time for you to use the energy we have given you. The fine-tuning is complete. Your awareness will grow, as will your understanding. The circle is completed. This is the point I have chosen for you to mention me in your book. I have now made you aware of the true privilege you have been given from Spirit."

A thought came into my head. This is magic, very magical.

Did not the word magic come from the word Magi, from the Bible? This must be one of the truths of the Bible. One that remains from the original text: not tainted by man's hand as they had told us. She came back with a little musical laugh and said:

"Yes, I am a Magi. Now you understand exactly who I am. You are blessed, child. Goodbye, until we meet again. I will be with you, always."

I am not ashamed to admit it, but while writing this, I have tears coursing down my cheeks. Not tears of sadness, but tears of joy. For a couple of minutes they would not stop.

Then suddenly they did. Like turning off a tap.

I felt the love and peace she was giving me.

I know I am blessed.

I know she is here.

Watching.

Always.

Chapter Nine
– The New Beginning
and "Shairi - Lah"

It was two weeks before our next meeting, which was held on 8th November 2019 at Irene Harthill's house in Shotton, as the schools had been on holiday the week before.

This was our seventh meeting and I had been buzzing all morning with the energy of Spirit. My voice and my insides had been quivering during the last hour as we took our places around Irene's table. I informed Irene and Freeda that I had the number "137" burned in my thoughts. The number of creation. The one, not as God a deity or being, but as the energy of all things in the cosmos. Three, the triumvirate. God the Father, God the Son, and God the Holy Ghost. Seven, the days of the week and this is why this meeting now is important but divinity does not come into it. After a brief hiccup with the video camera, Freeda tapped the bowl with its vibrations echoing in my body. We said the Lord's Prayer.

Freeda started us off by saying, "Welcome, Friends. Thank you for coming and joining us today and I am aware even before we came today, you were around us, surrounding us, and perhaps a lot to come today to join us. Bill is here with lots of energy around him; so much that he wants to give out today. It is bursting to come out."

We agreed that Freeda should ask the first question. Freeda said, "I was told journeys and journeys leading from lifetimes to lifetimes, trying to create a circle of light. The time is not right yet, but I want to know what the circle of light is and what you mean by it. Could you please be a bit more explanative on it? Thank you.

"I want my guides to come in and explain a little more about it. Thank you and thank you to Bill's spirit guides and helpers for coming in and empowering him and making him the one who is helping us showing evidence. Thank you."

We then started our breathing exercise to calm ourselves, and open up to Spirit.

Freeda very quickly had the weird sensation of a spirit coming close as if it was sniffing the air like sensing what is here. She remarked to Irene that she knew when Freeda had a cobra with Hariharinanda. She demonstrated what the sensation felt like by quickly sniffing the air in small intakes of breath. She could not help doing it as he was sniffing the air. Sniffing again, she said it was more like that snake, that cobra that came through, Bill.

I said, "It was a bear", as I had the impression of a bear in my vision. He was sniffing the air. It is a bear. "I could see it," I said.

"Right," Freeda replied. "Thank you, Bill." Freeda continued sniffing, saying, "this is weird" before sniffing again.

I knew that Freeda had Spirit very close to her as I could now sense just how close he really was. I said to Freeda to go with it.

Freeda said very quietly, *"Come now"* before taking a deep breath making a fast sniffing sound through her lips before slowly exhaling in a much slower but similar action. This action repeated three or four times before I welcomed the friend, whom I knew was there. Freeda took a slow deep breath and slowly released it whilst making a moan like the hoot of an owl but without pause, until the breath fully exhaled. This repeated on the next inhale and exhale with the pitch of the note having a wavering quality, both up and down. The guide started to speak, saying:

"You wanted me to talk today. I am here. I am here. I am here. I am here. Oh the strength of me, the strength of me. I am here today when you wanted, oh so much of me. I came today to talk to you. I hope I am explaining and bringing my voice through better. I am aching to learn all about you: also, you are asking so many questions. On your first question, we will explain. It has been long awaited an explanation for this. You have asked at the right time. Yes, we are taking about journeys and journeys and more journeys but it is time now. It is time for you. We are here now to complete it. Suddenly all will change.

"Yes, we have engaged in communication. Now, imagine, imagine we are looking at you. You are oh, a light to us, a light to us. We can see you. Yes, we have been trying to bring the final light in. It has taken time but we are now bringing the final light in. Do you realise that it is time to complete the circle of light. We see you as light, generous, generous, happiness. This is what we want. Generosity and happiness, right? Explaining is hard. It is hard for us but now is the time. People will be coming to the light. You understand now. They are coming to the light. We need them to complete it by coming to the light. That is what we are doing. Bringing people to the light: and when we get people to the light, the circle will be completed."

I thanked him to which he replied, *"Thank you."*

"I understand," I said to him.

Freeda replied in her own voice that she was stepping back.

I immediately knew I had a spirit with me as in a soft voice, speaking quite slowly, he spoke the words, *"Today is a special day".*

Freeda replied, *"Thank you, Master."*

My guide said, "Yes, there is a Master."

"The energies are very close. Many faces. I recognise the faces from the Council."

I was breathing very slowly but quite deeply when Freeda requested, "Come forward, friend, come forward, friend. We welcome you."

He said, *"Thank you. You have a question, Freeda, many questions: many, many questions."*

Freeda said, *"I would like to ask your lady to come through. I would like to bring her through because I feel as though she is already here. Because I am playing with my dress, and feeling the material and feeling the physical. I think she is starting in me then going to step over to you. She is quite anxious at the moment. Quite anxious. There is an urgency. An urgency she said, (yes) and you are feeling the urgency, right? (Yes, I am.) She is worried, worried, so worried about. She wants to get it right with you this time, Bill; she did not get it right with you last time. Right. (Yes.) Now I feel you are very close to her. Maybe on a relationship level, you know. It could be either a husband and wife or a son and mother but very, very close to her or even a sister or her mam. She is very ready to come through and discuss things. She is telling me ask him about. I cannot ask that. Sorry she has asked me to ask you about the day she died. This is what you have been feeling, very emotional and please ask him about the day I died; ask him about that. I feel as though this lady wants to get it out, get out her feelings and she was definitely: unjustly burned at the stake, if you want to put it that way. To me she was just gathering some herbs in the fields before she was taken and she is getting–"*

I interrupted by saying, "Mixed emotions."

Freeda continued, "She knew it was going to happen. She knew they would eventually come for her. She had a lot of good friends. Can you feel her stepping forwards towards you, Bill? Just relax and let it come through."

I replied, *"I feel she had another life. She is making me sad. It is her anniversary on the 18th. Of her last life on the Earth Plane. Her name was Catherine."*

Freeda asked if I could see her other name or not. Come on. Keep breathing.

I continued, *"Oh, so sad; Catherine Raine."*

Freeda said that she was definitely part of your family.

I replied, *"Yes."*

Freeda said, "She looks like you."

"But she is not of me," I replied.

"She looks like you," Freeda repeated. "She had lovely black hair."

I replied, *"No: well. We never saw it black."*

Freeda saw her with lovely black hair (*Yes*). She was beautiful when she was younger, beautiful. Absolutely beautiful and I feel that what she is telling me was a bereavement, a loss that made her very, very, sad. (*Yes. Yes, her brother.*) It made her very, very sad. I know that they say witches have cats but she definitely had a cat because I just want to stroke it here.

I said, *"There was a one at home."*

Freeda asked, "Do you feel as though you deserved to die?"

"No," I replied.

"It was unjust," Freeda stated (*Yes*) "and no matter what you said, it was going to happen. (*I know*). The fear must have been terrific," said Freeda.

I said, *"I see a circle, a hole in the clouds."*

Freeda repeated, "A hole in the clouds. Welcome, friend. Come on. Step through. Let us get past your bereavement. Let us find out about who you really were and the happy times that you had and the people that you helped. You know, I felt that she helped a little girl."

I said, *"Purple, purple."*

Freeda said she could see this little girl.

"Start again," I said.

To which Freeda replied, "Yes I know but I can see the eternity sign going between us as though we had been together before."

Very quietly, I whispered, *"Start again."* They are just telling me to start again. It is out. Freeda said, "Thank you, thank you, friend."

I reached into my pocket for my handkerchief then tried to remove my spectacles, but realised when my hands reached my face, that I had actually taken them off at the beginning of the session.

I remarked, "Stupid," and as I wiped my eyes, all I could see and say was "green, green. Green stars. Right, thank you. Right, I do not know why I am saying thank you for the emotion, but I needed it. It had to come out".

Freeda agreed and said, "Yes, it had to come out, it had to come out. I am actually seeing, you know with Greece there were two pillars of like where the God used to stand, was it Hermes? Two pillars, anyway, well I am seeing that, two pillars in Greece or you know, Greek pillars like as if it was a gateway, a gateway. You know like–"

I interrupted by stating, *"Hercules brought down the pillars."*

"Who did?" Freeda asked.

"Hercules," I replied.

Freeda continued, "Well that has got the pillars right. We have the two pillars, right. To me that is representing strength and somebody who is really, really, strong. Really strong. Because I can see the two pillars and somebody standing there Right, ready to push them, if you want to put it that way. Now I am being taken to a desert, with an oasis in it. That is weird. They are saying we have had a lot of rain but there is going to be a dry spell. It is not a dry spell; it is like a desert. You know we are going to lose the rain and have a lot of dry. It is daft to me but that is what they are saying. Extremities."

I said, "*I can feel the energy building. Two faces go backwards, going backwards. Backwards through the clouds, slowly. I can feel the energy, it builds up but it is not yet with me totally.*"

There were many purple energies about and Freeda could see them between us.

"*I felt them stepping closer,*" I said.

Freeda remarked that it would not be long before I would see and hear them.

"*I can see Spirit,*" I replied. "*A form, very close. A bull elk looking out in the cold. Welcome, friend. Freeda, you have a question?*"

She replied in a tight voice, "Your lady is coming through me."

I replied, "*I have someone with me but I do not know why. They do not want to speak yet. This is strange. I see the eye of an eagle, very close. No, now a face, the face of a woman but it is changing all the time. It is just purple.*"

Freeda said, "*The lady is trying to show herself but it was very hard for me because she keeps smiling, and then she is going away, then she is mentally trying hard to talk to me but it is hard to talk. She is very quiet, very composed. She keeps on fading but she is trying hard to come to you, Bill. She tells me she comes and stands beside you, talks to you. She is very happy she can talk to you. She has been waiting a long time to be able to use someone who could compliment you on your good work. You are amazing. She is so gentle and loving, loving thoughts with you, please take them. She is sweet, she is funny and she is making me laugh because this keeps coming in and going out and she is very wise. Sometimes she is interested in your technology. She finds it very fascinating but I hope that when this comes through you might be able to see me a bit better. Because you know that if you can see me it will make it more possible for you to understand me. Dearest friend you are my. Dearest friend I am here because you want me to be with you. You have journeyed so long on a lonely journey and I am here because I am working on you, with you, and together we will do a lot of work.*"

It was clear at this point that the energy of the guide was very up and down. The dialogue was a mixture of the guide and Freeda telling what the guide was mentally passing to her. This was making it difficult to understand who was actually speaking, the guide or Freeda. The rest of this dialogue I am trying to write as clearly as possible, but I have removed a number of words and repeats that are present on the recordings to try to clarify the thread of the conversation.

Oh goodness, that is not funny. She is bringing her face back in. Do you understand about watching the clock, watching the clock because she is telling me that you watch the clock (Yes) and she watches the clock with you. Because that is good, watching it together. She sits by your side, sometimes on a nighttime she will sit with you. Be patient. It is not your energies that fade. It is mine. It is difficult sometimes to come and help you. Just talking to Freeda about January because January is important to you. You will be starting the year in a better space. (Thank you.) She tells me that and this is a mixture of me and of Freeda. Have you been having problems around your chest area? (Yes.) Because she is giving you special herbs that is good for you, and a nice blanket. A nice blanket will help you as well. Goodness, your knee. What is wrong with your knee, Bill?

I replied no, that it was ok. Then she asked me if it was my lower back please? I replied I always rub my knees.

Ok because she is on about your knees and your chest. Oh, God this is a mixture of me, and her. This is me not her. This is me. Not Freeda. As you would understand, she would gather something not from the grass, but the bushes. Like an infusion.

She was talking to Freeda about the bluebells and the wild garlic: and the woods are absolutely, beautiful, and the bluebells. She always liked that. The trees and the walks through the trees. She had a little path and she loved to walk along the path through the woods and the fields.

It was sheltered and the trees were meeting over the top and it was lovely just walking along there but she used to go to a place where there was bushes and you could get things, it is not blackberries. I do not know. There is a different kind of berry; she used to pick off the hedges, for your chest. She used to make potions like creams, you know, lovely things like that. She was lovely; she would always attract the birds. The birds used to come and be her little friends. Magnificent view from where she was.

She was like on a hill where you could look right away over, right away, over where it was beautiful and she did not deserve to leave that beautiful place.

That was her routine every day walking along this little lane picking whatever she needed: and go back home with this beautiful view: and then it was all gone. She is pleased to come through you and work with you. (Yes, thank you.) *She feels this is why you have been feeling so emotional.*

I said, "She had been on my mind."

She is with you. I do not know whether she was, ducked first with the water: and then burned: because that is, what she is telling me. She is saying, with the bath, you know the water; it brings back memories, and then, burnt. Her hands were in a terrible state. Her hands. That is where it hit her, her hands. More than anything else, she remembers the feeling of her fingers hurting. That was the worst part, her hands seemed as though the pain was extreme in her fingers. She is saying get another blanket luvvie. That is the way she is saying it. Get another blanket luvvie. Get another blanket luvvie.

I interrupted saying, "The energy is really cold."

She continued about the rosehip syrup. That is good. Perhaps that is the bonus, she wants from the bushes. We do not have them now I do not think. (We do I said.) *Why are you getting the healing sensations in your hands? She is telling me that you are getting the feeling of healing because she is working with you.* (Yes, I could feel the energies.) *Yes, you can feel the energies in your hands. That is why she is coming in. She is working with you. You know something, when she steps into you she feels so peaceful, so peaceful.* (I replied that she makes me very peaceful.) *She says she could sit with you and just observe everything. Why she is telling me have you thought of writing a book?*

I gave a little laugh and said, yes, I had started.

She is saying that you have put pen to paper. You know in her time it would have been candlelight, you know that but things have advanced for you, technology. You do not even have to write it on paper now. You can just put it into your computer but sometimes it is nice to write. Would you please look and see if you can find her name in the records because she is showing me a big book with her name in the records. There was an Elizabeth as well, Raine. Around that area, you will find her. You know, Bill, this is daft: you know when we said about the Quakers, she looks like a Quaker. She was not a witchy type person and I feel she had a bonnet on and things like that, but she is lovely. She is lovely. She is knocking on the door for you. She is knocking on the door for you and I do not know if you have heard her knocking but she is trying to open the door. She is sneaking to have a look at you, check you and get that book wrote. Will you please and can it be about her, as she gave a little laugh.

I replied, "It can be."

She was not a witch; she is a very gentle soul who loved everything, the birds, the walks and the beautiful sky. The sunsets, she loved it all. She is walking along and I feel there is a dog following her, freely.

I said, "She has a wave in her hair."

She was beautiful (Yes). *I am going to leave it there and step back, Bill, because I think she wants to step into you. Just relax and sit gently because she is going to sit into you. She is leaving me and she is coming to you.*

I could feel the energy.

Freeda said, *"So Catherine, do you feel more settled now you have settled into Bill? She knew about the Ley Lines and everything else. She knew about the energies* (Yes). *She is talking to me still here. She knew where certain things would grow and certain things would not grow because she could feel the energies and this is what you are feeling."*

I said, "She is showing me the pulsating energies: a bit like a heartbeat, but slower."

Freeda remarked that she was so pleased that she had come today because she has been waiting around to get with you.

I said, "There was so much to arrange."

Freeda remarked, I have gone quite cold, quite cold, and I know it is not cold; it is right around my shoulders. (Yes.) Is there anybody else that who would like to work through Bill? Does Yellow Cloud want to come in? Can we change energies?

I said, "They are around me but I do not know which one would like to step up."

Freeda remarked, "Make up your minds, come on, we have got this time to spend with Bill, thank you. Just go with the flow, Bill: keep the breathing going please: or they will not be able to use your energy?"

I could feel the energy getting closer.

I remarked, "They are showing me flying machines. That is cold."

"Welcome Friend," said Freeda.

I returned, "Welcome, it's ok."

"Welcome Friend," said Freeda. "Let them use your body, Bill, keep your breathing going."

For the last few minutes, it had been impossible to maintain a steady breathing pattern. The cold feelings and occasional shiver were disrupting my breathing and had resulted in sharp intakes of breath as the coldness had washed through my body. After a sharp intake of breath, I said, "I am trying, Freeda. Just walk in, friend. Right, so."

We have a yellowy green, a circle, darker yellowy green. Yellowy green with a light mauve centre. It is slowly moving, anti-clockwise. It is circles within circles, circles within circles. That is a tree. No, it is a man. It is difficult to describe what they show me. I can see, yes, faces of the elders.

Freeda said, "Good, you are being helped, Bill. Welcome friends, they are encouraging you."

I remarked, *"It is quite misty."*

Freeda said, *"Good, let us see what is behind the mist."*

I replied, *"Pale yellow green. Yes, I can see Spirit. It is moving all the time, slowly going round anti-clockwise."*

Freeda said, "So, it is turning back time."

I replied, *"I don't know. The face of a cherub. There is energy moving. It is like looking through a cave mouth. The sides of the cave mouth keep changing. Show me that again, please. No, clearer, clearer that side, clearer that side. Bring it in, in the centre of my vision. Bring it in please. That is an elephant. That is an Indian elephant. It only has small ears and small tusks. A cat, no, then that changes. A small cat, not a big cat. Not a tiger or a lion."*

Freeda asked, "What kind of cat is it?"

I replied, *"A tabby cat with dark eyes, long whiskers, gone."*

Freeda prompted, "You can see a cave."

"Yes," I replied. *"It is in the mist. I want to go to that cave."*

A question from Freeda: "Did you do any ceremonies or did you live there?"

I replied, *"I am looking out. I am looking out, that means I am within. It is high in the mountains. There is mountains below me but not so far below me in the distance."*

Freeda remarked that it must have a wonderful view. I replied, "Yes."

Freeda continued, "Welcome Friend, you are giving us a good description of where you are from."

I continued, *"It is very rugged and there is snow on the peaks. There is no trees: no, there is no trees. A valley down this side."* (From the video, I had gestured right.)

"Was the cave special to you?" Freeda asked.

I replied, *"I live there."*

Good, said Freeda. Many people have lived in caves.

"There is only me," I replied. *"There is some pots left, with food, left for me; but I see no one. I do not see who leaves them, but they know I am here. It is the middle of nowhere here."*

Are you happy, asked Freeda.

"Yes," I replied. *My vision is a bit like a torchlight. When I look, it has a blue halo. It does not make it look any clearer but it is like a torchlight. There is a doorway through the mist.*

Freeda asked if I would like to go through that doorway.

I replied, *"It is a black doorway."* (A black one? Freeda asked) *"No, no, no, I can see it. It is forbidden to go through that door."*

Why is it forbidden? Freeda asked.

I replied, *"No, it is forbidden. No, I must not think about that doorway, no."*

Freeda said encouragingly, "Welcome friend. Keep your breathing going and relax into it. Just keep going, Bill.

I struggled to get my breathing relaxed and steady as I once again was holding my breath then gasped to regain composure. I said, *"It is the head of the elephant again,"* as it came up in my vision. Freeda remarked that I was definitely in India as you have an elephant and a cave. You might have been a hermit up in the Himalayas.

I replied, *"Yes, I feel it."*

Freeda remarked, "Unless it is a different energy coming through, totally different, totally different."

I stated, *"It is difficult to work with. It is much mmm: twisted. It is not level. Things keep going on their sides. I cannot keep it straight."*

Freeda prompted again. You must be high up in the Himalayas if there are no trees. (With a beautiful view, remarked Freeda.)

Back on track I replied, *"No, there are no trees. Snow, rock."*

Freeda remarked, "Definitely solitude needed by this person, or this guide that is coming through. A deep thinker."

I continued, *"It snows. I do not talk to anybody."*

Would you like to talk to us? asked Freeda.

He replied, "I have never talked to anyone in a number of years. I sit here on my own, contemplating."

This is definitely a different guide coming through Bill. He seems like a gentle soul. The energies are very nice around him.

He interrupted, *"Very old, no hair, almost emaciated. Very thin arms, spindly, as are the legs."*

Freeda broke in and asked, "Does he have a name at all, Bill?"

He paused and said, *"I cannot pronounce that, Sha, Sha, Sha, Shari–"* (Sharu? Asked Freeda). He went on, *"Shari."* (Shari? Asked Freeda). *"S.H.A, Sha."* He started again, *"S.H.A.I.R.I."*

Freeda repeated AIRI. That is a different name. Welcome.

After a slight pause, he continued, *"L. L.A.H".* *Welcome friend,* said Freeda.

He remarked, "That is a strange name."

Freeda continued, "Very lovely energies you have brought through, very nice, very–"

He finished Freeda's comment with, *"Peaceful".*

Freeda said, "Peaceful, a wise man, wise man."

He continued: *"Yes. I have a golden white aura.* (A golden white aura, that is lovely.) *It is like a highlight on my body shape, because I can see myself sitting. I am over here.* (He indicated to his right with a hand gesture.) *Perfect peace.* (It is beautiful.) *I can see the clouds that bring the snow."*

Freeda said, "Clouds with the snow, it must be very peaceful. Do you feel the cold?"

He replied, *"On the outside. It is cold, it is very cold on the outside, but I am protected; with my golden shield. Shield, no, not* shield. *It is not a bubble neither.* (Not a bubble.) *It fits like a suit of clothes but it is only one. It surrounds me: there is no gaps. It does not fasten. It is just there: and it envelops me and keeps my inner calm, my inner peace.* (Which is wonderful, Freeda remarked.) *So that I am one with the world.* (You must be, said Freeda, you must be highly evolved.)

"*I need no company. I was only a child, when I came, and the Master brought me.* (Freeda remarked, to become enlightened.) *I have been here since I was six years old. Now I am very old and I have sat here thinking all these years.*"

Freeda remarked that he sounded very, very peaceful.

"*I am,*" he replied.

I think Bill needs this at the moment, suggested Freeda.

I am at one with the Cosmos. I can see the pure white of Spirit. (Excellent). *Very soon, I shall become one with Spirit.*

Freeda remarked, "Wonderful, total peace."

You cannot describe; there is no words, in the languages of Earth that can describe this peace. It is like floating away as the mist disappears with the sun.

You have no form. You are just an energy. There is no.

Freeda interrupted him by saying, "Would you be prepared to work with Bill?"

You have a consciousness: but you are not there, you.

Freeda interrupted him again by asking, "Would you be prepared to work with Bill?"

He replied: *There is nothing much that I could say to him.*"

You have brought in lovely energies of peace, Freeda remarked. It would be lovely if you could bring the energies of peace and stillness in. So nice, isn't it?

"*Transcendental,*" he replied.

How can I explain it? When my time finally comes on this last time on the earth plane, my Spirit will join with the energy of everything. I will not exist in any form.

You are an energy, and a lovely energy, said Freeda.

He continued:

I am but a speck but I am at one with everything and that speck of everything can become everything. It is only a thought away.

Freeda asked him if he would like to leave as he had given this wonderful message to Bill and there was another guide around him, thank you.

He replied, *"My vision is closing. Goodbye friends. One day after transition, you will see me."*

I could tell that Freeda was quite excited. When this happens, she tends to interrupt the guide and can lead them off what they are actually trying to tell us. At the same time, Irene, who has extensively studied Yoga and the associated religion, was also very excited as she was furiously writing things down, rustling the papers; and trying to show Freeda what she had written. This had been going on for the last few minutes and I have left out a number of comments to help with the flow of the words from this Guide. As it was close to the recorder, it did make it difficult to follow all the conversation. When he restarted, it was clear that all the commotion with questions and noises had disturbed the flow somewhat.

He said, *"I can see purple. No, nothing in it, just purple. No shadows, nothing. There is a light. There was a light. Yes, it is back again. It has gone again. It is like a beacon, winking in the dark: oh brilliant, brilliant blue, iridescent blue. An iridescent blue that sparkles: on a coat. On a coat that buttons down the front. Spreads out a little. There is a white head covering, a turban with a spray on the top. Fine gold threads like a fan and a red jewel in the centre, with a gold pin. Clean-shaven: not clean-shaven, no hair; no hair. No hair. There is a tree in the background, very big tree. It is much wider than me. There is no branches, until you get to the top and it spreads outwards with elongated, rounded leaves. It is a strange tree to me. I have seen them before but Bill has not seen these, not in real*

*life. When he was in, in India, he was not in the right place to see
these trees. It is said that this is the tree that Buddha sat beneath.
There is a hole in the mountains but this is where I need to be.*

*"It is written and so I have contemplated my life from a child to
now. I have had many visions. I have been in many places. I have
been shown many things. My time is almost done: and yes, I must
go now. Oh no, I cannot stay any longer."*

Freeda said, "Your energies might be fading, or Bill's energies
might be fading now. You have had a lovely, relaxing Spirit side
come through today, Bill. That lady was very, very peaceful and
this man has been very, very strong and meditated lovely, and we
even have his name, lovely. I would just like to say thank you to
your friend for coming through. I do not know if Bill would like
you to come again but I think you have a lot to say to Bill. Thank
you friend."

With a long sigh, he started to speak once more.

*There may not: probably not: any more time for me. I cannot
foretell the future but I do not think that I am here for Bill. I needed
to come to give him peace, but the message: no not the message: the
demonstration, no, not the demonstration. There is a word. Yes, the
evidence is for Irene. God bless you, my child."*

Very quietly, Irene addressed him: "Shairi-Lah; do you feel
that you came to give Bill peace *("Yes")* and evidence for me?
("Yes"). Thank you Shairi-Lah. *("You are welcome child")* I would
like you to come again however, maybe, it is not meant to be."

He spoke once more.

*You have all that you need, child. There are other Spirits with
you, Irene, but sometimes you do not listen hard enough.*

Irene said that maybe she did not have the capacity.

*Yes, you have, child. You have everything that you need: but
like Freeda, you get too excited. You get an inner, like the bubbling
of the hot springs inside you. You bubble up, you get excited and*

then you do not listen with your ears. You hear through your ears but you cannot hear Spirit, because it is here, child.

He placed his hand just below the top back of his head and the nape of his neck: the occipital, tapping it slowly.

Spirit is here and sometimes, which is not really your fault, because you are human, and humans have traits. You were given these traits because you are human and this is the quest: is to put aside human traits to become one with Spirit and cosmic energies. Then you will find true peace. Like I have shown Bill, but Bill suffers sometimes because he has deep feelings: which makes him, not sad but, his eyes water. He has a great sadness because he has been through so much in other lives. We must try, with other guides, to take his sadness away.

Both Irene, Freeda and the Guide tried to talk at the same time.

Freeda sad that she thought he had helped Bill today.

Yes, chimed in Irene. Irene won and said, "We have got so much from this. Shairi-Lah I think, I feel so blessed that you have come through Bill today, very blessed. That my eyes may water."

Freeda jumped in with "She is ready to cry".

The guide replied, *"It is human and you must have these, child, but it is fine tuning of the energies. The energies that we tuned so that you can feel: yet not so intensely. Bill has been given a lot of energy. Perhaps we have given him too much, too quickly."*

Irene and Freeda both agreed and thought perhaps that the energies that had come today were to slow him down. The guide continued.

We must keep pressure on so he can be where we would like him to be. Also we must show Freeda different things that she has never experienced so that you can all work together and move not as one, but as a group yet move as each, as an individual: but the co-operation of the three is required: and the three is the middle number of creation.

Freeda remarked to him that he had made Irene very happy today. He said once again that he must go now.

As Freeda continued to speak, he repeated, *"I must, I must go now. Goodbye friends. We have joined the circle. Wheels within wheels. Circles within circles and lives within lives."*

Thank you, thank you, Freeda remarked. I think that Bill is coming back now. Thank you, Bill, for allowing this guide to use your body to come through. Thank you so much. Are you back now, Bill, are you back? Open your eyes for me. Bring yourself back into the room. Just take your time. Take your time. It has been a very powerful energy that has come through. You will not remember much of it but you have done a marvellous job for Irene today. She had a few tears; and still feels quite tearful.

Irene said, "Well not too bad really. It was just the emotion of it. Yes, Shairi-Lah I think is a Yogi. When he said his time was almost up, I did not know whether his time in this lifetime was nearly up or his time to come to this planet was over. I am not sure."

I asked what, what is she talking about?

Irene replied that she was just talking to Freeda about Shairi-Lah.

"Who?" I asked.

Shairi-Lah was the reply

"Who is he?" I asked.

Irene thought I had been channelling.

At this, Freeda started to laugh.

I said, "Sorry, Irene, have I missed something?"

They were both so intense in their discussions about the guide that they had forgotten about me and we had not closed our session down! We closed down properly and told Spirit we were so amazed that they could plan everything and put it all into place at the right time. Freeda remarked to me. Bill, I have to say that

I have a weird thing. I have a ball of energy off him and it is like, someone is yanking my arm. It is so like a magnetic pull. I can feel it. It is ok. It is just that I can feel it. We said they were marvellous with their planning again.

Freeda thought that it had been very intense today for us.

I said it was just like stepping through an extremely thin curtain of light, the Veil of Forgetfulness.

It was now that we found out that the video battery had gone flat some time ago. I had charged the battery that very morning. Thankfully, the tape was still recording.

It is a wonder to me how the guides that come to us in these sessions always seem to be pre-planned. It appears that Spirit knows better than we do about what is in our thoughts. When we have questions that have developed over the week between each session, they have an uncanny knack of bringing in specific guides to address the problems or questions we want answering.

The video always seem to show large dips or increases in the ambient light from time to time. Whilst I can appreciate that ambient light does change with the sun and the clouds interacting, the room we use has only east and west facing windows. The camera is set in auto for both light and focus. Changes should be minimal but they are not. It is not only the light that changes but also the focus. I have tested the camera repeatedly by sitting in front of it as we usually do and it never changes: only when we have our sessions. There are some things that happen, that defy explanation. Thank you, Spirit.

My thoughts on this chapter reinforce my belief in some type of reincarnation. The previous chapter has an ending of a conversation with a Spirit that appears to be able to come to us in two different guises.

Two lives, 423 years apart (in 2019), yet somehow linked to me in both lives. This belief is described in two books. These books:

"Journey of Souls" and the "Destiny of Souls" appear reinforced by our session evidence given by the guides that come to us. We are only scratching the surface of what lies beyond.

Chapter Ten
– Reunion. A lesson and Shairi-Lah returns

Almost half way through November 2019, the Fourteenth to be exact, found us once again at Irene Harthill's for our eighth session with Spirit. Our preliminary chat had raised our senses and we were feeling quite happy. This continued as we took our customary places at the table. With a laugh from Freeda, she thought it was just like school as I asked her, "What does the teacher say?" Settle down now, that will take a lot of doing, was the reply. With the video checked and aligned, we commenced. Freeda wondered what we would get today and I replied I did not know. We recited the Lord's Prayer then, one strike at the brass bowl with the nerve jangling tone and slowly pulsing sound as the ringing subsided.

Freeda as usual, started the proceedings with a few words. She felt that there was a lot of energy in the room with us today. She welcomed our friends as she said she could see them already. She asked me if I could see them to which I replied that I could see purple. Freeda could see them queueing up down my right hand side. There is a good crowd in today she remarked. She said you know what they are singing when she broke into song: Come and join us: come and join us, humming the rest of the first few bars of the song. We are lifting up the energies she stated. We lapsed into silence as we prepared to welcome the first energy.

Freeda said she had a name, Marion Johnson. She did not know who she was. I felt the tide of spirit coming in as cold energy was creeping over my feet and lower legs. Marion Johnson, related to Ann Johnson were Freeda's next words. I will leave that and see what this is. Marion Johnson related to Ann Johnson. Freeda was hearing a noise from the fan on the fire and asked Irene to switch it off, which she did, as it was a distraction to Freeda.

I remarked that my toes were like blocks of ice. Freeda said even if I wanted to move, I could not move now. I said my toes were starting to curl up as Freeda remarked her right foot was lifting. The cold was affecting my breathing pattern as the sense of coldness lifted and lowered, making me shiver. Freeda said, "Just go with it, Bill." She remarked that her right foot had lifted, but not her left foot. It was still stuck to the earth but her right foot was away. I said that I had the impression of me scratching the sand with my toes curled up. It was a strange sensation. I said that I felt many energies flying about. Freeda said her left foot was now elevated.

I voiced, "It is like the cold water of a mountain stream."

Freeda said, "Welcome friends." The energy was now swirling round my knees. It was affecting my attempts at a steady, rhythmic pattern of breathing by interrupting my in-breath to holding my breath, then releasing after a few seconds into a slow exhalation.

Freeda remarked that her fingers were starting to grow. (Which happened quite often as I have observed in her trance demonstrations.) I remarked that I thought Guy was here, one of Freeda's guides. I remarked, "He said we could call him Guy. He is a hard worker."

From the video, Freeda had raised her hand in an open ball shape as she remarked that she just wanted to hand out so much energy into this room. "Oh dear," Freeda said as I remarked, "welcome friend". At this point Freeda's hand had enlarged to tighten her rings around her fingers. She was feeling pained by this event and thought she would have to remove them telling Irene in a whisper of what she planned to do.

The video shows Irene approach Freeda and without touching her, hold her hands close and open to try to reduce the swelling and allow Freeda to remove her rings. After a short while, this appeared to work and the rings removed by Freeda herself, but with some difficulty. It took almost five minutes to complete.

After a few seconds longer, it became apparent that Freeda had a guide with her. His voice in a singsong tone repeating: "Come. Come. Come. (Pause) Come. Come. Come." Then a lilting tune with unintelligible words: then a reasonably steady note with a slight lilt, three times, sounding quite eerie to me.

He continued, *Oh Dear. Can I say, today it is my day to talk again with you. You wanted me, and my friends to come: and we are here. So we would like to welcome you today. You are my friend. Honestly, you are so helpful with us. We want to work with you liking what you are doing. It is right. It is good: it is time to work properly.*

Bill there is working very nicely. At times, he forgets what to do but we help him. He is a very mature student. He understands a lot but sometimes he is difficult because we know him and we will: and he answers a lot of questions but sometimes he is many miles away. His thoughts are not always in tune with us. He needs to be, say: Fine-tuned.

This will do. Today, honestly, he is my friend with knowledge. We work on him to give out the knowledge that we want him to give. You help him. We help him. Why do you not take ordinary photographs? That would be good. Sometimes we need to do a freeze frame rather than this erm, camera. It is good to see us just standing still. You know, sometimes a photograph is better. Bill is better sometime: to be frank, (laughing) rejection, he gives us rejection but we are trying to work with him and stop this rejection. He makes me laugh as we give him things and he goes no, I do not want that. Well, I am sorry: you are going to take what we give you. Right. Maybe, maybe want you to work with the other side of your brain. Right, ok?

Yes, thank you.

Why is it you always get yourself into trouble? He said laughing. You making me laugh you getting yourself into trouble. You give yourself too much trouble.

I said I do not know why, but I do. I am sorry.

He immediately replied, "*But you do. If you get rid of the trouble, we will help you more.*" *He continued laughing as he said,* "*It is good today.*"

Bill, there is a man here called Joe, Joe. Do you know Joe?

"Yes I do," I replied.

He is here saying, "*Tell him. Tell him, ok, that many people are waiting to talk through you.*" *Right, ok.*

Yes. Thank you.

Many. You will say some things you do not understand but you will start with A, then you learn B, then you learn C: so much to learn, like going to school again. Right, ok. Chuckling again as he said, "*So if you do not understand the words we cannot give you them.*" *He continued, I know and heard you talking about the black door. The black door, you have never knocked on it yet, right.*

This took me by surprise, as the black door was a vision from the previous week. I replied, "No, it was forbidden."

No, No not always forbidden, not, not always forbidden. Because you are curious, about what is on the other side.

As I replied, "yes, but" with a small chuckle, he also chuckled.

Saying, But yes, you know what we have said, yes it is, forbidden, for now.

As I replied, "Yes, I know", he countered me with, *"You are curious"*. I replied *"Yes", I understood that*. Again, he remarked, *"But you are curious. The sky is your limits. You can go where you want to go right, ok. Be like a child, learning the, a: b: c's: of it all. Rewrite your script right. Make it a blank page and work with, as a child learning from the beginning. It is a blank page with a long journey.*

They are showing me, I first thought it was an eraser, but it is a rub out, a rub out ok.

They are showing me some things you have to rub out and start again. Scrub the paper, take it, take it and start again, right, because you are writing a book, yes. You scrub the papers and write it again, Correct?

I answered, "Yes, I will start again."

Well we are helping you with the, a: b: c's, right. Ok.

They say you are doing very well with this book.

You must be quite a way on. (Yes, well.)

You are. You are. You are doing good, doing good. Why do you not get your eyesight checked?

I replied that it was due in April.

They are saying perhaps before now, perhaps before now, right, ok, right.

I said, "Well, ok: but is it eyesight so that I can see them or eyesight so I can see on the earth plane?" Laughing as I said it.

Yes. It is eyesight so that you can see them, right, ok. Right.

I replied, "Yes. Ok, I need to concentrate more. That is a C. If that is concentration: that is a C."

He replied, *"Yes it is"*, whereupon I reminded him that I must start at A, in the beginning.

Bill, do your hands hurt you?

Odd occasions, pins and needles.

Yes, they are showing me your hands hurt. Right, I am going to go back into myself, Freeda, right. Who is Jen, Jen? Do you understand somebody called Jen?

I replied, "Yes, I do."

Who is Jen, Bill please?

My cousin, I replied.

Because they are talking about Jen. Has there been worry around Jen?

I replied, "I went to see her. *(Good boy)* Because, because I felt that she came and asked me to visit her so I did."

"*Ok, good boy*" was the reply from Freeda.

"I was given it in a sequence of pictures," I replied.

Freeda interjected, "*Good, good.*"

"But she has more: She had a very bad stroke and does not move, or see, or speak. *(Sorry, sorry.)*

Well perhaps she does see but we are not aware that she can see us. I felt a small grip of my hand when I held hers and I felt that she knew who I was and that I was there, *(Brilliant, brilliant),* but I could not communicate with her using thought or, or bring, or bring her through like she came before.

Freeda said, "*Bill, I have a terrible pain in my chest here. It is not indigestion. It is something to do with. Was there a gentleman who passed with a heart attack or something because it is a really, really, bad chest. I have it on me. I do not know what it is, but honestly, this is not indigestion. I know this is not indigestion. It is not from.*"

I interrupted saying that I could not think of anybody off the top of my head.

I am going to ask them to lift it because it is quite painful.

Not a gentleman anyway, a woman, yes, I offered.

Right, perhaps it is a woman but it is quite painful. Right, if I get this it will leave me. Ah, God, I am just going to have to breathe through it. This woman, she was not married twice was she or had, widowed and met somebody else, or something like that: you understand that, Bill? (No). I am trying to get what she is telling me. Did she have a son please?

I replied I do not know who it is, Freeda.

Well, this Lady is coming through. Do you understand of a Margaret? Margaret. Sorry she is not coming through but the pain is terrible off her. This is not off me.

I commented, "It is now my left eye instead of my right eye watering now so we are working with the other side now."

Freeda replied. *That happened quick, didn't it.*

I replied, "It did. That come all of a sudden, that one and I do not know why."

Freeda said that she was going back into breathing to try to get this lifted off me. (Referring to the pain.) It is right up into my throat.

I commented, "Well, if it is right up into your throat it is a man."

Freeda said, *Ok, thank you.*

I remarked, "And I know who it is. I know where you are at."

Freeda said, *do you understand about two relationships with this man then, please, or a son? Do you understand of a son please?*

"Yes, that is me," I replied.

Freeda said, *so it is your Dad.* (Yes.) *Oh dear, mind he did not half have a lot of pain. Because it is on me, oh, goodness me and oh, it is right in my throat and up to me ears and everything. He is on about money. I do not know that he did not have a lot of money, can you understand that, Bill please?*

Yes I do I replied.

He always wished the best for you. He was lovely, mind, wasn't he, nice man.

Yes, he was a nice man I replied.

Very smart right. Smartly dressed, right, ok. I wish he would lift it off me. It is hurting.

If I tell you how he died will it lift, I asked.

How did he die, Bill?

He choked to death I said.

Thank you, right. Well I will tell you: I have to explain this to you, right. It is right up into my neck, but you know like when you get something stuck right up into your stomach: it is like that, you cannot swallow it. It makes it like bad indigestion. That is how he felt, right ok. It felt as though it was his throat then ah, stuck right in his back and he could not move it if you want to put it that way. It was very, very painful right, and he wanted the best for you, right. Ok. Sometimes he comes through to you but you cannot hear him properly. Well, he is. Oh God, he is sitting here very strong with you, Bill, mind, right, ok. Now he is telling me of a man who lost part of his finger or something, do you understand: or part of a finger or a limb? Do you understand that at all, Bill?

I replied, "No, I do not quite understand that."

Well he is showing me a finger missing and something to do: did he have a brother please?

(Yes). *Right, something to do with his brother.*

I replied, yes, his brother had what you call a bett finger *(Ah, right. Thank you)* so it looked as if it was missing, but it was not.

Right thank you. He is with his brother.

He is the one I owe the fiver to, I remarked. We both laughed as Freeda said that is why he is saying about the money again you understand.

I said yes. I understand. I know who it is.

Freeda said, yes. They understand but he: your Dad: that is why he wanted the best for you and his life should have been longer and sometimes you missed him a lot and you wanted him to be there with you, right. Can you understand about doing a dog kennel, or a shed or something?

Yes, I replied. We put a shed up.

You know that man used to work very hard and when he got into his bed, he appreciated bed. He just wanted to get into that nice bed and go to sleep but then he had to get up and graft the next day, right. Grafting was his life. He was always out to make a bob or two ok: but for his family. Oh, I wished he would lift it. It is right on me. He is keep going to his throat you know and then I to tell you and he is repeating, he said the worst part about it was not so much his throat because it went right up into his jaw and into his ear. It is his stomach where it got stuck.

Like it felt as though something was stuck there, right, ok: and it was like bad indigestion. Well I am trying to lift it off us. Oh, he is lifting it. I am starting to get it lifted a bit and oh, do not do that. He is going up through my jaw and out through my ears, ow.

Sometimes did he have a little bit of a beard on?

Only when he did not shave, I replied.

He is rubbing his face at the moment. Right ok.

I remarked, he used to do that.

Well he is rubbing his face and he is saying you are his hero. All he taught you: has worked out for you and are you still polishing those shoes?

I laughed as I said that I still do.

Freeda said, "He is a bit of a taskmaster isn't he? I do not mean in a nasty way, but he always kept you cracking. He always had something for you to do. You never got time, you know when he was there it was always busy."

I remarked that he always appreciated it.

Freeda continued. *Why is he bringing you a lovely big cabbage? Did he do his garden? Well he must eat cabbage because he is bringing you a big cabbage here, right. He is still rubbing his face and he is still very much with us, right. What was this about rope? He is showing me a rope. Did you, I do not know why. Did you tow or something, or did a rope or something?*

I replied, yes, we towed.

Right, ok, because he said about towing, but it had to be a really, strong rope. He is on about the Wednesday, what day did he pass, Bill? I know it was a long time ago. Mind I have to say it was not very nice to see him after he passed, mind.

I replied that I did not see him because it was better not to.

It was good that you did not because it was awful, awful. All of his mouth was down to one side, not nice but anyway after that: have you been looking at his picture, been looking at his photograph?

I had as I have a photograph hanging up on the wall.

He is a handsome man, isn't he? He was handsome, mind. He had the bonniest eyes on him, bonniest eyes you know how you see the old-fashioned pictures and it seems like the eyes stand out, you know. His did. You know, like Charlie Chaplin when the eyes stand out, your Dad's eyes are like that. Did he ever go to the war? (Yes. He was in India and Palestine.) *He is saying it was no good to anybody. No good to anybody you know. He lost some good friends, one close friend he lost, right,* (He did, very close. I know who he is talking about) *and he is still rubbing his chin, right, and he is still rubbing his chin as he is talking, right. By, the pain, it was bad: it was bad that pain, Bill. I will tell you he was a strong man. His fists you know, he had big hands on him.* (He did for his size.) *Yes, he was a strong man, right.*

I remarked, "My right ear knows all about it (laughing) yes but he did, very rarely hit me. *Well I will tell you: you know how they had the belt outside the trousers, well he is showing me his belt outside the trousers,* (going to work) *but he was ready to go then. Always had a bite to eat before he went and I will tell you what, he loved your mam. There was always a kiss before he went, right, that was the right way to do it. He is on about a little black and white dog. Do you understand about the little black and white dog?* (Before my time.) *There is a little black and white dog though. I do not know whether it was a little collie or like a cocker spaniel but it was black and white.* (Asta was the name of the dog*). and There was a dog with a human name like, you know when you get a dog with a human name, like Ben or Sam or like well. There was a dog with a human name and who is Billy?* I said me.

At this comment, Freeda started laughing. "That is so funny" as she laughed and laughed again. He is saying Billy. Did not call you Bill, did he? (No.) *He called you Billy.* (Yes.)

This is making me laugh, she said, still laughing. Oh, he is still here mind, Bill. Freeda was still laughing.

He liked his jam and bread. Bit blackcurrant jam and a nice fresh crust. Right, ok. He is so much with you, Bill. Oh, he is saying to me, not Bill, Billy. He is so much with you, Billy, ok.

He is proud of your family and he wants to, err, I do not think he is going to go yet because the pain is not lifting yet, but he is saying he wants to go with you today. He will walk out of here proudly with you today and he has waited a long time to come and see you, properly, right. He is with you here, today.

I replied, "He has. Thank you."

Corned beef pie. A big corned beef pie and mushy peas. He could eat the mushy peas on their own. (He could, yes.) *Make a feast out of that and can you remember when your bed broke, your bed broke. He is saying that bed with the headboard broke or something.* (Headboard I think.) *Well he is just laughing about it, ok.*

He is hurting me like. He is saying you did not half miss him the first Christmas. It was such an empty space, right, but he was there with you, right.

I had missed both my parents that first Christmas because they had passed within eight weeks of each other, Mam passing first. Her birthday was on Christmas Day.

Did your mam have big boobs on her? Freeda asked, with a laugh. Excuse me, she remarked.

For her size, I replied.

Well he says, to him she was a voluptuous lady and he loved her. They used to laugh together, didn't they and it used to make you laugh as well, right. I will tell you what else he is saying: you hated them short trousers, hated them, right. It was not for boys, short trousers and you must have done what I did; go down on skates on a book. Yes, he is saying going down on a skate with a book and your dad used to be off to work with his belt round his trousers there and away off, happy times. A big pan of broth on the go there, lovely, lovely cosy home there.

*Well if you ever want to talk to him, go to the house right: go
to your old home and he will be waiting there for you right. There
was an old chair, that, he used to sit in. It was not posh, but by God,
it was comfortable. Do you understand that please? (Yes.) That is
where he is sitting, ok. I am going to ask him to step back, Bill and
we are going to see who you are going to bring through today. I
might get something in between. Your dad has dominated this. Ok
are you happy with it?*

I replied, "Yes I am, very happy with it. Thank you very much."

*We will say bye to him. He is on about Tommy, Tommy. Do you
know a Tommy or Tom?*

I replied, "Well yes, I know three."

In fact, I knew four, plus a great cousin from Durham, killed in
the Second World War. This man, Lance Corporal Thomas Barker,
is a little story about what a Spirit and an extremely receptive
Medium can do.

One Sunday evening at divine service, around Remembrance
Day 2019, we had a Medium/demonstrator, named John Clarke
as our guest. Near the end of the demonstration, he came to me
and asked if I knew someone who had been shot. I said yes, I did.
In fact, I was looking through old family photographs and had
found a Christmas card from him, to my parents, which I posted
on the Family website.

He then asked me to explain what I knew of the death, as it was a
known story in the family. The story goes that he was washing in
a stream at Monte Cassino when a sniper's head shot killed him
instantly. The Durham Light Infantry did play a large part in the
battle and incurred heavy losses.

He had been interred at Monte Cassino War Cemetery.

John informed me that I was to do some research. He said that he
had Tom with him and he was shot twice in the upper left body,

the first killing him instantly. He had died with his best friend in his troop, the only ones of his regiment killed that day. He was not in the DLI.

He was interred twice in the same cemetery. It was not Monte Cassino.

He (Tom) was just there that evening to say thank you for remembering him.

To say I was amazed is an understatement. I duly did the research and I eventually found the following information.

Lance Corporal Thomas Alec Barker Number 4452691, was killed during the fighting on the 10th September 1944, aged just 21. He was not buried at Monte Cassino War Cemetery.

He and his pal were the only two killed that day serving with the Sixth Lincolnshire Regiment, not the D.L.I.

He was buried: twice, in the same cemetery. Plot 7-D-11 and then re-interred in 18-J-7. Both men fallen together, side by side and laid to rest, side by side: twice. Together always in life and death, with his pal, Private H. C. Gislam at Monte Cassiano Ridge War Cemetery. God bless them for their sacrifice.

Freeda continued. Well, he is on about those. Do you know a man called Jones or Johnson?

Johnson, I replied.

Well, he is on about Johnson and Brown. (Next-door neighbour.) *Do you understand about a door number eight or a ten? What was your door number, Bill? Was it eighteen, no?*

I racked my brain and I thought it was eight. (Our Shadforth address was eight, Church Villas, just after I was born.)

Well, he is on about the door anyway. I will tell you what, there was you born and there was another baby born quite quickly or vice-versa; wasn't there. There was a baby ahead and then you were born. There was two babies born quite quickly together anyway. Do you understand that, Billy? Not for us, I replied. *Right then now where is he? Is it within the family, has there been two babies being born quite quickly?*

I commented, "You are asking something now, Dad."

Well he is just saying that there was a baby born then another baby born.

I said, "Well yes, in the extended family there was, yes."

Ok, thank you. Right: and Ronnie. Who was Ronnie: Ronnie, Ronnie or Robert?

Ronnie, I replied.

Right, Ronnie. I am rubbing my chest because I want it to go, but it is still Ronnie: and did you know somebody called Dixon? (Yes.) *Mind he is talking about a lot, mind, isn't he. Ok.*

I replied, "It did not matter where we went, we always bumped into someone he knew.

Was there not, what is he on about the pulley man, pulley, pulley man?

I commented, "That was Tom (Great Uncle). That identifies which Tom it is."

Right, ok. The pulley man.

I said, "Yes, he was rubbish at it as well."

Great Uncle Tom operated the colliery winders. He was a bit heavy on the brakes on the man-riding shaft. This heaviness on the brakes allowed the cage to "bounce" at each stop level. This was very disconcerting to the miners in the cage and often cursed by them. He was well over six feet in height and a nice quiet, kind man.

Who had the old car? It was an old car, old car.

We did.

Ok, but it was a good one. A good one. He used to talk to it. (Yes we did.) *Come on. Let's get cracking here. Howay, let's get cracking, right.*

Who is the man that had only one eye, or problem with one eye? You know I do not know whether he had lost and eye or whether it was a lazy eye, but he had a funny eye.

Laughingly, I said, "Me", at which point Freeda burst out laughing herself. I had never noticed it she remarked.

I replied, "No, you do not notice it now."

But you did.

"Yes, you would have when I was little," I said.

Yes, because there is that: and was your mam good at knitting?

Oh, yes, tremendous, I replied.

Because you got some lovely jumpers off her, right. Much appreciated. I can see, like a grey one, a grey one and she knit that one for you. (Yes.) He is giving me lovely times here and I can see this dog with a slipper in its mouth, right. The dog had a slipper in its mouth. It used to run around with this slipper in its mouth, right. This is daft you know. Where you lived, did you have, like a rabbit hutch in the back yard? Am I at a different place now? There is like a hutch in the back yard. I do not know whether it was for dogs, like greyhounds. (No.) Well, somewhere he is showing me. Right, ok. I can see allotments, but you walk up the path and there are quite high fences. Do you understand he used to have an allotment where you would walk up a narrow path, Bill? Because he is showing me a narrow path and there are allotments.

Do you understand where he is? (Yes. I thought so. I think I do.) He has a barrow here and he is pushing it. Freeda laughed.

I said I knew where he was at then. I know which allotments it was.

With the barrow?

"Yes," I replied. "It was not his."

Well you understand where he is.

We were both laughing!

Well, Bill, I am going to ask him to step back because he wants to talk to you all day, right, ok. He said roast potatoes, lovely roast potatoes. He had a thing about potatoes. Lovely new potatoes you know, nice taste, lovely. He liked roast potatoes, He liked new potatoes, He liked potatoes and turnip mashed up. He liked his potatoes. By God he could eat, could he not.

I replied, "Yes, he could put some stuff away."

Yes, he could, and you know something, he never put on an ounce. (No, he did not.) Never an ounce and it annoys Billy he says. It annoys Billy, laughing. You know it annoyed our Billy.

I replied with a laugh. "It does now."

He said, I did not think that he was going to grow into big lad; like you are but you take after your grandad. (I never knew my grandad.) *Well you take after him, your grandad. You take after him, a big lad your grandad. Big lad right. A big strong lad. What he is saying is; and it is nice of your dad; he is saying that the biggest thing you have is your heart. You have a good heart on you Billy.* (Yes, thank you.) *He is talking away here. One of the reasons why you wanted to do this work was to get your dad to come through, right:* (Yes) *and he has come through lovely for you, today. He says it is time you know. It is time for you to have things, to appreciate things. Right, ok. You were really good at maths, weren't you?*

With a laugh, I replied, "Is he not laughing?" Freeda said yes, he is laughing, as we all were.

Freeda remarked, "He is rubbing his face again. He is back again here, back again having a good time today." Higher maths was not my favourite subject I must admit.

He liked a bit mustard on ham. (Yes, he did.) *Laughing again, as he said more mustard than ham. Ha-ha, can you remember that, Billy? Lovely sandwiches, more mustard than ham on* (I take after him), *and a nice cup of tea with two sugars: he liked a strong brew.* (Yes, he did.)

Who is Robbie or Robert? I replied, "Son, or my son, or his brother." *You understand where we are on, right. He says our*

Robbie used to come around but there was a big fallout in the family, wasn't there. There was a fallout in the family he is telling me. I do not know if it was before your time but there was a fallout in the family. I can see this paper and it has green leaves on it, you know like, it was quite detailed paper with green leaves on it and white. A nice paper and he is on about this paper, right. (Wallpaper.) *I will just leave it, like green leaves or something but it was nice though.* (Yes, it was nice. I could picture it.)

What is he on about Easington Village? Did he have a connection with Easington Village?

I replied, "He did used to go to Easington Village."

He is on about that. I have your, this guide, who came through last week with me, see what we get here. He is showing me, you know when you really: you know when you see the pictures of the Chinese paintings on the teacups, willow pattern; well Shairi-Lah is showing a house like that but on stilts. You know when they had them lifted up like that and that is where he started his life, before he went on the journey. He used to love to sit and watch the sunsets and you do, you do. (Yes, I do.) *He is working with you a lot and since you come last week, you have gotten a lot of peace.* (Yes, I have.) *A lot of peace. He said you will, you know how we have done the bell today; you will hear a bell when he is coming, as though to make an entrance for him. He is making me laugh as he is walking, he is lifting; you know that Buddhists would have a long gown on. He is lifting his up to walk and he has sandals on and he has something wrapped round his shoulders.*

I feel as though he is carrying a bag of stuff on his back as he is going on his journey. You know like, Dick Wittington, and he had his little bag on the top, on a stick, he is away with that. He is away to the top of the hills, to the mountains. He is telling me he met somebody on the way, a Master, who helped him. The Master was sitting and he talked to the Master, then he went further up. I feel as though: I feel as though this Master; I am going freezing cold: this master was from Spirit to teach him on his journey. Every step he made up that mountain there was a different Master and he actually had eight in all, eight Masters on his journey until he reached enlightenment. It was eight Masters before reaching enlightenment. He is pushing you and rounding you up to go on the journey. He has wanted to do this for a long time with you. He says; oh, that is a bit naughty: forget your other Masters. Forget your other Masters and he will work with you. He has given you his name. He has given you details of who he is and he says you will be famous. You will be famous, He means famous with yourself. You will be happy with yourself. You will be famous with yourself. You will feel as though you have achieved things.

This man sits with his finger like that. (The video shows the forefinger up to the lips.) When you see this film, you will understand he sits like that while he is thinking. You can put pen to paper about him because if you do not, you will forget it. The colours that we were talking about before we started: was meant: for you. The top one will be your gold. It will be your gold. Yes, it will be gold: the highest achievement you can get.

We will settle now and I will let you, see if he is going to give you anything else.

I said, "It is very cold." Freeda replied. "It is freezing, right round your legs and up to your tummy. Your dad is gone because my pain has gone, thank you. He is still here. Who is Edward? Your Dad is on about Edward (Edward is in the extended family), you will find out about Edward anyway and John. He is just going so I will leave it."

I replied, "Ok, thank you."

Freeda remarked, "It is so cold, the air around us. It is so cold."

I did remark, "Yes, making sure." This remark is on the sound recording but there does not appear to be any connection to Dad or Freeda. Freeda then asked Irene not to forget to ask us to step back as she felt that we were going to go very deep today, more so Bill than me. We sat quietly for a few minutes.

I suddenly quivered and knew there was someone very close to me. Freeda echoed my "Welcome, friend" remark.

I said; *"I am finding it difficult. Why? You are welcome to step into me."* Another quiver went through my body. I kept holding my breath for a few seconds as the feeling of abject coldness came and went.

Freeda said, "Welcome friend. Welcome friends. Come on." Another involuntary shiver shook me again. "Take your time," Freeda remarked. It felt as if the energy was trying to blend with me or trying to speak as I was taking a breath; but instead of speaking, I was holding it for a few seconds before exhaling. After a few more breaths, I said to them, *"I am trying to let you in. Why are you struggling? It should be easy."* Once again, breathe in, held, and then exhaled.

Freeda remarked, "Welcome friend. There is some lovely purple about, lovely purple colours."

I was struggling with my breathing. Interrupted time, and time again from a steady breathing pattern, it was like small electric shocks hitting my body as Freeda remarked, "Take your time." I replied, *"I don't: I don't. I don't think he wants to channel."* Freeda remarked, "Fair enough, fair enough."

Another couple of interrupted breathing cycles then I said, *"Right. Good afternoon, friends. Is that what you wanted, just to talk, right?"* I sensed an affirmative answer. *"Ok. Yes, thank you. A very peaceful gentleman,"* I remarked.

Freeda said, "Welcome, friend. Perhaps a little bit shy. Come forward."

I replied, *"He has let me breathe, he is welcome. Welcome to channel."* One more breathing cycle, then, back to square one. More of the involuntary jumps: like small electric shocks that catch your breath and interrupt your mental state. Then, quiescence once more. *"Yes."* Just as Freeda said, "Your lady is here, Bill. Witch, she is here. I don't like saying that."

I remarked, *"The energy is changing. It is so icy, icy cold".* I took a deep, deep breath as I tried to take her energy within me. I realised there was more than one energy as I said, "You cannot fight, one at a time please."

In a strained voice, Freeda remarked, "Your lady is still very strong": a pause: "She has stepped back now. Bill, I think she is going to come to you." My breathing was normal when a quiet musical voice came out of me saying, *"Hello. Hello. Can you hear me?"* Freeda welcomed the friend. It went on, *"Say you can. You have been helping today: there is lots of energy."*

Steady breathing lulled me into a false sense of security when suddenly a shock and an involuntary start elicited me to remark, *"It is me, I do not want to play games. No, I do not want to play games. I do not want to know who is the coldest,"* as I was jolted repeatedly and given icy cold feelings all over my body. Freeda broke in saying, "I think there are too many wanting to step into you, Bill." I continued, *"Fog in the air, I cannot stand on one leg,"* as my foot was involuntarily raised off the floor. I said, *"They are just playing with me,"* as I felt such a penetrating draft of indescribably cold air which made me scrub my hair repeatedly as if coated with itching powder: while they seemed to be blowing this icy cold air around me. *"Howay, guys and girls; come on,"* I said.

Irene said she thought that they should not be with me. Freeda asked them to "Step back. Step back please. You are not compatible. Go back to your appropriate place please: and step forward the one who is compatible please."

I said, *"There is another energy there, Freeda so let's–"* stopping in my tracks as my forehead had become so very itchy that I was trying to rub the hair into my skin to alleviate the itch. After thirty seconds or so, the itching subsided; and I returned to a normal pattern of breathing once more.

Freeda asked, "Is there anybody who would like to step forward and use Bill as a channel today but it has to be someone who is compatible please. Step forward, not all at once; one at a time: please."

I answered, *"There was no malice intended. It is awareness, isn't it? Yes, thank you. It is awareness that there is lots of them about and each one has a different way of letting me know they are there. It is like blind man's bluff and I have got the mask on."* The breathing interruptions started again with varying degrees of coldness striking me from different directions. I asked, *"Is that two different ones or the same one?"*

A deep breath and then a pain in the back with an icy draft was my answer.

Freeda remarked, "So they are playing games today."

I replied, *"I can feel the energy and yes, I can feel the energy and it is swirling about my legs and it is getting up towards my knees; and it is really, really cold: and this is what I usually get: but the: I am not getting purple."*

Freeda remarked that she had seen the purple.

I replied, *"No, I am getting; it is like a dirty yellow, it is a dirty yellow."*

Irene queried the colour but Freeda had just seen the same colour, a dirty yellow. Freeda said, "I don't think that is good that. I think they are trying to get somebody to step in who is not supposed to step in here, right: and I think what is happening here is that you, Bill, are struggling against it because it is not supposed to be in you: Right and a dirty yellow is not good. I am seeing it as well, no."

Irene remarked that with the coldness there must be some angelic type energies around. Freeda said, "I feel as though this dirty yellow is blocking it. I think this is a lesson for you to learn, Bill: to say no. You know as soon as you see this dirty yellow it is not right, it is not right. I think this is not a progressed soul this one.

You know you usually get the purple. This is not right. I can see it. That is why it is not getting any further with it because your body is saying no, this is not right. It is very persistent. It is a time waster."

.

I replied, *"Yes, well it is, but the, it's purple trying to move it, but it is not moving. It is coming back again, right. Ok."*

Irene said that it should go back to the place with the same vibratory level.

Freeda remarked, "Definitely not you, that is why you are fighting against it."

Irene stated, "It has to go if you ask it, Bill."

Freeda joined in, "Just ask if it will go back to its appropriate place because it is your body that it is stepping into. It is not at your vibratory rate. I can see other nice things. I can see the waterfall; you know what he had before, the waterfall coming down and that is lovely and it is more the place he wants to be than in this dirty, mucky yellow." Irene remarked that they would try, these energies, to barge in.

I said, *"I can see the water but the water is dirty, a dirty yellow and it is coming from the side. No, it can go away. I have asked you politely now, yes, on your bike. Definitely get on your bike."*

Freeda asked, "Prepare the way for somebody to work with Bill but I think you had to experience this, Bill, because he is blocking you totally. You know that usually you are able to go into it but this is not and this is what you are seeing. I am seeing a lot of purple in the dirty yellow and I am actually seeing an eye. I can just see all the others trying to push him away. It is a male energy. Push him away but he feels that he has something to say but it is no good because Bill is not the type of person to come through. You cannot, you are not the same you need to go somewhere else."

He was still making steady breathing a problem.

Freeda said, "Concentrate on your water clearing, Bill, the water that is coming down and I think that will wash him away you know. Instead of a mucky yellow, think about a colour, clear, clear spring water coming down."

I remarked, *"I can see the energy coming back. The river, there is more than one. Dirty yellow, the light is too close. It is coming back again. No, that is it. I am finished. Go away."*

Freeda said, "He is blocking you totally. Totally blocking you."

I returned, "Here endeth the lesson."

This battle of wills between these incompatible energies and I had taken almost twenty-five minutes of shocks, pain, and unsteady breathing in an almost continuous assault of my senses. It has tried my will, my patience, and all the things I had tried to remove it. I was ready to stop the session and admit defeat. Now it did not seem like a lesson to me, more a punishment. I only had one question in my mind. Why?

I said, *"Right, I am coming back, back out of this. If they are not going away, I am. Right, goodbye: head for the light."*

Freeda remarked, "Thank you, Bill, God bless. God bless. Do you feel as though it is lightening up now, Bill?"

I said, *"Yes, it has started to get a bit more yellow, but it is not much. Right, ok. There it is. A hole in the clouds. Now I have a tiger, yes. The energy is dropping away."*

Freeda remarked, "Do not worry about it, Bill. It is a lesson you have learnt."

I said, *"It is slowly pulsating. It is very slow. I have a ringing in my ears. It is two tiny green cylinders, just lifted and then went. Yes, green, two little green cylinders, yes, they are off this side."* Indicating to my right.

Freeda said, "Which is good. Very good. Is there anything else you can see, friend?"

I replied in a whisper, *"The Cosmos. The cosmos and millions and millions and millions of stars. Pinpricks of light. I wonder what that is. I know what that is, a spiral galaxy."*

Freeda remarked, "The first step off your first Master. You have a few to go before you get to the eighth. So two green cylinders. What else was there, Bill?"

I replied, *"Stars and the Cosmos and a spiral galaxy."*

Freeda repeating what I had said: "This is better vibrations than the other one that was in," she remarked. Different altogether.

I said, *"Why do I see a doctor in a face mask? Somebody lying down. I have a pain in my eye, left eye. That is a pedal car. Yes, indigo blue with light blue flashes. That is better, purple oh yes. It is nice that. Purple and clouds. Yes, now we have the circle open in the sky. Yes, yes I can see the feathers sticking out all round. Yes, it was a lesson, thank you. Okay, it was a hard lesson. It has opened up now. We are not going to get the letters in rotation. A crow. We had a "C" before. Now we got a crow, a black crow. I do not know what the crow is saying. I do not know crow. Is the black crow the Crow nation? It seemed as if the crow was laughing. We got it right. Yes, the sun is shining through the clouds. Peace. It is a summer's day."*

Irene said, "The galaxy, would you ask whether that galaxy was the Milky Way?"

I replied, *"It is the spiral galaxy, I think of Andromeda."*

Irene commented that it is the next one to us because we are a part of a spiral galaxy are we not.

I replied, *"It is part of the Milky Way but it is just pinpoints of light. All stars are suns. The spiral galaxy is at this side"* indicating to my right. *"This side,"* indicating again to the right. *"I have the eye. It is a human eye. It has just gone past looking at me. He is looking right at me now, brown eye. The sun is smiling. The song: "The sun has got his hat on; hip, hip, hip, hooray." Yes, big smile on his face. It is very peaceful. A lot slower than what it has been in the past. Yes, that is energy: a big ball of energy just appeared. There is lots of it around. I can see many different light clusters of energy all around, passing across. It is like floating in the sea. It is very calm. It makes it cold again.*

"Yes, it is a new lesson. It is like the priesthood class. They are showing me things that I have seen before but I have to forget before. Start from here yes.

"Oh, there is a window. It is in a house. The house is white, standing on a hill. It has a roof on. Strange shaped roof that. No, it is not a house. The roofs are at different levels. It is on, ah, yes; I have seen that shape before, on the TV yesterday. That is Lhasa. That is the palace at Lhasa and the sun is shining through the clouds: mottled cloud and you can see the sun. Well you cannot see the sun but you can see the radiance of it through the cloud."

Irene remarked that it looked like our friend Shairi-Lah was back. Freeda remarked that it looked like he was here to teach him (meaning me) the first lesson of the dark energies. Muddy, yellow, dirty. Bill could not work with that. This Guy has a beard. He is stroking his beard.

I continued, *"This is where he started from, Lhasa. I have a picture of a child with a staff in his hand and he changes hands because he is walking up many steps. Like a spiral path in the mountains. It is not very steep but it is steadily uphill.*

"There is a valley down the side. He is already quite high up but the path seems to be never ending. It goes around corners and disappears then you can see it higher up, just for an instant then it disappears again.

"He does not know where this path will lead him: but he knows he must follow that path, through all the twists and turns. It is his path: he is showing me in the beginning, yes, from Lhasa, on the path into the mountains. He has come to a temple, like a big shrine on the side of the road but there is some people in there and they have; they rotate. Make a noise when you rotate them, big cylinders, prayer wheels. Some he just moves his hand to move them and others he must spin them; but they do not spin on their own. They

*are heavy for him: some take two hands to move. They are very old;
the wood is almost black with age.*

*"His first Master. The boy gives him some food from his bag that
he has at this side to the Master, who thanks him with his bowl and
his stick down this side of his shoulder held."*

(The video recording shows the bag at the left side and me going
through the motions of the offering and receiving of the food
with deference. The master is holding his bowl with the stick in
the crook of his right shoulder, held firm by his elbow tucked in.)

*"Thank you, my child," the master said. "I am accompanying you
on your journey. I will take you the next step. Will you follow me?"*

Irene repeated the question to me, "Will you follow him?"

*I replied, "Yes, I will follow him. He has kind eyes. He is an old
man, like my grandfather, perhaps even older. A very weatherworn
face, bare head, but a kindly smile. We leave tomorrow, early in the
morning, just after the sun comes up: after prayers. Tonight we must
rest. Yes, the weather looks fine. It is a long way, a long, long way
to that peak over there. There is peaks before that but we are not
going over the top of each one because the trail goes round the sides,
gradually climbing. There is stops along the way, sometimes two
days' journey, sometimes three days. We must take a bigger coat,
something that is warm because as you get higher up it is colder,
because this garment is too thin for the cold. I can feel it eating into
my bones, my jaw is quivering; my teeth are chattering. We must
go inside to the Temple.*

*"There is two rows of Monks sitting cross-legged on cushions, on
wooden pillars. They sit with little cymbals between their thumbs
and forefingers. They sit very upright and cross-legged, with their
hands on their knees. They look like statues. You cannot see them
breathing. I want to ask the question but the Master says no, shhh.*

He is telling me, I must not speak, child: you will learn as you progress but at this time, it is not for you tonight.

"You must rest from your journey because tomorrow is hard for such a young one. We must walk, but you have young legs and I am old. Because you are so small, we can walk together and we will not slow each other down. You have little legs and with my long old ones, we have the same pace, child. We shall journey together."

Freeda remarked, "Would you like to go and rest now?"

He replied, *"It is time. It is time to go."*

Both Irene and Freeda thanked him for his time and the lesson we had learnt from the day and said goodbye to him until the next time.

He replied, *"Good night, Master. Goodbye friends."*

Freeda thanked everybody who had come today and she felt sorry for the soul who had tried to get in: and that we could not help him. The vibrations were not right for him to fit into Bill.

She said God bless once more as we visualise them going through the hatch until next time we come. Amen.

"Why wake me up with a tear?" I asked.

Freeda remarked that until I was speaking as Shairi-Lah, my energies were about six feet behind the chair I was sitting on. Once the energies came though, they brought me forward. Both Freeda and Irene could see energies around me from Shairi-Lah. As I returned, Irene said that she had put a protective bubble around me to shield me from the dark energies, the dirty yellow that I was seeing.

It suddenly made sense as I realised that the protective bubble she had generated had trapped the dark energy between my own aura's and the bubble. This did not allow the nice energies to come and move the dark energies. Eventually I had broken through the outer shell Irene has created around me to expel the dark energies and clearing the dirty yellow to a far more inviting colour.

These were valuable lessons learnt today and I am forever grateful to Shairi-Lah for his calm, measured voice and the clarity of the visions he gave me. Most of all he gave me a true sense of peace in the whirlwind of life.

This is the reality of our journey. We must keep going, even though the path may be hard. We can rest awhile, but must continue to the end of the road wherever it leads us. One thing is for sure. One way or the other, we cannot escape our destiny.

Chapter Eleven
– "Tootsie"

Thursday the 21st November 2019, at Irene Harthill's house in Shotton, session nine, started with Freeda laughingly saying she had to remember the words exactly: because of her brain you know. We all laughed because Freeda is usually ten steps ahead and is always on the go. She is like a whirlwind and always thinking ahead. We started almost immediately with a single strike of the bowl with the strange pulsing, ringing tone, shaking my brain cells. A sound that shivers your spine, leaving a tingling feeling.

We both removed our spectacles and I asked Freeda if she wanted to remove her rings. She replied yes, if she could get them off. The reason for removal is when Freeda channels, her fingers quite often swell to the point of pain, in the ring fingers. As a trance Medium, her hands and fingers tend to enlarge and there are visible changes to her facial appearance.

The Lord's Prayer followed as the ringing faded to a slow pulsing vibration.

Immediately after, we could feel that the energies in the room were very strong. Freeda thought that we had built up the energies just by talking before we sat down to begin our session.

We had another laugh, as I needed to finish a boiled sweet. Freeda had removed her's that made me feel like a squirrel chewing its nuts, trying to dispose of mine as quickly as possible.

Freeda said that Spirit knows we are having a bit fun here and it does lift the vibrations. Laughter is one of the best things to lift the vibrations and we do have a good laugh.

Freeda started by thanking Spirit for coming and joining us this day. "The three of us are gathered today here saying to you, please come and help us. We enjoy your company; I hope you enjoy ours. It is a bit of time of laughter, light, and love and this is what we are sending out to the universe. We are trying to help the universe, just the same as you are trying to guide us to help them. We have some questions to ask today and I hope you have the right people around, arranged to give us lectures because we will not be doing the lectures, you will be. We are actually filming you and talking to you so we will see all our film of today. So, Bill, have you eaten your sweet?" Yes, I had. "Good lad," she replied. I am going to get started and there is questions I would like to ask to you today from Spirit. You know we go away from here and we study on lots of things.

"Why have you showed us this: why have you showed us that, like our George coming in and he is just saying, George taught listening, right? We do listen: we are listening. Sometimes you have to get the right interpretation, but we will do it: we will get there. Thank you everybody for joining us today and I think it is a full house so let us get cracking."

"One hour," I said. Freeda replied, "Spirit we have one hour. I know that people say you have no time over there, but you do because when we come to you and say this time coming it is valuable to us to know it is earth time. So one hour please from now. Thank you; well it might have been five minutes since, because I have been talking so long."

I could hear the electric fan running in the background, as Freeda piped up with, "that is another thing, Bill, when your spirit guides come through, ask them to talk up because I was told from Spirit one time, they cannot hear you, so talk up. Often Spirit will talk into your ear or give you the words in thought form. Sometimes they shout as if you cannot hear them and other times they will talk in whispers. They can read our thoughts but we use language so we need to talk normally, so they can hear us and we can get the words out using our vocal chords in normal speech form."

I replied that my problem is that I felt so privileged that I talked in deference to Spirit so I was quiet in my speech.

I had asked them to speak up a little but they had told me that the volume was up to me. The privilege they have given me still causes me to whisper or speak quietly. I have a lot to learn.

Freeda replied, "Yes, you do have a lot to learn but you are doing it really well. I am really over the moon with what we have done within this time. We have had some really good answers to very heavy questions you know. What we are doing is channelling, and the channelling is good. Thank you for what you have given me, Bill, in the past: and I hope that I have given you and Irene some good stuff as well." We thanked each other and Spirit.

I said they are coming through quite quickly, as there is purple there already. Freeda remarked they are using me as a vessel and that is all we are. Just a vessel used. I remarked that there is spirit there already. Freeda replied, well you bring them through what you have, Bill. If Spirit is there already and I will ask my question after you. Your turn.

Spirit was standing just in front of me, just waiting.

Freeda replied it was my turn this week so get cracking. I replied that I am the pupil.

Freeda said that she was a bit funny with Spirit but they know what I am like. I say to them get cracking, as I am in life, fast forward. That is how I work. With a laugh, she said sorry about that, Spirit. Welcome friends and I am pleased that you have come to Bill straight away. We are dying to hear what you have to say. Bill does not know what you have to say, he is just going to start it, thank you, Bill.

I said, *"Dark eyes. I have a face with dark eyes and then I am seeing a white energy in a purple background. My feet are cold: my legs are cold. The tide is coming in. Yes, it is washing round like standing on a sandy beach with the waves coming in. They will be a little while yet. I will wait.*

Freeda replied that she would go into it and ask her question; as long as I reminded her, how it was worded. It is how could we help people come to the light? Is that right, she asked. I replied *"Yes."* She asked how we could help. Right I am going to go into it. She lapsed into silence and steady breathing as I had.

I knew Freeda had someone with her, so I welcomed the friend. I could feel that it was her hard working Guide, Guy, once again. I said, "Good afternoon. Welcome." He immediately replied with "Dear" and then some hums and ahs. "Take your time, Guy," I offered.

He said, *"You ask again many questions. We knew before you were going to ask this. You asked how you can be doing a big job. A very big job that sometimes is hard, hard to do. Yes, we can help you little by little informing you of what you should be doing. We are giving you information all the time. I am getting a bit restless about how you want so much so we are here to understand your needs to facilitate you. This is hard for me to give to Freeda. Right, you do not have to worry. We are pointing you in the right direction. You do not understand at the moment, which direction we are leading you: but we will prepare you. You will understand a lot more. As I have told you before it is all happening, all happening and what you are asking is how we can help to bring people to the light. There are many people who are in the dark at the moment. When they have seen all this darkness, and not much understanding of how it is happening, they are going to ask questions. Questions: they will ask more questions. Why? How? We need more. We want to be better, a better world. We want generosity, kindness, love, in this creative world. It is a creative world. We help you: oh dear, right. My eyes are hurting. We help you create a lot of things. There are so many people that understand now that we must create. Get better. Be kinder, more generous. Do you not see how the world is changing? It is changing.*

"More people are coming to the light but we will help you. You help them in the way that Bill asked Freeda last week. How can we do it? How can we do it? As we say, you can help by doing: talking, spreading the word, right: but also, we are doing it. We are doing it. We are bringing people to the light, but you are helping. Some people just do not evaluate things and the word evaluate is right because what do they want. Do they want a life that is not evaluated? What value is on it, in it? They want a better life so this is my answer to it today from my friends in spirit and to you.

"We are helping you as well. Understand that: please understand."

I replied, "Yes, I understand."

Guy continued. "Oh dear."

Freeda in her own voice remarked he was getting frustrated, so frustrated because we are wanting it so quick. It is happening, it is happening and he is keep saying it is happening. Can I just go back into it please because he has more to say? As Freeda was reconnecting, I asked, "Can I just say something, Guy" to which I received an affirmative "Yes" from Freeda.

I said, "*It may feel that we are wanting things very quickly, too quickly for Spirit; ("Yes") but it is because I think from me, as Bill, that last week with Shairi-Lah, he told me to forget everything that I had learnt in the weeks before. ("Yes"). Which seems a backward step to my human mind: ("No") and my question or my thought was, could this be explained today as to why this happened?"*

Freeda said, Yes, I will answer it. Yes, I will go into it and answer it for you, right. Ok.

Thank you I replied.

Freeda asked that Spirit please step forward and answer Bill's question please.

Freeda was shown mental pictures that she did not understand so she said that she would tell me what she was shown.

They are showing me a full field of corn on a summer's day and it is ripe and it is ready to be taken. If you want to put it that way, harvested. They have a lovely field of corn, which is beautiful, but everything has to be, harvested. They are saying to me, it had to be, harvested. All the stuff you had learned had to be cut and a fresh crop had to start to grow. It could be a different crop. It could be cabbages, it could be turnips, but it was not corn. That crop had to be stored in a different place. Now you are starting on another crop, which has to grow. It is not that it has to be forgot about, it has to be stored, then, we start afresh, so that is another book to be opened and another lesson to be learnt, right. This is what they are showing me and this is how they have done it, symbolically.

They are also showing me, and I am just going to explain Bill by doing it this way. They are showing me a river now but you need that river because the river is the energy for the field to grow. Now you need Spirit flowing through you before you can get the next crop. The river is there and it is absolutely a lovely sparkling, fresh, clean river. It is not muddy, it is not dirty; it is feeding the new crop and this is what Spirit is saying to me. It is even sparkly, it is lovely and even sometimes they tell me you feel this energy flowing through you (Yes, I do) and it is sparkly and it bounces off you.

Can you imagine fireworks? They are showing me when the water is sparkling it is bouncing off and there is fireworks and it explodes and you see a flood of colour. That is what he is trying to say to you. It was not that you had to forget all that or push it away. It had to be, cropped. That was; put aside and grow a new crop but it is being, fed. Shairi-Lah was right: you have to store the first crop.

They are explaining to me you also asked about why you have done this at this time in your life. You know the crop said that was summer, as you know. Guy was saying, "As you know." Freeda said that she must slow down, as she wanted to get this right.

Every crop has its season. That crop was chopped in the summer. Now you are at, not the autumn of your life, you are at the winter of your life. As you know, wintertime is the time to retreat, to go into retrospection of your life. What you have done with your life; reflection. You could not have done that up until now. You could not have done it up until now so that is why they are showing me it is now for you. They are actually rolling a carpet out and I do not know why they are rolling a carpet out. They are rolling a carpet out and they are doing a lovely room for you. A really, nice room for you and they are even saying they are making everything comfortable for you to do it. A comfortable room and done out nice for you. That is what they have done: give you everything that you need.

They have given you the time, they have given you the comfort and they have given you some lovely spirit guides that are coming through. Shairi-Lah, how could you wish for a better guide than him? You should be so happy and he has took you on to the first step but he wants you to store the other knowledge because he has knowledge to come through for you. He is showing me a great, big book. Have you been getting a great big book, Bill? Shairi-Lah is leading you to the right books, to the right people, to the right new thoughts, and the stored thoughts are there. Does that answer your question?

Yes, it did answer my question clearly and unequivocally. Thank you very much.

Guy was still talking to Freeda. He said you know when the tide is too strong, you cannot go upstream, and I do not know why he is saying this, but you have to go with the flow. Go with the flow because you cannot force it. Whether you like it or not, you cannot force it. You might think that this is daft and might sound stupid to you but they are telling me that mint will be good for you. Mint, you should look it up.

You know when we talked about the turtles and the energy lines; we have not done that yet and we should be looking at the map and seeing where the energy lines go. Flow from that island round and it should be on the world map and see where those energy lines go in that circle.

I said, Yes, it is wavelengths.

Freeda replied yes, wavelengths. Oh, God, you are getting wrong here, bloody hell. Excuse me for swearing.

Your wavelengths are up and down, and not tuned into the proper channel. Will you stop just getting on to the channel then taking it off to somewhere else. You will get static. You will not hear things clearly. Just continue with what we are doing and listen to your spirit people coming through. Spirit people, not spirit guides, spirit people. Why are they saying spirit people? Perhaps it is a lot of your family, people you have met in this life that are helping you as well: not just spirit guides, but people. You are getting grandads, other people, your dad because you have so many questions to ask about your life as well Bill. Why has your life been, you are just getting there and knocked back and you feel as though with this work we are doing now, you do not want to get there, and get knocked back. You want to progress, are progressing, but Shairi-Lah is good for you right.

I replied, *"It is not in my mind, my conscious mind, that I have these feelings. It has been hard at times but it has also been very good and that is life. We need, I have, I have accepted my life but I sometimes think; from what I have been told in these sessions and from feelings that come through from Spirit, that I do not know whether I have missed flags in the past* (Which is correct) *that I should have seen.*

Well, said Freeda, you are not doing that now and you are here. I am sorry that I had to do it this way but they were just showing me everything. They were not talking through me; they were just showing me pictures of what I should tell you so we can see if we can go into anything else. Oh, there is a little girl running around here. She is not half-giggly. She has ringlets in, she has a blue dress on, and she is running around here having a good time. Freeda laughingly said she had just looked at you and me, Bill and wondering what we are doing. We are meditating, channelling, pet, so do not worry about us, we are all right.

I am sorry if I am gobby but I have Ginger Rogers; Fred Astaire and Ginger Rogers dancing. What was one of the songs that they danced too? Does Irene or Bill understand this song it goes de, de and they are dancing away to this though, and the song is relevant.

Putting on your top hat, remarked Irene.

Yes, Freeda replied. I can see them and the top hat and the stick, everything. There must be some kind of celebration coming on here, from Spirit anyway. Putting on your top hat: did de, dee, dee. As Freeda sang and hummed the tune. They are complimenting us and they are quite jolly about it as well. Christmas is coming.

I said, *"Yes: I am seeing a lot of energy. There is the odd flash of bright iridescent blue. It is just keep flashing in and out. Now I have a pulsation in a cloud with Spirit gathered round. A hole in the cloud and I know there is someone very close to me because they are making me jump. The purple was beautiful. I just do not know who it is. They do not seem to want to channel.*

Freeda interrupted asking, "Bill, do you know someone who used to make homemade bread? This is the person who is coming to you, mind. If you want to talk to this person and they want to talk to you. Will you please understand that not just your spirit guides are coming: some people from Spirit were coming? So who is the person who made the bread?"

I replied, "My mam."

Well she is here and she wanted to talk to you. Understand that the purple is floating right around you. I can see it. It is beautiful.

I replied, *"Yes, it is cold as well. It is putting shivers up my back. This is where it is mixed up. Because. So. Yes."*

Then nothing.

The channelling was starting and I was no longer in control of my thoughts or voice. Somebody was coming through as I mumbled yes. A few groans and noisy breaths, a few more moans then a slow deep measured voice spoke through me.

Good afternoon friends. (Freeda welcomed the guide.) Thank you very much for the invitation. I have not been here before but the, the energy; is very, very strong with you all. You, you, as he started to laugh.

You could hear he was trying to control the laugh but was fighting a losing battle as he continued to laugh for a few seconds. In a higher, almost falsetto voice he continued.

You have so many questions, laughing again. Oh dear me it's: as he laughed once again.

We are all laughing here. He lost his composure as he laughed and laughed again. Oh dear me, oh. Mirthfully he said we need more time for all these questions but we can only answer one at a time. Laughing again as he repeated, oh dear, oh dear me, oh dear. Oh, you are so (Lovable, Freeda said) ah, you send lots of love. You demonstrate it to each other. It is good. It is good the way you work but you are so inquisitive and you ask questions which you; which you need to listen to and, and to discuss between yourselves and then quite often we will know, exactly who to bring to you. Today, (laughingly) today, it is like being in a theatre and everybody wants to ask questions.

Freeda, you got a question, an important question. You need to think about this child. It is in your head but you must dig it out because I have been, (as he laughed again) I have been nominated to answer you. He finished with a peal of laughter. This is going to be fun. Oh dear me, dear me: as he and Freeda laughed together.

Freeda said, "This is the question that I have to ask. I know you are going to laugh at this because the question I am going to ask is. "Why does our communication always have to be so serious? Can we bring a lot of lighthearted energy into us that we could perhaps leave with us this lovely happy energy? Does Spirit always have to be so serious?" That is one of my questions.

The guide started to laugh uncontrollably which had Freeda laughing freely as she stated she knew it was daft but could he please stop laughing at her. It is all right you are going to ask Irene next.

The guide then gave a calming motion with his hands as if settling the conversation down before saying in a quieting voice, *"No, serious, serious".: Turning to Freeda, he* said in a loud voice, *"RIGHT"*! Which had Freeda and him laughing uncontrollably as he slapped his thigh. Freeda said she thought we were going to get some bangs and claps in the house after this where we are going to be laughing.

The guide resumed with calming hand signals saying, *"Calm, calm"*, as Freeda repeated, we were going to get some bangs and claps in the house after this. That is why we are going to be laughing.

The guide turned towards Freeda and continued in a low voice, "Right, silence. It is up to you, what you want to do. That rhymed, didn't it," as he burst into laughter again.

Laughing, Freeda remarked that is not funny. I asked a question!

Do we have to be serious all the time or can; He interrupted with, *"It is serious, child"*: or can we have fun? *"Yes."* He replied, *"Sometimes, sometimes."*

Freeda interrupted asking, "Can you leave some of your energy with us?

He paused then replied, *"You can have a little bit. You can have a lot."* Can Irene have a bit? Freeda asked.

He replied, *"Certainly, Irene. You need quite a bit child, so you take that,"* as he waved both his hands towards Irene. *"I have not heard you laugh. I have not heard her laugh. She sits very quiet, doesn't she? She is like a little mouse sitting on a little chair,"* merrily laughing at his remarks, as Freeda was.

"No, seriously, sometimes we need to be quite serious so that you take it in, but it is quite a, it's quite a happy day today so we will have some fun, but it is still all truth; so you must bear that in mind."

Freeda remarked, "Well, Can I. Can you understand?" As the guide silenced her by asking her a question.

Have you had your answer, child?

No, not fully, Freeda remarked with a laugh. Can you please stay?

He replied, *"So you were not listening when I was talking to you."*

Freeda replied, "I was listening. I want to ask another question."

He replied, *"So you were trying to fool me. One at a time, one at a time."*

Freeda said, "Can I ask another question please?"

The guide said, *"Wait, the little mouse in the corner."* He had a few attempts to talk as he laughed at his own thoughts. He raised his arm and extended his index finger in the direction of Irene.

"You, you: oh, this is a serious question. That is putting a bit of a damper on things, isn't it? Irene, child, lighten up. Lighten up, be happy. Ask your question."

Irene asked, "Will I become enlightened in this lifetime?"

The guide laughed and asked, *"In this lifetime? How fast do you want to go?"*

We were all laughing aloud. Well not that fast said Freeda as both her and Irene said, Zoom! Zoom! Zoom. We have zoom in here.

He asked, *"Full enlightenment, child?"*

Yes, replied Irene.

"Oh, takes forever," he replied slapping his thigh. *"Takes forever."*

I have been at it forever, Irene replied as both her, and Freeda, burst into peals of laughter. That sounds quite rude, Freeda commented between laughs.

The guide, straight faced, replied, *"Isn't it always the same with young spirits. That is all they think about."*

The quick repartees between Irene and Freeda had the guide laughing with them. They were all helpless with laughter. Freeda said that Irene had said it, not her. She did not think about what she was going to say before she said it, did she?

The guide remarked, *"Because she opened her mouth before putting the brain into gear"* as they dissolved into laughter once again. Eventually the laughter subsided and they settled down again.

He was becoming animated using many hand gestures, head and body movements, to emphasize his words and serious explanations.

The guide resumed, *"No child, listen. Seriously, seriously, shh. Seriously. There are many, many souls everywhere and it takes many, many, many, almost uncountable lives in different places, not just here on earth, but in other dimensions; what you would say, other worlds out there and it goes on forever. Each time you learn little lessons. You are here, Earth, what you call this ball floating about, is the most difficult place we have to earn: no, no, no, no, no. Not earn, learn. Learn. It is extremely difficult here on this earth plane to learn the lessons. Because you, no, not you. We as Spirit, when we join to one of these* (He laughingly pats my waist area) *bodies there is quite a bit of queer stuff inside this shell* (Pointing to my head) *and it takes a while to blend with it.*

"Because we cannot, once we are here, as Spirit, in here, (pointing to my head): we cannot really change it to the way we would like so we gain our points when we go back. Cannot do that. What we have to do is to work on it, with it, in conjunction, so it is seamlessly as one. From that, we then hope. We hope. We try. Sometimes we do not try hard enough; sometimes we try too hard. Nevertheless, we try hard to complete the learning, the lessons, yes, yes, the lessons, more than one; that we came onto the earth plane to learn. This, this, ah, yes. (Pointing to my head with his right index finger.) This grey matter fights with your spirit and it is always in battle. Because the grey matter rules the body and the spirit has to try to get the body to follow the path that you need, the path to get the points that you need, to get a bit higher; when you go back.

"It is fun and games. Sometimes it is really good and we can have a good laugh. (As he did.) You can rebel, you can question, and the paths are there; left hand, right hand; and up and down. You have

not the memory of which one you should take. So, it is a competition between the grey matter and Spirit. Depending how you have blended and reached an agreement with this piece of matter, (as he waved his hands down my body), whether you will actually learn all your lessons or not. The fun is, you get to come back down again, until you have learnt all the lessons that this world can teach. You could say you can reach enlightenment on the earth, with the earth, as one set of lessons. Then you go somewhere else".

He laughed at this point in his dialogue. He was using his hands and arms to great effect in describing what he was trying to inform us. Only Irene could see, as both Freeda and I had our eyes closed. He had fashioned a globe as he described the world and used gestures to point to my head for grey matter. It was almost like sign language as he reinforced all that he was saying with hand gestures around my body.

"You can go where there is not a body and you are just thought. That is fairly easy, as you just float about and learn a bit. Yes, but it takes a while, probably in earth years, maybe three to five thousand, no problem".

"Then there is other strange worlds and there you have to learn how to manipulate things. How to grow mosses, because those up there, the big guns, shall we say the ancient ones, they decide shall we have a little solar system here, or shall we put one here. When you get up there, when you are finished with Earth, for the time being of course, you can go up there and start to learn how to make mosses and leaves, see what they look like, and put them on the world".

"There is another one like this. It is like a vacation place because there is no fighting, death and destruction. There is none of these stupid humans on it, so it is like a playground. The sun always shines, well, during the day. It gets dark on a nighttime of course. (He laughs). Yes, it is like a holiday camp you could say. You learn

of course, you always learn. As you get higher, it gets that little bit harder and then you have got to work, as I work".

"I have to teach, teach people. Well not, teach, no, you have to make them aware of what is going wrong and what is going right. You cannot tell them too much because the head goes. (He indicates a swelling of the head and makes a humming sound.) *You have to be, serious* (Laughs) *and very careful how much, and what you tell them. It is their choice in the end anyway. It is your path, your path, this guy's path (referring to me); and it is a big path with this boy. (He laughs aloud as he indicates my body.) Cannot tell him I said that."* As he laughs out loudly once more. *"Well half-serious, so does that answer your question little mouse?"*

He laughs loudly again.

Irene said, "It absolutely does. I am absolutely, fine with that." Both Freeda and Irene are laughing.

Freeda remarked, "You will never guess what I am getting for you: "TOOTSIE". Yes, Tootsie; you know like the Charleston."

Irene replied Dustin Hoffman I thought you meant. No, Tootsie. Freeda replied.

A short discussion between Freeda and Irene ensued about Tootsie and men dressed as women in the film between the laughter of them both.

Freeda mirthfully said to the guide, "I am sorry, I should not have said that about Tootsie. I am not making game. I am being light hearted. Mmm, better shup up."

In a very calm voice, the guide asked, *"What am I thinking?"* As he pointed to Freeda and Irene.

Freeda replied, "That I am naughty", as the girls and the guide erupted into laughter as he dropped my arms down.

The laughter subsided and he raised my arms, pointing to Freeda and Irene and once more, in a very calm voice the guide spoke. *"Serious, what am I sending you?"*

Freeda replied, "Lots of love."

He replied, *"No, other than that."*

"Energy?" replied Freeda.

"No," he replied. *"You are talking about Tootsie. What goes with Tootsie? Come, come. Come on. Hurry, think."*

This question had Freeda and Irene confused, and undecided. Eventually Freeda admitted she did not know and could not tell him.

He dropped my arms and slapped my thigh, lowering his head in resignation and looked right, as if seeking guidance from the unseen energy.

"Is it rude?" as both Irene and Freeda laughed once again. Irene remarked, "I do not know, we all have different parts." Freeda agreed.

The guide remarked, *"Black and white shoes."*

Black and white shoes: exclaimed Freeda and Irene simultaneously. Well, that goes with Ginger Rogers said Irene. Freeda remarked, yes it does, yes it does. Irene laughed loudly.

He was still looking left and waving my left hand as if thumbing a lift but referring to Freeda and Irene. The guide remarked, *"Two crazies here."*

He appeared to be talking to someone on his right hand side.

"Two crazies here. Have you heard them?" Still waving my hand in a thumbing action.

Irene was still laughing. As the observer, she could see the actions of the guide: as Freeda remarked, "Well do not bring your friend in."

The guide was chuckling, *"oh ho, ho. No, no, no",* as Freeda remarked there is your friend wanting to come in.

"He is a little devil," he remarked.

Freeda remarked that she could sense a friend wanting to come in.

Irene said, "Can I ask another question?" as Freeda remarked, oh here she is, the little mouth. Another exchange took place between Irene and Freeda like two giggly girls in the school playground. This was turning into a comedy show!

The guide interrupted with, *"I said Mouse."*

Irene said, "Would you consider this whole experience to be a cosmic joke?"

Freeda once more dissolved into laughter as she replied "Yes".

Irene replied, "I feel it is a cosmic joke", as both of them dissolved into laughter once again. Irene continued, "Sometimes it is very light, other times it is very dark. It is very lively. I am just asking for guidance on that one."

Freeda remarked that the energy was building up, as everyone was happy.

The guide replied, *"Guidance, to where, child?"*

Freeda laughed.

Irene said to see if it was a cosmic joke or not or I am demented?

Freeda interjected, "You asked, mind." Once more resulting in laughter as the guide replied, *"Demented".*

Freeda remarked demented, no, diamanted. Always diamanted.

The guide remarked, *"See, we were just having fun and then the damper is on again."*

Irene burst in, "How is that? It is a joke. I feel that to me it is as I am only asking for guidance" as laughter reigned once more.

Smiling, the guide replied, *"Guidance, she wants all the answers."*

Freeda with a laugh remarked, "I know, that it's unfair. I am going to ask a question."

"Serious?" the guide asked.

Freeda replied yes, "A serious one. Please, I am asking a question," as the guide tried to calm her voice making shushing sounds. "This is for Bill, right. This is for Bill, right."

"This fellow?" he asked.

This fellow. Yes, right, ok. Freeda replied.

"Will he find more, spiritual awareness? Is he becoming more spiritually aware?" I know you are using him but we want to know, right. Thank you." The guide spluttered a little as Freeda requested, "Do not laugh at him. Now, come on", as she laughed. "Will Bill become more spiritually aware?"

Using an old TV advert quip, suitably changed, he replied with a little snigger.

"Course he is, Malcolm."

Freeda erupted into laughter telling him he had all the answers. No, seriously. Freeda said.

"Seriously?" he questioned.

Seriously, Freeda replied.

"It is not a joke?" he questioned once more.

Freeda replied, "No, it is not a joke so do not think it is."

Calmly the guide replied.

If you reach full enlightenment, whatever they do up there, I do not think there is any fun in it. Sorry, that is just my opinion.

This remark raised lots of laughter.

"That is good," remarked Irene with a laugh.

Freeda, laughingly asked, "Is it a bit boring?"

He replied, *"Don't know, never been. Don't want to go in case it is"* as all broke out in laughter. You would rather stay as this, Freeda commented.

"Well, yes. It is good. So good. Yes he is," he replied.

Thank you, Freeda said.

He said, "That was easy done."

Yes. Freeda replied. I just want to know that Spirit understand each question because I think, sometimes, he worries about it. The guide was laughing. Freeda said, "Shut up you. I will ban you." In the silence, you distinctly heard one of Irene's dogs break wind. Which was, perhaps, what he was laughing about in the first place. Freeda continued, "I am not going to talk to you anymore as you are laughing at me."

"Freeda," he said.

"What?" was her reply. "I am being nice", she commented.

As the guide started to speak, he burst out laughing. I am not going to talk to you anymore as you are laughing at me, Freeda told him. Through the laughter, he said in a whisper, *"What you want to know"* as Freeda replied, I told you what I wanted to know.

"When that dog, (What?) W*hen that dog breaks wind, you want to know which way the stink blows."*

Laughter erupted before Freeda managed to reply, "Well I am not going with the nasty side of a fart, excuse me. I will go with a pleasant smell," as she laughed again. "I will go with a pleasant smell: and do you know something?"

I want to ask Spirit.

The guide interrupted saying, *"By the hair is getting thin."*

He was feeling my hair at this point after he had scratched my crown.

Well behave, she retorted. I want to ask Spirit this question as he said, *"It is not stuck on".*

He was pulling my hair on either side to see if it was actually hair and not a wig!

"Listen," remarked Freeda, determined to ask her question. Is it correct when we smell bad smells that it is a dark energy or a negative energy about? Well, we talked about it. It smells like rotten *("Fish", he said).*

Yes, you know like rotten smell.

"Rotting fish smell, rotting fish," he remarked.

Freeda continued, and you know when you get a whiff of it and oh, something that is around me is a bit eggy, stinks. Laughter erupted again as they all thought this hilarious. It is a horrible smell that one. Freeda asked through her laughter, but how do we get rid of it? Laughter again as Freeda asked, stop pumping? The laughter burst out again.

"Nosegay,", was his reply, *"nosegay",* as the laughter continued.

Freeda remarked that she was not being funny. More comments flowed between Freeda and Irene before Freeda laughingly said she was pleased that I had brought this lady through today: or man. "Whatever the case may be," remarked Irene.

The guide replied, *"Well sometimes: wouldn't you like to know."*

Freeda was laughing again as she said it did not matter now, to anybody.

He replied, *"It does not matter to me"*, as he chuckled to himself.

Freeda replied it does not matter whether you are a man or a woman as long as you are happy (He replied, *"AC-DC"*) it does not matter nowadays you know.

He pondered this exchange with a, *"hum, well, yes. The simple questions are always the hardest, aren't they?"*

At this point, he appeared to be addressing the question to his right as if some energy was listening or perhaps guiding his dialogue.

Freeda replied, yes, it is simple. In a way, it is simple because we could go into depths about this, you know. We could go into the depths about the rotten smell, the bad energies you know like hanging over, a cloud hanging over you, with the negativity. I would like to say, I would like to ask you complicated questions like, how do we get rid of it?

"That depends what it is,", he offered.

Well that is exactly right, replied Freeda. That is exactly right.

He continued. *"Is it, is it, well from my point of view, up here. Well here, here. This thing has one of these, and it, a smell organ, and this grey stuff in here responds to what this does."*

He had stuck my right index finger up my nose at this point and then pointed to my head, index finger extended. He then used both hands, the left to indicate my nose and the right to indicate my head.

"If you have rotting fish, stale cabbage, perfume, this responds here.

(Pointing to my nose and head once again).

"Sometimes inside, yes, inside, inside. Not sure exactly where the damn thing is."

He patted various parts of my body with both hands as if looking for something before pointing back at my head.

"Inside, inside there is one of us, and sometimes we get the feeling, that this, one of them funny spirits running about in the dark. It has not come to the light. No, it has not come to the light, been naughty boys, sometimes very naughty boys and then so, so, what, you have to put the protection on. Tell them to go first, then, put the protection on. Because if you put the protection on, you keep them in the middle, nearly swore, or this way you keep it inside the box. Then you cannot get rid of it."

Freeda replied, well the thing that you said which was resonating with me was, that you did not say, this entity or this body. You said this thing. So do you feel as though when these entities cross over they no longer have an entity they are just a thing: just a thing, you know or something that hangs around you. It is not an entity anymore; it is not a person any more. It is just a thing.

He said, *"No, no, no, no, no. From our side. People who follow the human and it overrules the Spirit so they do nasty things, very nasty things sometimes. When they transition, the doors shut. We do not open the door."*

Freeda remarked yes, you keep the thing out.

He replied, *"No. We keep the spirit out, the energy out. We do not want it contaminating the next level up so it goes into quarantine, English word, yes. We keep it out, the other side of the door."*

Freeda said, good advice: really good advice. That is excellent.

When they come to terms with it because they have a guide: who will go and tell them why they are in the dark, but the guide cannot stay with them. It is up to them to come to the light. Dependent, no, no, not dependent. Depending on the seriousness of their, on their, this is difficult, on their level of disobedience.

Freeda interrupted stating, Right, how naughty they are.

He replied, *"Well, yes."*

Disobedience to whom? Irene asked.

He answered, *"To the sanctity of life."*

She understood the answer.

He resumed his dialogue. *Then they might have to stay there a long, long time; but we will send well, well no, not we, the guide will check every so often and reinforce the erm, the, the nature of the misdemeanor to see if this spirit has realised how bad he has transgressed. Once he comes to terms with his transgression, then he will be allowed to come to the light and receive further alignment of his thoughts. In very severe cases, the Spirit will be isolated and sent back to the beginning, to be realigned to what is expected.*

Irene said, so he will be, sent back to the beginning, and start all over again?

Yes, said Freeda.

The guide said, *"Not quite. They still have the memory of their lives but it is a change, a change? Yes, a change, not DNA, no, no, no. It is a change in how the energies, are aligned. So we do not, the spirit cannot be destroyed. It is not brainwashed, but it is realigned."*

Freeda stated, basically, if they were not in the right vibrational energy, they would not be able to enter into his level. They have to be realigned to vibrate at the right level, to open the door to come in.

Irene asked, is it true to say that, and I need to ask this because it is quite important to me to understand this. That it is when they decide, they go to a place that is appropriate to their vibratory rate. Putting it into that kind of terms. They are the ones that have to decide if they wish then, to come to the light then they can get the help to be realigned.

Well, yes. In a nutshell, yes. You were told in a previous session, how these things happen. It was slightly different because the question was tortured souls.

Freeda said, yes, I remember, it was me: that asked that.

The guide continued. *It is not torture like pulling fingernails, chopping fingers off and legs and sticking things in people, like they did in the old days. It is a case of them being in, you could say, in the darkness between the earth plane and reception. So they are out in the street, the hotel door is shut but the bed is inside. They must make their mind up that what they have done is against the laws of the universe and request, not forgiveness, because it is written, it stays with them all the time but they must request that they can come to the light.*

They will be interviewed by their guide: to determine whether this is truthful. He will report, back to the Council and the Council will make a decision on whether we open the door or it remains closed to them.

Both Irene and Freeda wanted to comment.

Irene asked: is it the Great Karmic Council that you are mentioning?

He replied immediately.

Irene, there are thousands and thousands of councils. We have a council for so many groups. Then we have a council for so many more groups. That council has a council above it and then the ancient ones and they probably have someone again, almost close to everything: that decides on their behaviour. It is, you could not imagine until you are over here and aware of what it is. I can only imagine the levels above me and there are many. Many, many, many.

If you think that here, we have the souls of everyone who ever lived, just on the earth plane. These people are constantly going backwards and forwards, living lives after lives after lives, to reach a level on the earth plane so they can become, in their way, Guides for the new souls. Because of the population explosion on the earth plane, there is more and more, new souls coming, and these souls are very young. They have this grey matter, which they are blending with difficulty. We have our junior guides who have done this a few times, to help them: but because of their human traits, their base desires, they can lead Spirit, especially new Spirit, on strange pathways.

The organisation of the transitions, up and down, in and out and across to the groups: the schools, the teaching, the healing and the planning: It is much larger than the population of earth. People like me who is only a tiny cog, grain of sand, tell the truth: a grain of sand with little teeth on is part of this huge machine that we call, base one.

Irene remarked, "I have so enjoyed this session and can only thank you for coming through and just being so candid about things and giving us, great joy."

Freeda agreed saying it has been lovely. It has been uplifting and thank you for coming. Thank you and thank you for your advice on Bill that he is getting there. Thank you.

The guide remarked, *"Joy to you all. It has been so good. Makes a change, doesn't it?"*

He was quite jovial whilst saying this as both Freeda and Irene were laughing with him and having fun. Thank you repeated for how much they had enjoyed the session and how uplifting it was. The guide broke into the joy they were sharing by saying, *"I think I am being called. I saw the warning signs. It is like bright blue flashes like little stars."*

Freeda remarked time is up. You are being called. Thank you again. Irene said she could not see it. Is it like an electric blue?

Through a smile he replied, *"Signals for me. It is like cobalt blue. It glows with an iridescence. Bill has seen it before on the earth plane. Ask him, he will tell you. That is the Master, I had better go, goodbye friends."*

Freeda said goodbye until we meet again. He laughing replied, *"Should see you again for this"*. With laughter from both Freeda and Irene, Freeda retorted, you are sneaky! You had better go back. They are calling you and do not forget Fred Astaire and Ginger Rogers, Tootsie, right: as Irene repeated Tootsie then gave out a loud peal of laughter. Freeda said laughing, bye Tootsie.

All you heard from him was, *"Black and white shoes"*.

Freeda broke into song: Putting on the top hat: them humming the next line. Just enjoy what we have done together, today. Thank you very much for coming, very unexpected lovely visit, thank you. Absolutely, remarked Irene.

Freeda asked, Is Bill coming back. Just take your time, Bill. Trying, I replied. Freeda remarked, she does not want to go, does she. Freeda said, you have to behave yourself, you have to go, pet, Tootsie. Until we meet again. It was lots of fun.

You have to let Bill come back through now. Are you back, Bill? You are partly back.

As I looked at Freeda, her face appeared to me very suntanned and younger. I asked, "Have you been on your holidays?" Laughing she replied No, I have not been on my holidays but do I look nice, as she laughed again.

I replied, "You look a bit like Sandra to me."

Freeda laughed and said, "You know, I had Shairi-Lah come through for you and he said, he has to listen to the music. There is some music and he said you would understand it. I do not know what it is but there is some music and you have to listen to the music so there you are. That is another step on your journey. Right, ok. We have had a lovely time, haven't we?"

Irene said, "Yes, if you were not aware of it."

"You will enjoy it," interjected Freeda.

Still bemused, a one-word answer: "Vaguely".

Freeda replied, you will, because you are still coming in and out of it and then you see bits and pieces and then it goes, you know. We have had a whale of a time with Tootsie. Laughter and a discussion between Irene and Freeda as Irene did not know it was Tootsie. Freeda was only carrying on with her but that was what she had heard.

I have black and white shoes, I remarked.

Irene and Freeda simultaneously, yes, that is right. Fred Astaire and Ginger Rogers used to wear shoes like that in those days.

I agreed, yes they did. In fact, my dad had a pair but they were brown and white. The image of my childhood as a young boy looking in the bottom of the wardrobe for Christmas presents and seeing these light brogue brown and white shoes came into my mind. I must have been only seven or eight years old at the time.

Well, there you are, said Freeda. It has been lovely but anyway as I say, Shairi-Lah said you have to listen to the music so that is another step on your way up.

Is he going to tell me which music, I asked.
Freeda replied, I think, he has just said you will find out. I will probably be the one that tells you. I was trying to tell Freeda that I have a wide range of music in my collection but she would not allow me to talk.

No, No, No, she said, this is special music.

Well I have special music, I replied.

You will listen to it right, affirmed Freeda.

Irene reminded us to close properly.

Freeda thanked everybody who had come today and would they please go back out through the hatch in the roof, because I know there is quite a few of you, it is like bus trips today. So goodnight, God bless. I could see Catherine wheels like fireworks but felt good. You do not know what you are going to get until you start, but we must have needed that today. We must have needed the upliftment. We all agreed it was wonderful and uplifting. Thank you, Spirits.

This session had been different from previous ones, as "Tootsie" appeared to be both a comedian and able to speak with a normal voice and a girlish voice through me. The gestures and animation of my body had never happened before to this extent. He made great use of my hands in forming what he was trying to describe with a variety of gestures to both calm down and draw in energy as Tai Chi practitioners do. His conversations with an unknown entity that appeared to be watching and conversing with him on his right hand side were quite remarkable when I reviewed the video recording. His visit was totally unexpected, but we were so pleased that he came to us with information about the other side of life, beyond the veil.

Chapter Twelve
– "Tootsie" and the Table

The following week, Thursday November the 28th 2019, dawned reasonably clear and bright. Session ten, and I felt energised and a little nervous, as I usually do before our weekly sessions. I always wonder what we will get and what surprises Spirit has in store for us that day. It seems to me that they already have our session prepared. They seem to know before we arrive what questions we are going to ask and whom they will bring forward to answer them. Freeda, my mentor, has two or three regular Guides who have helped me enormously and brought me twice as many to channel in nine short weeks. After last week with "Tootsie", we were all still on a high. Our initial conversation, peppered with laughter would no doubt, lift the energies even higher.

Irene asked if I had a tee shirt under my jumper. I replied, "Too right have I." Well, you can always take your jumper off if you get too hot, because I feel that the energies are going to be a lot higher today, she replied.

Freeda remarked yes, the energies are good today.

I replied, "That is why I put my jumper on."

Freeda replied, "See Irene, he knew before he came."

"Are you clairvoyant?" she asked me.

Both Irene and Freeda burst out laughing at this remark. I replied, "No, no I am not", as both said, Yes, you are.

"I do not know what I am," I replied. "I do not get a lot like, a Medium does. I only get bits and pieces but this is where, yes."

Irene interrupted me saying, "Neither do I but yes, this is where it is good. This is what you want because if you are evolving all the time, you can never do better: Then you can help people."

Freeda said, "Well, honestly I think you are coming on a lot."

I can talk to people more about what is going on, I replied.

Freeda agreed. She laughed as she told us her guide was having a laugh as he said no, he is not a medium, only a small. When he gets bigger, he can be a Medium.

Laughter prevailed at this remark. You are not a medium: you are a little cog in a big wheel: just a small, at the moment. When you get bigger, you can be a medium. Well, Tootsie said he was just a grain of sand with a few little teeth in.

My feet were getting cold.

Shall we start, asked Irene. It is red hot in here so there you go. Ok, here we go, said Freeda. Are we starting Mr. Small, Mr. Small, asked Freeda laughing.

I replied, I was thinking more of Mr Blobby but never mind.

Laughing herself at this, she remarked, see what the energies are like today.

Sitting at the table, we recited the Lord's Prayer. A stroke of the bowl to vibration immediately brought the energies around us. I knew we were late in starting which would be why they were immediately present, waiting impatiently for us. As Freeda went into her breathing pattern, they showed me a monk with a cowl on and a beard. Irene said that she had a black leaded, windowed front door stove, set in a high fireplace and she did not know why they had shown her this. Freeda could also see it but she thought it was the kitchen of a stately home. She felt that the door was open to allow the sunshine to come in.

I could see a pot-bellied stove with a coffee pot on the top. Then a cabin, with a single iron bed in the corner on the left hand side. It is a one-roomed trapper's cabin. There is a dressing table on this side, like a dresser with drawers. One long drawer and cupboards underneath. Three or four shelves. It is a wood floor. I have not the right colours so I think I am been waylaid here, I remarked.

Freeda's guide, Guy, was near me. I commented, "Although we are their guides it is a partnership." He called my name, Bill, over a dozen times to focus my attention. I said welcome friend. He addressed us.

Now we have come to terms with you. Do you understand these terms means that you can now understand us. You know the rules, the regulations, and the terms. You are like a baby in a toyshop with, like lots of sweets but you do not like the bitter ones.

Sometimes you are attracted by light. The light fascinates you. Sometimes I think as though you want to go through that door but you cannot, not yet. You make everybody fun at this side. It is fun for us to watch you struggle. It is so much fun (he laughs loudly) to watch you struggle.

I remarked, "I am pleased you enjoy it."

He replied, *"It is good because when you are struggling we know you will get to the other side. It might be a struggle but it will be honest work. Honest work and no easy way. Masters of all time have done this. Masters of all time have always struggled to get to the other side. They want to do lots more right, but they are the Masters. Yes we can say it was easy for the Masters but it never was, ok. Contemplation, contemplate everything you do. You do not contemplate things. Sometimes you do act before you think, right, ok.*

Get those scales out and weigh up what is hard for you and what is nice for you and I am sure you would like the lighter one. Do not go onto the heavy stuff yet, ok. My God, naughty, you are naughty with things. You know he sits and he stews and he thinks, but in the end, you are only chewing yourself. You know. Oh dear me, chew yourself. Can I do this: can I do that, can I think that, and we laugh. We laugh. You know Bill, oh, if you get an elastic band, it only stretches so far then snaps. Will you please control your thoughts and stop stretching them.

That is you told today, Freeda remarked, laughing. Put that in your pipe and smoke it!

Irene asked, "Would you say that we learn much more by our failures than we do by our successes?"

Freeda asked to wait until she brought her guide back. She asked Irene to repeat the question to ensure she got it right which Irene did.

"Is it true to say that we learn much more through our failures than we do through our successes?"

This is a difficult question to answer. Everybody has tests. Some have simple tests; some have hard tests. This journey is how educated you are, right. Educated in the fact that if you have difficulties, you know easily how to get through them. Some people make it hard to get through them but yes, you are right. Sometimes bad sometimes good is good for you. You get through this life with lessons. Each lesson taught by being, not introvert, no that is not the right word. Not introspective, it is not like that at all. It is more watching, watching. Not inside watching; seeing how other people react. If you watch other people react, then perhaps you will not take the journey they have taken. If you do not take the journey they have taken, it is a much easier ride for you. Observing is the answer.

"Watching and waiting?" I remarked.

The reply was *"Yes"*.

Right Bill, you are getting a lecture here, Freeda remarked.

The guide asked me: *Do you read the Bible?*

"I used to," I replied.

You please read the Bible and just open the page to where it comes to you. There is some lessons to learn for you, in the Bible.

Some of it is biblical truth, but as you know, and have worked it out; there is two meanings to you. Do you understand that please?

Oh, he is saying you have to get back to your writing. He is saying why don't you do your writing more. Why don't you do your writing more, get your head sorted. Do what you think, not what you want to do. Do what you think about: he is a naughty child, he wants hitting. He wants putting back at that desk and writing and writing and writing, Ok.

January (2020) is a very important month for you, January ok and you will understand it when we get it.

Freeda said that she would talk about what he is saying, as it was important to understand what he is saying.

If you give a dog something to eat, it will come back. With you (Me), they are feeding you because they know you will come back. Feeding you again because they know you will come back but you can understand: this is what he is saying. If you are kind to this dog, you get much more love and information from it. You can get the dog to do what it wants or what you want of it; and this is what they are doing with you. They are giving you little bits and pieces, little enticements, and you will keep coming back because you love it.

I said that they asked me for commitment and that is what I gave.

Freeda replied, but you were doing it obediently like a dog. If you feed it and give it a nice little bit stuff, it will want to come back again. This is what they are doing with you. They are giving you little titbits to bring you back, more titbits to bring you back.

I replied that I did understand. In one of the previous sessions, they said, "All religious, all religious books were tainted by man." When I open the Bible and see the text, I will question what I read, as to whether it has been; tainted by man; or is in fact, biblical truth.

He continued. Well as you can understand, there is two ways, some is truth, some not.

I remarked that some is like a philosophy. It has hidden meanings.

He answered, yes, right. Some has good meanings, good meanings. These men, who wrote this were, ascended Masters. They knew a lot more about the time, the future. Well, very connected, very connected and some of the things they knew long before us. They knew about life, they knew about sorrow. They knew about love. They knew about; everything you need to know, devious people. They knew everything and in that book, there is a bit of everything that is within us. We are all capable of what is in the Bible. It is man that is capable of it all but it is finding out what you know is right and what you know is wrong.

Freeda remarked that I was getting it today. You have to develop your senses, you know, develop your senses. I could see sunlight pushing through the clouds I could see in my mind.

She continued: The taste, the smell, the hearing, the feelings, and mainly use your third eye.

It is time you were using it more. I can actually see your third eye and two eyes and you are developing it more. It is time for you, that tunnel vision coming back. You can tunnel, you can see and you know you can do that. They are showing me a heart. Have you had problems with your blood, Bill? I replied, "Yes, diabetes." Does the light affect you? *(No)* Because there is a light here and it is affecting you. I do not know what they are doing with the light, but they are showing me that, right.

I replied, "It is really bright and it is making my eyes water."

Freeda said she was going to shut up because he wants to have a go at you all afternoon. I cannot keep going like this. It was not fair. Freeda said that they were showing her a chair.

I gave a sudden start. It felt like an electric shock, over almost instantly.

Freeda asked if I was going to come through. Is there somebody coming through you? Welcome Friend. I replied, "The energy is building and I am getting these shivers up my back and it is a different colour."

Are you getting purple? Freeda asked.

I replied, "A little bit of purple but more like a pale yellowy orange with purple round the sides."

Freeda said she could also see what I was seeing.

I shivered again.

Freeda said, "Bill, you have got to bring this: It is a man that is coming through you and I can see it is like that man we had last night but he is standing at the table.

"You know, like, you would stand at a table with a bread knife. He is cutting some bread. He is standing at the table but it is exactly like that man we had last night and I think he is very much with you."

I replied, "Yes, there is somebody with us. I am not used to the different colour. I have a frosted glass window and there is something on the windowsill. I do not know whether it is seashells. Why am I thinking of Poseidon?"

Irene and Freeda both said was that the ship that sunk.

I broke in saying, "No, Poseidon was a god, a Greek god. Right, now it is going very bright: really bright but pale yellow. Right, ok. It is strange, this energy."

Freeda said she thought it very good.

I replied, "I have never, no, not like this, I have never felt like this. It is very gentle. It is almost as if. Are you in the water or are you not in the water? It is more like a: It is like a very, very gentle: not even a swirl. It is just."

Irene broke in asking, "Is it loving? Do you feel the energy is very loving?"

I replied, "No, it is fairly neutral. It appears to be quite neutral. It is as if we have the legs in the water but it is not water, it is

thinner than that. It is almost like a mist but it feels like water."
Another shiver. It certainly made me jump and say "Oh dear me".

Freeda said, "I can see it like a hole with half of me in the
water and the other half at the top. I am seeing it like that."

I remarked, "I have got a column. A column in the centre of
my vision. There is something in the centre. It is a very indistinct
face. Bring it back, please. It is a yellowy green now." Another
sharp shiver shook me. I remarked, "You are not sure whether
he wants to blend or beat you with a stick because you are not
expecting it when it comes." Another shiver, then a slow deep
breath.

Freeda remarked, "Isn't it nice to be in the energies though?"

To me, the colour was changing to purple.

Irene asked if she could say something. She remarked, "For a
while I don't see, I cannot see."

I remarked, "It is not switched on." Even though there was
nothing to view from the lens side to tell me this!

For some inexplicable reason the video camera had switched
itself off. Further examination afterwards showed that it had
also failed to record from the start of our session. We eventually
managed to reset the recording mode and the camera was once
more indicating that it was recording.

Freeda remarked, it was meant to be. It did just not want us
to record. As long as we are recording it, that is great. (This refers
to our base audio recording, which runs parallel to the video
recording during every session. Just before the video restarted,
a big shiver went through me then the video came to life once
again.)

I said, "Right. Now I have got purple."

Freeda was seeing the same purple.

I remarked, "It was like a big golden keyhole there."

Freeda remarked, "I can see it like a hole in the floor as if you were dropping through it. You know there is half up and half down."

I replied, "Yes, there is a horizon. I am seeing a horizon and it is a darker purple, and then it gets lighter as if you are looking at the tops of mountains, far away. You can just see them as a darker purple outline. I have the sensation I am floating towards it. Because the mountain does not come to me, I have to go to the mountain."

Freeda piped in asking, "Bill, was there a lady who wore a scarf because she had cancer because of her hair?"

I replied, "Yes, my wife." A big shiver went through me causing a sharp intake of breath. Freeda continued, "I did not know, but I saw it. I am seeing a beautiful garland of flowers like what I have at the door off Irene. There is like, you are putting it on a grave but there is nobody dying. I feel as though it is about the time of somebody's passing and this garland placed on the grave. I do not know what that is about but it is the time of a passing."

I replied, "It is only the male side of the extended family that passed round about this time."

When did George pass? Freeda asked.

I did not know, as he was not a relative of mine, I replied.

Freeda said that they were talking about George passing and Edward. Do you know an Edward?

"Yes, I knew an Eddy. That is on Maureen's side. He was a nice guy, him," I remarked. Freeda said that he connected well with me, to which I replied, "Yes, he did. I really liked talking to him. He was a nice guy to talk to. Well, they all were really."

Freeda asked if he ever played music. I answered that his son did, he played the accordion. Freeda could hear the music, she said. I replied that he was a good singer. Is it not happy times, happy times that we should be able to bring back into our lives. It is the company, isn't it. It is what I was trying to explain here, before we started. It is the company. It is the bouncing off each

other. The things we have to tell each other. It is lovely to bring
Spirit in and the lovely memories, Christmases and everything,
you know.

I remarked that all the colours were changing as I was
listening to her.

Did Maureen have to get another ring? Freeda asked. "Yes,"
I replied.

She is funny, Freeda continued. She likes to cling on to
everything, possessions like for past things. You know she keeps
everything, doesn't she. Because they are saying, it is all precious
to her. She is a very sensitive lady that likes to feel secure and she
has all these bits and pieces that she keeps.

She is very determined, I offered.

Does she have problems with veins? Freeda asked. "Yes," I
replied as Freeda reiterated they were saying about her veins, like
varicose veins. Mind she is a strong woman. She is your backbone.
She speaks up for you as well.

I agreed all the points mentioned.

Freeda remarked that she was hearing that she is a good lady,
a good lady. Yes, I replied. You call me at your peril with Maureen.

Freeda remarked; she is like a Rottweiler when she starts and
when she gets hold she does not give up. Freeda continued, "This
is funny, has she got a blanket you know how the bairns (Children)
have a special blanket or something because I am shown the
blanket, ok.

We have two I replied.

Freeda was seeing a ball, a globe like a bauble. A baby toy or
something similar that I had to remember, with writing on, or a
name on.

I had white roses in my vision. I knew what they were showing
me but what they were showing me was slightly different to what
Freeda was seeing. It is now in a clear, perspex box. It is a posy of
white roses. It is too: they are not showing me the inscription. It

was given to Maureen and I do not know whether it is Nanna. Yes, because the feathers we find in the house, we put on the roses and she did not want it to discolour with age so we got a clear perspex box that it sits in.

That is lovely, that is beautiful. Freeda remarked. She said they are telling me to put my hands up so that I can feel the energy coming off it.

I could see Spirit floating about, purple white shapes. Well they are not shapes: more like little fluffy pieces of cloud. It is getting cold. We were all feeling cold and said so.

Freeda said there must be a cold breeze going right around us.

Yes, I replied. "It is not water, it is air. It is air swirling round as I could see a real purple colour in my vision. That is purple with white edges."

Another strong shiver and I remarked, "Right, there is a hole in the cloud. It is very small that. It is an intense purple. I am coming back from that because it is going into a face with an eye and now it has gone to clear purple again. No, there is a dark purple, white edge around it. They are itching my neck. Another shiver. They are making me hold my breath a bit and I do not know why."

Freeda remarked, "Go with it because I know why." Freeda said they were showing her sniffing up as she was breathing two or three sniffs in quick succession as she inhaled. There were two balls of energy in her upturned hands and the energy was very strong that they were giving off."

I said that her first sniff was a white with a golden edge to it, like a thick gold rope wrapped around it. Freeda replied, "The golden rope you are seeing is a gallows."

"Somebody was hung," I replied with a shiver. "They are making my neck itchy. I wonder if that is where the rope went as my head tilted back, and the edge of my left hand indicated a vertical path in front of my left ear, that side."

Freeda asked about an engraved watch, which belonged to my dad's brother. The energy in the two balls she was holding was getting stronger and she felt that her fingers were growing, especially the left hand little finger. It was starting to pain her.

Another big shiver and I could see a very pale colour.

Freeda could feel a lot of energy.

I remarked, "Yes, it is like a cloud. What it that? You know it is a bit like a searchlight on a moonlit night and the searchlight is picking up these energies, like these little clouds. Well it is like a wisp of smoke but it is picking them out and they are glowing in the light as they go in and out of the light. It is nice and restful. There is a peace about it."

Freeda commented, "Perhaps you are picking up on the really celestial energies like angels."

I remarked, "My legs are cold. My feet are freezing. Absolutely freezing. They are making me: oh, my toes and the backs of my legs, I can feel the muscles going. (Into spasm.) I have a ringing in my ear. No, it is not. It is in the back of my head. It is like a tuning fork." Freed removed her rings as they were hurting her fingers.

I remarked, "I think I am getting wrong for not tuning in."

Freeda said that she felt the table pulsing as she had placed her hands flat on the table.

I remarked, "That is a woman's face that and it seems half familiar."

Freeda asked me if I would do her a favour. "Can you put your hands on this table please? Just keep them steady. Can you feel the table? It is pulsing. Go with it."

I replied, "With my fingertips."

Put you full palm on, requested Freeda. She asked Irene to do the same and she stated that she could feel the energy.

Freeda asked her if she could feel the table pulsing.

Irene replied she could feel the energy very much so, going up her arms really strongly.

I said, "It is making my stomach quiver, shaking."

Irene said that she thought we should leave our hands on the table.

Freeda replied, "It is not half pulsing."

I felt that it was shaking, really, really shaking.

Freeda remarked with her, it felt like it was pulsing, as if it were alive. Irene and I both remarked that we had felt it pulsing.

I said, "I felt as if I was trying to stop it shaking."

Stay with it, Bill, Freeda asked. Because I am telling you now, I feel that this table is going to move. You know as if it is becoming more flexible.

Another shiver went through me as I remarked, "Made out of rubber". I could feel the shivers change into shakes, as I fought not to hold my breath. My arms had stiffened up with my shoulders raised.

Freeda and Irene both encouraged me to keep going, as I was repeatedly subjected too uncontrollable shivers.

In a pause, Freeda said that she knew what this was for, like the table tilting and that is how it feels. The shivers and shakes started with me again.

Irene commented that she felt the energy was building up to plug us into higher realms. Freeda said, "Just go with it, Bill, because it is shaking like anything."

I was trying as my whole body shook and my breath came in deep gasps of grasping a lungful of air. I gasped out, "I know it is but I have got my feet off the ground".

Freeda said, "The table is rocking, it is away. Goodness me! We are away, away".

That is fine, Irene remarked.

My breathing was now in short gasps and moans.

Freeda asked if I could feel the chair shaking.

I managed a deep gasp. "Everything is (another gasp) locked up".

Breathe with it, go with it, was the advice from Freeda and Irene. Freeda remarked, "It is getting violent though, isn't it".

"Oh dear," I gasped out.

Freeda said, "Go with it as we are going to get some knocks here, mind. It is going to build up then it is going to go back, right".

It was over. The water in the glass on the table was still moving but I was able to breathe more normally as I recovered from the exertion of blending with this energy.

Freeda remarked, "Oh, it is gone", as the energy subsided. "It has gone, mine's gone", whilst Irene remarked she could still feel the energy. Freeda confirmed hers had gone as I remarked, "It has stopped. The table was out of sync", as I lapsed into incoherent mumbling for a few seconds.

Freeda said, "Welcome, Friend. Welcome, friend", as I groaned on my exhalations.

For three or four breaths the groaning exhalations continued. Freeda repeated, "Welcome, friend, welcome, friend" as a deep growl of a voice from me said *"Hello"*.

Freeda replied, "Hello friend. Thank you for coming, hello". Another breath, then he started to laugh. It was Tootsie back once again. Irene and Freeda both laughed with abandon and the table started to shake again. Tootsie remarked.

"What do you think about that? As he laughed aloud".

Freeda remarked, "It was great. I think we should do some table tilting.

"Do you want to do some table tilting"?

He replied, *"Oh dear me. It is great to be back".*

Irene asked, what is the point of table tilting? Freeda replied, "Ask questions. Two for yes and one for no." Tootsie slapped the table twice. Freeda exclaimed, "Oh you bugger. Stop it, Bill. Oh goodness, this lady. Wicked. This is a wicked lady. Welcome, friend".

"I am not wicked. I am absolutely terrible", he replied.

This remark caused laughter from both Irene and Freeda. Are we lifting the energies again today? Freeda asked.

"Oh dear. What do you want to do"?

Freeda replied laughing, "See what is knocking about". Tootsie slapped his hand four times on the table as Freeda repeated, "See what is knocking about." Have you brought your friends with you? She asked. Tootsie glanced to his right and said, *"Nooo"*.

Freeda said, "That is a bit disappointing. I like your friends. I just want a kicking. Why have you gone silent?" As she laughed loudly. Freeda was really enjoying this. "Why have you gone silent? Come on." Tootsie glanced again to his left side as if talking to someone and turned back asking:

"He just says: "Am I getting fixed up"? He turned back and said, "It is up to you. She is weird, you know".

Freeda, creased with laughter saying to Irene, "He is asking am I getting fixed up"! Tootsie was laughing, as he said, *"Sounds like the Three Stooges, doesn't it",* as he in turn laughed aloud at his own remark. Freeda said that she was going to sing a song to him. Right, you have to listen as he composed himself.

"It is going to be weird this. Wait until I cover my ears", he remarked laughing.

Freeda began singing.

"Daisy, Daisy, give me your answer too. *"Ooo, hoo",* he added.

I'm half-crazy, all for the love of you,

it won't be a stylish marriage,

we can't afford a carriage.

"Tootsie" was chuckling to himself.

But you'd look sweet upon the seat, on a bicycle made for two. That is for you, right".

Tootsie asked, *"Have you ever seen square wheels on a bike"?*

Freeda laughed again as she said, "I do not think it will work very well.

Neither did the carriage when the wheel fell off, he replied laughing. Ah, dear me. That took a bit of doing.

Right. Freeda said laughingly. We want your wit. You have to be witty today.

Tootsie laughed, as Freeda asked, "What is that saying, when wit is in, something's out"? Irene remarked, "No, when something's in, wit is out".

Freeda repeated. When something's in, wit is out, laughing.

"Witty? If wit was [blank], you would be covered in it", he said, with knowing laughter all round.

Now that is naughty, Freeda remarked with a laugh.

Tootsie turned to his friend and remarked, *"Stop that. You are getting as bad as them. Are you sure you do not want to come in"?*

Freeda asked, "Is it your birthday?"

"That's difficult. We do not get birthdays up here, man".

Ok. Freeda replied. I have been told, it has been a birthday.

"Nothing to say really."

Freeda said, "Well at least you have come in."

Irene commented, "It was you with the table demonstrating that you were around".

"Yes," said Freeda.

It was your idea of fun, remarked Irene.

Tootsie, with a grin, held up both his hands stating, *"Guilty"*.

Everyone dissolved into laughter.

"Frightened the life out of this fellow though," he remarked as *he patted my chest.*

We can move mountains, never mind tables, Freeda stated.

"We can do anything. Well, within reason," he replied.

"Oh, I have given him a bad neck. I did not mean to do that," he said. As he rubbed my neck. Freeda said to Irene, "Mind you have to watch it because I am lifting."

Tootsie said, *"When he comes back tell him I am sorry. I will try not to let it happen again".*

Behave, said Freeda.

"No, it is serious this. Can he not keep his head still? Ah, that is better. Right, shall we begin?"

Yes please, said Freeda, as Tootsie chuckled.

He turned towards his friend saying, "Earwig hoe! Have you got a coin?

As there was no reply, he motioned a flick of a coin saying, *"Heads or tails?"*

Tails, called Freeda.

"It is your question first then. Sorry, Irene, you lost out there, flower. You should have called first because you had tails in your head. Well, I can let go of this table now, can't I?"

No, replied Freeda. My question is, "What was your view of the energy that was coming out of the table. What was the point of view? Let us put it this way, because there was a lot of energies."

"Good, wasn't it?" he remarked.

It was good, Freeda replied.

"Called concentration," he said

Yes, it was making it possible for it to move, Freeda remarked. The energies flowing through it were terrific.

"There is some funny people about," he remarked.

This made Freeda laugh.

"We had to, sort of, mmm: open the path."

Yes, right. It was very good, said Freeda. I enjoyed it.

"They are the opposite to burglars, you know; when they see the light, they think there is nobody in. Oh, there is just a couple of pains in this man's back."

He stretched and twisted me as he tried to take the pain out.

"That is what he is telling me anyway. He has cold as well, hasn't he? Still, he tries his best I suppose."

God loves a trier, commented Freeda.

"Yes, he does," Tootsie replied.

"Howay then, Freeda."

What do you want to know? She asked.

"No, you had the question. You won the toss."

Freeda replied, I asked you. What did you feel about the vibrations, of the table? I asked you that and you are not answering me.

"What did I think about it? Well it was not for me."

Irene and Freeda both laughed as Freeda remarked, "Yes, but you enjoyed it."

Yes, she did it, remarked Irene, or he, whatever.

Tootsie held up his hands stating, Male.

Ok then, Male; remarked Irene with a laugh. Freeda remarked, Bill, I am getting this song and it is like, right.

Ok. If you want to call me Tootsie, that is up to you. I answer to most things.

Well what it is, I am getting Rock a bye baby on the treetop, and I think we should try the table tilting because I think we will make a very good group together.

There is a lot of stuff on the table and then the camera will roll over and then it could break and then. It is just a party trick.

It is, remarked Irene.

Freeda replied I know it is. I have done it and I do not think it is a trick.

Irene said that it was for people who could not plug in to the higher energies.

Got it in one, Irene, Tootsie replied.

Freeda retorted, No, no, no. How do you know if you do not try? This is what I am being told. How do you know until we try together?

Right, try it. Tootsie sat back and folded his arms.

Not with this table, Freeda stated.

What is the matter? Too heavy for you, flower?

Irene started to cough and splutter.

Freeda said, "I like a round table."

Look here. Just about choking Irene there.

Irene remarked, Keep it for a different group.

Freeda said, no. No, we are not. We are going to do it. There you are. We are going to do it and it is not what you think.

If you are going to do it, go ahead.

Freda asked, "Well you can join us and Irene can join us."

No. you go ahead. You have the energy. You can do it.

Freeda retorted. We do not know until we try it. I don't know. Your energy was not too bad there.

"Well, it was getting there," he replied. "It is a heavy table, you know. Takes a bit of doing."

It is a heavy table, Freeda retorted. I thought it was going to lift off the floor. The way it was going it was pulsing for me: you know when something is ready.

"Look, if we had kept going and we had gotten the table off the floor I would not be sitting here now."

Why? Freeda asked.

"I would be lying down recovering," he remarked. Freeda laughed.

"I came here for a day out, not for a day of work," he replied. "Did not half get wrong the last time, dear me."

Irene asked, "Are you still with us. Is it you that is talking through Bill?

"Why? Who do you think it is? I will tell you what: Doubting Thomas has nothing on this."

Irene and Freeda broke into laughter. Irene asked, "What name would you prefer?"

"I have told you."

Irene broke in, "Call me anything, I know. All right then, Anything."

"Right then. Tootsie will do."

Freeda chimed in with a laugh. All right. Anything.

Well, what do you want? Rastus? Ezekiel? Jebediah?

Freeda replied, "No, we want Poseidon." Irene creased into laughter.

No, he is the one with the trident, man. You have to watch him.

Well what about Zak? Irene asked. That could be a number of things.

Zak?

Zacharias, Freeda asked.

It could be a good few, added Irene.

No, just give me Tootsie, man.

Tootsie it is, replied Irene.

Tootsie will do for me. There is only one thing. I could not find no black and white shoes over here. I had to make them myself. There was nobody had any. Mind it was good of this fellow's father having brown and white ones. A man after my own heart that, you know.

Freeda asked, "Do you feel the cold, Tootsie?"

The cold: I think I am sitting on one of them Ice Thrones. My bum is numb: Hey, that rhymes as well. I will tell you what.

Irene broke in saying, you are a poet and you did not know it.

Yes, this is true. This is very true.

Freeda commented, we are getting to know your nature though, yes, cheeky: laughing.

I try my best, he retorted.

Freeda replied, "I know, but that is your way, isn't it. That is the way you."

Yes, I like just the way I am. I like a bit of fun like, yes.

You like to travel through life like that, Freeda stated.

A few lives like this.

That is good. We like the energy, Freeda commented.

That is why I do not make progress.

Irene jumped in asking, "Are you on the second or third rung or something?"

Number four, he replied, as he held four finger up to Irene.

Irene commented, "Number four. Well that is good to know, number four. Well you are with the right group, aren't you?"

It took me a long time to get here. I was knocked back twice, but they put up with me. They know what I am like. They cannot change things.

Freeda replied, I know but I bet you are disruptive, then laughed out loud.

Irene commented, I think you raise the energies.

Sometimes, he replied.

Freeda said she thought that he was a free spirit.

I do not know about the energies but I nearly raised the table.

Freeda said, I think you are a free spirit.

Ah well. Not exactly. They give me quite a bit of freedom, you know. I can just float about down here. Every now and again, they check up on me, as they did last week: so it was back last week to talk about the case.

Freeda commented, "They dare not let you out down here. You have too much fun. You love to come down and chat with us."

I do, I do. I do, I do I do. I love it. It is absolutely marvellous!

Tootsie was quite excited as he said it, showing that he was very happy to be here. Irene and Freeda were both laughing at the comedy of how he had said those few words.

"Guess what," said Freeda. You get a biscuit after; and a cuppa, chimed in Irene as Freeda joined in with: and a cup of tea. You cannot have that, Tootsie, she said laughing. Do not blame me for laughing. It is your fault.

You just, you have no idea, man.

No idea. I would agree with that, commented Irene.

He spread out his hands saying, "I can have a big cup like that, two handles," as if he was lifting a trophy cup full to the brim that was heavy, Just like that.

Freeda replied, "Yes, just make us jealous."

No, do not eat now. Do not need it. A bit like them electric cars you know. You just plug in then: broom! There is the energy back. It takes a little while.

Irene and Freeda liked the idea of plugging in to the energy. The energy of the cosmic oceans so to speak, said Irene.

Freeda asked, "Tootsie, can we have the table again? I want to have a go see if we can raise the vibrations on here."

"Oh, I do not know whether to do that. It is cold in here".

Just take your time, Tootsie, Freeda requested.

"Are they sending someone in to help us, as it is getting cold around here"?

Freeda commented, "Oh, it is starting off already. Can you feel it, Irene?"

I do not have my hands on it, she replied. "Put your hands on," Freeda requested.

"Oh, it is getting cold around here. Yes, my hands are warm enough". Tootsie had been rubbing his hands around then gripping them together.

Can you feel it already? Asked Freeda. Pulling. You know, like the waves on the sea with the tide coming in. Irene replied, "I can feel the energy as if it is much more. It is not. I am much more in sync with the energy. It seems to come in and run up my arms."

Freeda requested Tootsie to put his hands on the table.

"Yes, but it is not balanced. It is not balanced," he replied.

Well try, said Freeda.

"We need somebody over there", as he pointed to the opposite end of the table.

Irene replied that she would sit in the middle, at the back, right.

"What a good idea," Tootsie exclaimed.

Well, thank you. I have done something right, replied Irene.

Yes, you did something right, commented Freeda. It is weird, ohh!

"There it is shaking. Oh, I know what you want there."

Freeda said, "You know when the tide is coming in backwards and forwards."

Tootsie commented, "Aw, man, there is someone playing silly buggers here. Excuse my French."

"The energies are not in sync. It is erratic. Once you get them into sync, you will feel in it. Like totally in tune, you know." Whoa, whoa, whoa! It is weird, exclaimed Freeda.

There is somebody else.

Oh, it is weird. It is building up, isn't it? Freeda remarked.

Yes it is. There it is away.

The table started to shake and made knocking sounds. The knocks were slightly erratic and appeared to be quickening.

What are you doing, trying to get it apart?

Wait a minute. Just keep it going. Wait a minute and I will tell you, remarked Freeda. When I say stop it will stop. Stop! Stop please! The table did not stop. It had slowed to a steady, rhythmic knocking.

Tootsie burst out laughing which started Irene off giggling.

"Come on, stop," said Freeda.

"Right, there you go."

The table stopped.

Freeda said to Tootsie, "Stop it. That is naughty. Stopped. Right, we are going to try it again."

I do not think you will get it up.

Freeda replied, come on. Try again. What are you doing?

Just trying to get my hands right. I have all this side to go at you know and it takes a lot of doing on your own.

I am on my own here, replied Freeda.

Tootsie was looking to his right appearing to converse with another entity.

"He has just wet himself laughing, him," he commented.

Right, said Freeda, here we go again. Whoa! Can you feel it Bill, building up again?

We are getting Hardnut and I do not know who that is. Right. Are you going to lift it, like?

Right, said Freeda. No, we are going to get the knocks. Come on, Spirit, please keep it going.

You will break the joints, you know.

No, one knock for yes and two knocks for no, right, so can we have one knock please. Tootsie slapped his palm on the table sending Irene into fits of laughter.

Tootsie, behave yourself, said Freeda.

Well you asked for one knock.

Off the table, Freeda replied.

The table started to move. Whoa, we are away. Freeda remarked.

There is two knocks. Were you listening?

No replied Freeda. I am deaf in the right ear.

Irene said it was these, the things in the middle of the table.

"Your Knees?" Tootsie commented. "Well she said a knock from the table. You do not know what you want, do you?"

Now, now, said Irene.

Quite sharply, Freeda said, "I am feeling the energies." Then laughed.

"Feeling the energies?"

It is lovely though. Isn't it nice to feel the energies?

"A bit like feeling yourself to me."

Not it is not. Can you not feel the table, Tootsie? Freeda asked.

"Why yes I can feel the table. Who the hell do you think is pushing it? Why aye."

Well it is not me, protested Freeda. Are you pushing it, Irene?

No, I am not, she replied. I can feel the energy going up my arms and my head is tingling. At this Tootsie started to laugh and commented. *"Eee, it's electric!"*

Irene said, "I cannot vouch for anyone else, I am not."

Freeda's arm was tingling. Is your arm hurting, Tootsie? She asked.

Mine? No.

Well mine is, said Freeda; as the table was still gently knocking as it moved, back and forth.

"I was just thinking. Have you, got your hands on the table?"

Listen to the rhythm of that, said Freeda.

"Aye. Yes. I had better not think too hard. That is rude that."

Well, behave. Listen. You have to listen. Freeda said. No, but it is making a sound. Whoa!

"It is now!"

Freeda started to count. One, Two, Three, Four, Five, Six, Seven. Isn't it.

"All good children go to heaven."

Well, be a good girl and you will go, Tootsie, remarked Freeda. He is a boy, Irene reminded her.

Why, whatever, quipped Freeda. Then Freeda started to laugh.

"Please myself," whispered Tootsie.

I am sure you can, remarked Irene.

Let's see if it is counting, asked Freeda.

"Look, no hands", as Tootsie lifted his hands off the table.

No, see if it goes, One, Two, Three, Four, Five, Six, Seven, again. One, so that is yes. Two for no. One, two, three. Are you tired? Now, I am a bit bored with this.

"I am out of sync. Other hand. No, stop!"

Freeda remarked, "Hey, it stopped straight away for you."

"Why is it going out of sync? You are not doing nothing with this bloody table are you?" As if, he was talking to an entity on his right he said, *"I thought it was you. Freeda, the little devil has turned up."*

You? Freeda enquired.

"No, him. He always interferes. Because he cannot get the women, that is why."

Freeda said she wanted to try the table tilting even though Irene did not like it.

"Feel the energies!"

Well once maybe, said Irene. It is a party trick to get people interested.

"Feel the energies!"

Yes, knock for one.

"Victorian party tricks, man. Let us be honest. It is, man."

It is not what we are about Freeda, Irene said. They started discussing the value of table tilting against what we had with our sessions to date. Freeda was insisting on trying it and eventually Irene said there was a round plastic table in the garden Freeda could use. You know it is a democratic group, Irene stated. We will try it, won't we, Bill?

"No," Tootsie replied.

Freeda laughing said, "That is not democratic, that is No."

"It is two against one. Two against one. I am speaking for him," he replied pointing to my chest.

I will do it on my own, Freeda stated. I have a little table out there, Irene told Freeda and it is plastic and small. We can sit round that. We will do that next week.

"You are chuntering on giving him (Me) lectures about not listening and not doing it right. What else was there? I know what he was thinking climbing the mountain. He was frightened he could not get his fingers in the crack. He was going to fall or roll off, so he is taking his time".

Which is good, Freeda remarked.

"Yes, it is good. The thing is if you roll off. Once you get over half way, it gets harder. He was told that. He knows that, but the higher you go":

The better it gets, quipped Freeda.

"Aye, but the harder you fall. Argh, his nose is terrible."

Irene remarked; the mountain is symbolic. It is your enlightenment and you have to be careful how you go.

"The mountain is human. All we are going is dimension, dimension, dimension, dimension, dimension. It is dimension. Believe me. I tell the truth. It is dimension, dimension and they are only a thought

thick so you can go from here to there, and that could be the other side of the universe. Perhaps told you too much there. Mmm, sorry. You never, you never heard that."

No, said Freeda.

"The world is your oyster."

Out of the oyster you get pearls of wisdom, replied Freeda.

"Mmm, yes," he replied.

Pearls of wisdom, mused Freeda.

"Well that was a medicine ball of a pearl that one. I had better not say anything else."

Irene asked about the energy on her side of the table that he had brought through. She could feel it.

"I did not actually bring it through. No, I just gave it a little flick, man. It is just like a tuning fork."

Well I could feel the tuning fork very harmoniously going through my body, Irene remarked.

"You are thinking of good vibrations, you. That is a song. You know that. Beach Boys fellas."

Freeda broke into song again singing and humming the first two lines of "Good Vibrations".

"Well, if you start singing and you hold this table, there is a good chance of it coming apart."

I am sorry about that, remarked Freeda. *I just need to.*

"No, you do not need a table."

I do, man. I will do it on my own, Freeda replied.

"Do not be like a little girl. Grow up, man."

I won't, replied Freeda. I want a table.

"I know, it is all in the mind."

I want a table. I want a table. Ha, Ha, I want a table, remarked Freeda. I am having a table.

"You have to have a proper table. You do not want a plastic table."

Another discussion about the table between Irene and Freeda
and eventually Freeda left the table asking if Bill was back yet.
Further discussion, then she would go when we get Bill back.

Irene said she would look after me while Freeda went outside
for the table.

As I started to come back I asked, "What is she doing out there?"

Getting that table, Irene replied. She wants to do table tilting.
Do you not remember?

What? I replied.

Yes, she wants to do table tilting.

Well, she has it tilted, I replied.

Irene laughed, saying, "She is bringing it in."

Eventually, the table was cleaned, positioned and the chairs
arranged. The camera and recorder repositioned, and we took
our places around this little table.

This was something new to me. I had heard, but never seen, or
took part in, table tilting. I was quite apprehensive as I was about
to experience this phenomenon.

Freeda explained the basics. You put your hands flat on the
table as she was and close your eyes; and you will feel the table,
like an engine going backwards and forwards: or it might pull one
way then another, with its energy. Then you might get messages.

What is it going to do? I asked.

Freeda described one time that the table had rocked sixty
times. One of the table sitters had a sixtieth wedding anniversary.
Freeda stated that she just liked to close her eyes and just let things
happen. "Do not be nasty and do naughty tricks," she asked.

Who? I replied.

"You" she quipped.

Irene replied it was not him. It was Tootsie.

Freeda replied, "Tootsie, right, ok. You be a good boy or girl",
with a laugh. "Just let the vibrations build up".

I replied, "You are confusing me".

Freeda continued, "No one has to push it, just feel the energies building up".

I started to laugh.

Freeda asked me, "What are you laughing at"?

"I can feel the table shaking", I replied.

"I know," replied Freeda. "I am not pushing it and you are not pushing it".

It was the combination of, the feeling of water running around my legs and the movement of the table, which had caused me to laugh. A nervous laugh which often happens when I feel something strange, but pleasant.

Freeda said thank you to those who would come around us and thank you to Tootsie. It would build up and build up.

I remarked it was like a dough maker. Like one of those things going round and round making dough. It was strange but thrilling. It made me nervous, but pleased at the same time.

Freeda replied, "Yes. I would like to say welcome friends and those gathered around us and can you please build up the energies a little bit more?"

Freeda remarked to Irene, "I know you are not bothered about Jimmy coming through, but he is standing right beside me here."

"I was not bothered about him coming through, but", Irene replied.

Freeda interrupted stating, "Well I know but I will just give you some evidence because he is standing right here next to me. Do you still have some trousers belonging to him, Irene?"

Irene replied that she thought she had got rid of them.

Freeda said that she thought there was one pair that Irene had not, and would she please observe that. I know you would not like this but he is having a few tears. He has his handkerchief out and is having a few tears. He has no regrets about you: no regrets, mind, about you.

Irene asked, "Why are you having a few tears, Jimmy"?

Freeda replied, "He is having a few tears. He just is because he did not cry the tears while he was here and he is sad about it, ok? He is really starting to build up the energies now."

I remarked "Dear me", as I could feel the table starting to rock with more and more energy.

Freeda addressed Jimmy. "Thank you, Jimmy. Yes, I know you are getting; do not get in a temper", as the table bounced eighteen times towards Irene before coming to rest. Still slowly moving with a gentle swirling motion. Freeda asked Irene about eighteen, but Irene could not relate the number to anything, as the table started to build energy once more.

Freeda then suddenly asked me if I knew a Norman.

"Yes", I replied. Immediately thinking of my father.

Freeda asked, "Is Norman in the physical or in Spirit?"

"Spirit." I shot back, as the table started to bounce once more towards Irene.

This time the count was twenty before the table stopped lifting and resumed a slow, steady rock, but staying on its legs. I felt sure we had miscounted as the question about Norman had led us to miscount.

Freeda asked Irene about twenty, as she felt sure he was trying to pass a message to Irene. The table started to bounce the leg closest to Irene a third time.

Freeda said twenty before the table stopped bouncing and I broke in stating, twenty-three; as her count had started too late.

Freeda and Irene asked for confirmation from me as I repeated, twenty-three.

Irene understood twenty-three. She was almost that age when she met Jimmy! The table bounced three times. Freeda asked about the three years. Irene confirmed they had courted three years. The table started to bounce with a count of twenty-three once again.

Freeda remarked that Jimmy was telling her he would marry Irene all again.

"Would you, pet?" asked Irene.

Yes, he would, replied Freeda. Jimmy was making her laugh as he kept pulling his trousers up and Irene would understand this action of pulling his trousers up.

"Later on," replied Irene. Freeda agreed that later on, he did have to pull his trousers up. The table rocked again to a count of thirty-two, but I pointed out that it could be thirty-three if you counted the last motion of the leg as it came to rest.

Freeda said that Jimmy like jam sponge or cake with custard on as the table kept up a swirling type motion.

Slowly the table tilted towards Freeda six times. A very positive but slow tilting motion. She remarked that she knew it was her brother George. From the strong, positive way, the table moved towards her. Freeda thanked him and told him he was getting through. The table bounced four more times. Freeda said that she would have to think on that because George had five children. The table felt as though it was going round in little circles.

Freeda asked George if he could give her anything else, as I broke in with a question.

I asked, "George, are you on about the fifth bairn? (Child). So the first four, then the last one."

Freeda immediately stated, "Martin."

I said, "Just give us: yes, good lad"; as the table immediately rocked towards Freeda.

Thank you, George, I said, as the slow, confident rocking continued, to a count of thirteen.

Freeda commented, "Unlucky for some but lucky for others. Our George's energy is round in circles. Have you noticed that? It is not rocking. It is round in circles." The table was going clockwise in circles, then pulling backwards and forwards as it started to rock slowly and confidently towards Freeda, ten times. Freeda had to think about this one. Suddenly she remembered. "Oh, well, my bloody house, 10 Office Street. Am I thick or what, George"? As she laughed at herself.

I retorted, "Don't answer that, George. Whatever you do, do not answer that", as Freeda and I laughed together.

He did it twice, Freeda remarked. Ten Office Street. Do you come there? Can you show us? The table rocked purposely towards Freeda ten more times, as she said, Yes it is ten more so he does come there. Thank you, George, said Freeda. I know you are round me all the time and thank you to Jimmy. What about the wedding anniversary, Irene?

It was in March and Jimmy passed in the June. Their golden wedding anniversary.

Freeda replied, "That was good. That is how you will always remember him. A glass of wine in his hand". The table rocked to Irene five times.

This led to Ian and his wife Dorothy who had lived in a house number five, in the early years of their life together. Ian was Jimmy's best man and Jimmy, Ian's. Jimmy had gone back there, as it was his happiest times.

The table bounced thirty-five times as the table tilted towards me, once more. It had really tilted slowly over, almost onto my knees. This is for you, Bill, Freeda remarked. I thought, with the last tilt, it was thirty-six. "This is for you," Freeda remarked. As Freeda was saying you know how it always.

I interrupted, remarking thirty-six years since, my Mam and Dad died.

Freeda commented, "Well this is the energies you have with you. Your Mam, she is lovely. Isn't she gentle? Do you understand of her being gentle?"

"Yes I do," I replied.

Freeda remarked she is coming in nice and gentle. Isn't that nice, as the table slowly tilted towards me once more.

She is offering her love. Love you. Can we have another one? Freeda remarked. A name with "S" asked about. Sylvia, Susan or some name beginning with "S". I knew a Susan but this one referred to here, was at the circle in Horden when an old friend from my early years had come through. This was on an Angel board and quite sad as both her, and her older sister, Jennifer who was my age, were already in Spirit. Various questions I had asked about our early childhood answered perfectly through the board.

Freeda remarked that I had mentioned Paul and he is a little bugger. As I answered, yes, Freeda broke in with "He has been here before that one. He knows a lot".

"Too much," I replied.

Freeda asked that if it was Bill's mam, could you please tilt because we want to do a little more before we finish. You will have to get cracking before we finish so can you please tilt towards Bill, please. Can you please build the energies up? The table slowly tilted towards me once more.

"Thanks, Mam. I enjoyed the hug the last time. It made a difference."

We repeated the question with Jimmy and George, in turn receiving a responding tilt.

The table was still moving slowly, like the, "Rock-a-bye baby" nursery song. Freeda thanked all the Spirit guides and helpers that had come through today. I remarked that it was tipping towards Freeda and Irene in turn then flattening as it came round to me. The table had moved towards the alcove and I was bent over to reach the table. Freeda said that there was a vortex in the alcove and they were going out through there.

I remarked, "It is not a vortex, it is a doorway."

Freeda agreed. I asked, "Show me a doorway" and the table tilted towards the alcove.

Freeda felt the energy of her sister, Maureen, as the table had tilted towards the alcove. Freeda asked and pleaded for Maureen to build up the energies but to no avail. Freeda thanked everyone for the day and a safe return through the doorway. Amen. We all repeated Amen.

Freeda remarked that she had enjoyed the tilting but felt a strong desire for a cigarette, even though she did not smoke! This feeling, she put down to George as he had smoked. Freeda asked me if I had enjoyed it.

I replied that it was different. It does work but it is too slow, as you have to count and then try to relate the numbers to something. Fortunately, Freeda had been able to communicate with the energies around us. Without this communication, it is very boring as both Irene and Freeda agreed. What we all agreed upon was that there was a doorway in the alcove.

As Irene arose to make a hot drink for us and attend to her two dogs, Freeda asked me if we could do a little bit more by sitting towards the "doorway" and see if we could get anything more. We re-arranged two chairs towards the alcove. We discussed how to position the chairs. We finally decided on sitting as if to "go through it" with Freeda in the "driving" position. Freeda driving and me in the navigator position.

We sat facing the wall. Freeda said she felt a magnetic pull. A feeling of someone pushing her towards the "doorway". She asked me if I felt the same.

Closing my eyes as requested I had half of my vision in a yellow colour, split vertically to a purple colour on my right. I felt drawn towards the colours. Freeda asked if I could feel the floor starting to shake. I could feel the presence of tremendous energies around us.

Freeda could feel the floor shaking around us, and vibrations under her legs. It was slowly increasing in intensity.

I was not party to such feelings and remarked, "No. This is for you, Freeda, not for me. You have to go with this"."

There were a few whoas and ahs from Freeda as she felt she was riding on a rollercoaster. I remarked that there was no weight on my feet but they were still touching the carpet. Freeda replied that she felt she was on a rollercoaster as I responded with, "This is for you".

Freeda's rollercoaster turned into a bumpy train ride as she rocked in the chair. She was laughing, as she said it was so funny. She wanted to swap seats with me to see if I could feel it. Swap over my seat, Bill, she asked as she rose to change places with me.

Sit there, she instructed as I suddenly said, "I have the song "Road to Nowhere" in my head." You are not going on the road to nowhere, she replied.

I think I am perfectly in line. I think it is straight there, as she indicated a point on the wall in the alcove. Swap over my seat. Just sit there and relax she asked me. See if it builds up like a roller coaster.

Irene called in for our coffee or tea preference. We decided coffee for both of us.

As we resumed, I felt a shiver run right through me, as my whole body responded to the energy.

Freeda asked if I could feel it, as if you are rattling now, as if you are building up the energy. Wow, I can feel it again, she remarked.

"There is more energy on this seat than there is on that seat, to me," I replied.

"There is," she answered.

Another sharp intake of breath as energy rocked me.

Just go with it. Breathe through it, exclaimed Freeda. Can you feel it as though you are on a train driving you so it is a bobbly road, so your seat is bobbling up and down?

Another two shudders went through me, causing me to grunt and gasp.

Freeda remarked, "Strong, isn't it? It is hard to understand but weird can you understand. Can you feel it?"

I have a smell, a smell of flowers.
Oh, lovely, lovely, remarked Freeda.
Oh, I have smelt them before.
What kind of flowers?
Wallflowers.
Oh, that was my favourite. I always used to sing, wallflowers, wallflowers, because my Dad's garden was full of them.
"It is. There is," as a huge shiver shook my whole body. "There is a massive patch of wallflowers and they are all different colours. Ohh, the smell is just ohh!" As I breathed in the incredible density of the beautiful perfume of these flowers in my vision.
Beautiful, remarked Freeda. I could smell them as I walked up the garden. Can you feel the floor vibrating? I cannot think. Bloody hell it is hard.
I am barely sitting on this chair, Freeda.
I know, she remarked. That is what I am saying.
I am barely.
Do you feel as if you are flying?
I have barely any weight on me.
It is good, isn't it?
Ohh that smell. It is just. Ohh, smell it. I was wafting the smell towards Freeda with my hands.
Wallflowers, wallflowers, she was singing.
Can you not smell it?
No, she replied; but you will, because you are in that gateway, the doorway.
Ohh. I kept repeating as the perfume wafted in to my senses, time after time.
How do you feel the energy underneath you? Do you feel as if it is rushing past you?
It's. It is a glass floor underneath me.

How about that then, Bill? It is good isn't it? Just take it on.

Did he have a greenhouse? Tomatoes? It has changed to tomatoes.

That is our George, Freeda responded. Big greenhouse, good gardener. Irene, he is getting all sorts here. He is getting the wallflowers. "Well good," Irene replied.

Ohh. What is that one? Ohh.

This is brilliant for your clairvoyance, you know. You are giving me brilliant stuff here you know, Freeda commented. Our George has a lovely greenhouse, a massive one. He had a boxing ring as well. Just keep going with it, Bill.

Well, my first feeling is chrysanthemums.

Freeda turned, shouting to Irene, Chrysanthemums, he used to grow show ones.

There is carnations as well. Zebras. Zebras. Like a pale yellow with like red zigzags. With purple ones, zigzags.

Yes, show ones. He looked after them.

The chrysanths were in, like a, not hot, like tomatoes but was enclosed. It was big. Did he make it himself? He built it himself, didn't he?

Yes, he did. I will tell you what it was. It was covered with mesh, like fine nets. Can you remember that, Irene? Our George's garden. He is on about the chrysanths. Our George used to grow chrysanths.

Ohh. That smell. Ohh, you just think he was stuffing them up my nose. Ohh. Was he a biggish fellow?

Yes, he was quite stocky, our George, strong man.

He wore his belt outside his trousers. The top was always like a little "V" on his trousers with a belt underneath. He has his sleeves rolled up to just underneath his elbows. He is bending down and that is a chrysanth plant. He is looking up. Did you take a photograph of him?

I do not know, Bill. I cannot remember that. Everything you are giving me is spot on there. They are all spot on. You are giving lovely messages here, mind.

He built a wall, yes.

He did it all.

He used to put hoops round the chrysanths with sticks in and that was around the hoops to stop them falling over.

Freeda remarked to Irene, isn't he doing well. You are doing smashing, Bill.

Was he a little thin on top?

No, no. He was not thin on top.

Are you sure?

He thought he might go but he did have canny (reasonable) hair. All right. It was thick enough.

I was smiling and Freeda noticed. Laughing she asked me what he was saying. Howay, tell me what he is saying.

I have been here a long time. I have lost this bit. (I was patting the top of my head.) *There is only this bit around here.* (I was indicating the sides and back of my head.) *It is a summer's day.*

Yes, that is when he committed suicide. That is when he went, on a summer's day.

He has a smile on his face.

Ah, yes. He was always smiling. A cheeky smile. He is always with me as well, Bill. Keep concentrating going through the vortex or the doorway.

He is telling, he is telling me. Come on, George. He was not punished. He was not: left as your Mam was. It was part.

I said aloud, "This is me. I am saying, how can you say it is part of the plan?"

Freeda replied, "Yes, it was part of the plan. It was part of the plan. It is not you saying it. It is him. It was planned six months before, and he knows that. It was his time, part of the plan. It made all the jigsaw come together. I understand that, George."

Yes, all right. He is trying to tell me, Freeda.

I think you have done very well, Bill.

Look. It is like; it had to be.

It did. He is right.

It was all in the plan.

Freeda replied. Yes, it was all in the plan. It was.

No regrets.

No, he did not. No.

They let me fetch my garden.

Yes, that is all he would want. He loved his garden.

That is where he is now.

Yes, always there. He used to be there at three o'clock in the morning.

Could he see the sea from his garden?

Yes, definitely.

Did he have an allotment: but he was like, higher up? There was allotments below him, out to sea.

My dad's allotment. Our George used to go there, to my dad's allotment.

Is that the one behind the quarry, behind the church?

No, it was the other side. Em.

Back of the pit.

Yes, behind the pit and you could see over the top to the sea. He used to spend many a happy hour there.

The pulley wheels got in the way a bit. He could not see the ships very well when the pulley wheels were going round.

Freeda commented, I think he is doing marvellous, don't you, Irene? Irene replied he has done very, very well. Irene asked if she should go and make the coffee. Yes please, Freeda responded.

George, you are going to go and have a cup of tea. He loves a cup of tea.

I asked George if he had anything else to say.

Two sugars? White pot, two sugars and a bit of milk in.

Freeda replied, "Yes, that did him all right."

By, he has a sweat on. It is warm in here.

You just look like him, Bill, from the side now, Freeda remarked. Just look exactly like him. George, I am happy that you have come through.

Thank you, George. It has been a pleasure.

You have done very well, Bill. You say you cannot do clairvoyance and cannot give messages. That was brilliant. Everything you have said there was spot on. Spot on. I am telling you; and I would not say it, mind, if I did not know it. You did brilliant.

You can stand up, George. It is all right. He is saying he has to stay bent over because he has not finished getting the little fresh seedlings out for the pots.

Yes, he would have to do that.

So get yourselves away and leave me to it.

That would be him exactly, Freeda commented. Thank you, Bill, Thank you very much.

Oh, and tell her he loves you too.

Ok and thank you very much.

Do not make me cry, George.

He loved me, you know.

Yes. Yes, big men do cry.

My best friend, our George. Well, how about that? You did very, very well. If you had been on the rostrum, that would have been everything perfect. See how you have come on. Bill, thank you very much for that. It was excellent.

Our session was over for the day. Now for the coffee, a biscuit and a review of the day.

Chapter Thirteen
– A New Year

It has been almost six weeks since our last session. Freeda had been in hospital with pneumonia and Irene had spent a few days there. Christmas had passed and here we were, session eleven on the 10th January 2020, ready for a new start to the New Year.

Freeda was still pale and looked a little under the weather after her ordeal but was keen to start working with Spirit again.

Irene was very interested about today. She had a feeling about it. She told us she was starting to settle down a little so it was probably the energies gathering for today's session. Freeda had a little shawl wrapped around her like some pictures of the Native American Indians show.

I could feel the coldness around my legs as soon as I sat down at the table.

Freeda opened up the proceedings with the Kabala prayer, which is in some ways similar to the Lord's Prayer. She welcomed Spirits, Guides and helpers who were waiting and the fact of it being our first meeting in 2020. I remarked that 2020 is the clarity of vision.

I could see green, for Irene. Freeda was getting the name Jonathan. I immediately replied Swift. Then Jonathan turned to Corolla: I said, Toyota. This was like word association. Irene asked corona or corolla? I had a Toyota Corolla during my working life and on the last day coming home, I was involved in an accident and the car was a write-off. Now Freeda had a Bentley. I remarked Continental. Definitely word association! I could feel someone very close to me now.

Freeda then had a question from Spirit: why do we not travel through time?

Backwards or forwards? Irene asked.

Both, replied Freeda. She felt that it was ages since we had sat together and she was quite intrigued as to who would come through and what we would get. You do not know Bill, she commented as Irene said that she felt we would be getting something profound through today.

I could feel a lot of energy and it was very close to me. It was interrupting my steady breathing as I had the word "insidious" spoken to me; yet I did not feel threatened. It was slowly creeping up towards me and it asked about the new camera system I had set up. I remarked that it was ok. I had checked it.

It was a funny thing to say, "Check the camera".

It was now really cold, on my feet; as I remarked that my thick socks were not helping me. Freeda had it on her back, but felt it as a wind going around you. I remarked it felt more like a creeping mist to me.

Irene was feeling it travelling up her legs as I remarked it was like stage smoke.

Freeda felt so funny. She remarked that it felt as if she wanted to win a race and she wanted to knock somebody over before the end, so she could win the race. She said that she had cheated to get there. They were making her laugh because they were telling her, just give Bill a nudge and you will get there before him. Everyone laughed at this, as she added, just trip him up as you are going!

The colours I was seeing were turning purple and I was starting to shake a little. Ever the gentleman; I remarked, "If you want to go first, Freeda, you are welcome."

No, she replied. I think I will let you go first today. Freeda said they were laughing at us saying, look at that.

I could see the face of an old Lifeboat man with his Sou'wester on.

Irene asked if anyone else could feel it but she thought that Shairi-Lah was around us. Freeda could see him with a stick. Not like a walking stick but like a conductor's baton and he is conducting. He is pointing and nodding to each of us as if to say, your turn. Bill's turn, Freeda's turn. He is prompting; it is your turn now.

Freeda addressed Irene stating, "He is pointing towards your lower back saying you have to get something done about that." He is funny. He is saying get that done.

Get your chest done. Get your heart done. Sorry, she remarked. "I am not channelling, he is just repeating and he is also giving you a third eye. You are going to have an inspiration, boing. The tuning fork is going to tune you right in. He is pulling moss out of the rocks and saying some of the minerals in there are good for you.

"The micro-biotic plants that would grow like lichen and things like that. He is just picking it out and putting it in a drink. The properties of it and ginger. He is telling me you have lost more weight. He can see it." He showed Freeda blancmange. It was referring to Irene going through the curtain of energies and out the other side with the energies feeling like blancmange. "You can pick up the energy on the other side. You get this when you do your healing. You go through the layers until you get to where you need to be."

Yes, Irene replied. Well Shairi-Lah is doing this for you. He is going through your energies and getting right down to the core of you. The core of your being.

That is excellent, remarked Irene. Thank you very much, Shairi-Lah. He is going. He is waving. He has a walking stick as well. Not a proper walking stick, a stick you know. Like a piece of wood off a tree, something like that, a staff. He states he is going to the core of your energies to help you. Right, ok and clear some rubbish out for you.

That is wonderful, Irene remarked.

He is saying you are like Livingstone, David Livingstone who despite terrible health soldiered on to discover Victoria Falls. Freeda was laughing as they were asking, "What is this Geordie lad going to say, like? That is you, Bill," as both Freeda and Irene laughed together. Someone is having a bit fun here.

To prove I was still awake I commented, "Dr. Livingstone I presume, a Moody Blues Song. We are all looking for someone."

"Right," said Freeda.

"It is, one of the lines they have brought," I replied.

I could still see the Lifeboat man, with his Sou'wester and a black beard; and the hood of an anorak trimmed with fur. Well it was a black beard. Now I am getting an old Guy, a very old Mandarin with a wispy beard. Now I have a very old Native American Indian. He has white hair. I have the purple with the wispy white passing across. A face is starting to come up. They were telling me I had lost my touch a bit. I had not being doing what I should have been doing.

Freeda remarked that we needed to do some deeper breathing and see what we get after that.

There was definitely something around me close and it was icy cold. I had the feeling that they were not making any attempt or even wanted to channel through me, that moment.

Freeda remarked, "Well we are going to. You know what I am like when I get started. A bossy boots. We are going too and ow, my head."

We can call him Guy I stated. He is a Guide but we can call him Guy. "Right, ok," said Freeda. "Welcome, Guy."

Irene said, Freeda, your face has changed. I have seen that happen, before.

I retorted, "He has not been lying about like we have."

Irene described Freeda's face as thinner and sharper features, with the eyes slanting slightly. "It may be one of your guides coming through. Do you feel it?" she asked.

I am ready to channel. You know I am getting ready. I said that there were yellow orange orbs travelling towards Freeda in my vision. There is a lot of it.

Whoa, said Freeda, whoa. We know who is coming through then.

I remarked I could see a lot of energy travelling towards her, a lot of energy like big orbs of orange in rings of purple slowly going across to her. I could feel it and could see it.

Guy came though immediately stating, "*Well, here we go. We are back again. Yes, we thought we were going to stop working but we are not. As you understand, once I come through we work. I am saying today, we welcome you all on this New Year, this new adventure; this created visit. This created visit because it was, created. This created visit. We will show you today how to create new things. Once you get the hang of it, it will become much easier. Creating things is a good way to show people what we are doing. So let us put it this way; today it took a while before we start to create because your ideas were flat. So flat that they are unbelievable. Right. Ok. We are looking at you and saying; when are they going to create something? When are they going to come out of their box because you are just sitting there waiting for us to create.*

Well it is not us that creates it is you that creates and I am sorry if I am being a bit firm as usual. Bill, you should be creating in your mind; and you can do it and you will do it. You understand me.

Yes, I replied.

Yes, okay. Sometimes you waste time, you know. You wait so long instead of saying: let us get cracking, go. You can make the, the husky pull a sledge if you whip it, right. Pull the sledge and let us go right, because it is time to get cracking.

"Yes," I replied.

Yes, and Guy has been with you for a long time and I think Guy is here today to demonstrate his power through you. Honestly, you are a good channeller but sometimes you need knocking on the head. Now it is time to create. My creation today is a beautiful lake with a, it is gorgeous. A beautiful lake but it is night time. Nighttime and the lake is midnight. You can see so many sparkly things in the lake. Some coming out of the lake sparkling which you see reflections sometimes of them. Sometimes they are pale blue. Sometimes they are silver. Sometimes they are a very turquoisy green; but all these things are in the imagination of the lake. Just imagine creating your lake. Looking at it peacefully: watching the stars shining over the top and the moon shining a pathway to a different place. You can create this wonderful. I can see, at the end of my creation; I can see a beautiful Native American girl. She is waving and smiling, and she is saying, come, come. Walk along the lake and join us. Come on a light path; join us. Do not be frightened. Come along long, long, long. Can you hear the music in the distance and the sound of what they are singing? I can hear them. They are singing: Cona maa akaa, cona maa akaa, cona manaka, cona manaka and then I can hear the drums going slowly and they are pounding, and drumming, and they are dancing but it is nice. It is nice. It is echoing in the hills beyond. Oh, it is beautiful. You will understand now.

Oh, I have a child here who is asking me questions. This child is asking; ask the name of my Master. Ask the name of my Master. Mykea, no. Ask the name of my Master. I am asking, right, I am asking. Red, red, red, red, mmm, red. It is not a fox. This child is asking the name of his Master. Ask the name of my Master and I do not know but they are saying red something, red something. No, it is not Red Cloud.

Red Elk, Irene offered.

Yep, yep, yep, yep, so I have given that back to this child. This child wants. That is funny. This child, mm, wants to know, is it time? Is it time yet to play? Is it time yet to play? Now I will start the game. I am asking, what kind of game and he is saying the drawing game and what we have been doing before, Irene. The drawing game and things like that this child is asking. There has been children around when we have been doing our work. Here is my guide coming back again, Freeda commented. He is very inquisitive about things like that.

I remarked, "I can see the energies just floating towards you."

Freeda stated, "But we have to breathe them in, breathe them in. I am getting the daisies in. You know those daisies we had before. Pick the daisies. Does he love me, does he love me not. Does he love me, does he love me not.

"The daisies. Definitely, love conquers all; love conquers all. That has brought me onto thinking what is going on in the world here. It is like bouncing back, back and back. One is bouncing off and one is bouncing back you know. It has taken me back to when we first talked about showing Bill and me; and I was tripping him up to get to the end quicker. It is not who gets there first. It is not who gets there first, and it is not a fire warning, but it is not that at all. You do not have to have any competition at all. It is all competition. You know, what is all the competition about. You know it is ridiculous. Competition is not right. We should not have to compete. We should all be happy with our own lot you know. We should all be happy with our own lot.

"They are just saying as well, it would be great if we all could have just clear vision of things but sometimes it is not as easy as that. Sometimes people have clearer vision than others do. We just have to take it as our vision, our vision. How we perceive things and no competition at all, right". They are just saying, "Why do people do it? Why do humans do it, that they want to compete?" Better vision than the other ones."

I commented, "It is a human trait." There is pine trees around the lake and clouds in the sky going across the moon.

Freeda replied she could also see that and isn't it lovely.

Irene remarked that she could see it as well.

I continued, "I can see the ribbon across the lake off the moon. There must be a little bit of wind because there is a ripple on the lake. It is not very clear to me. It keeps coming and going."

Irene said, "Bill, if we can still the waters of the lake we will be able to see the past and the future." Freeda agreed. Irene continued, "Would you all agree while we are still within ourselves?" Freeda agreed.

I replied, "I came to the lake on the wings of an eagle. I was looking down on it just above treetop level, just floating. I can see a light, a yellowy white light on this side. (Indicating left.) Is that where the gathering is? The gathering."

Irene remarked she could see houses, made of wood. As if it was an ecological, living with nature, nestled among trees.

I could see little wisps of smoke coming out of some of the lodges. Like pine lodges as we would say now, but they are cabins.

Irene interrupted saying, "Right, exactly right." Freeda remarked, "Would not that be lovely, living like that, with nature?" Irene replied, "Yes, that is what they are trying to tell us, darling and it could be one possible future where we do not need everything we think we need. There would be no competition as such. Everybody doing their best of course."

Freeda agreed and remarked how funny it was that the eagle was quite curious. He is quite curious in fact, he is not going round once, and he is going round a couple of times to have a look to see. The countryside and all around it.

Lovely, my eagle, Irene remarked.

Freeda responded, There is something attracted him, I can see something attracted him, you know.

I said I could see the horizon now looking into the darkness.

Irene remarked that she thought he was looking for people to come to the gathering, people of like minds, definitely.

Freeda agreed. He can see from the smallest to the long distance as well. It is like, he is saying, come on, come. Come.

I broke in. There is shapes, like rocks in the darkness. The sky is dark, indigo. It is dark and the moon is behind the cloud but there, you can see the cloud lit off the light of the moon. Both Freeda and Irene agreed.

I said, "We are high up now. He is looking and there are no lights. There is no lights down there now. It is yellow, orange."

Irene remarked, "It is cold and people are lighting fires. That is good for me to see all of that."

It is lovely. Isn't it nice, remarked Freeda, because we are sharing the same vision here? We were all sharing the vision and the feelings, each one of us seeing different things in the complete vision.

Irene said it was good.

I remarked, "I can see the fires of Australia in the darkness. I am a long way up, a long, long way up in the sky. I can see the coastline and there is just fires everywhere. Little groups of fires everywhere. They are quite sad about this."

Irene remarked, "Really? Well, there must be a message coming about this, Bill."

They are asking me why and I do not know why, I replied.

Irene asked, "The sadness, you mean?"

I replied. "No, the fires. Why the fires? Because of the heat and the dryness and no water. No rain.

You have the lake though, Irene remarked.

I replied, "That is on the other side of the world."

Freeda asked, "So we are in Australia now, are we?"

No, I replied. I have come round. I can see the shape of the world coming back up.

Irene asked about the fires in California.

I replied, "No that was earlier on. They have gone. They are in the past."

Freeda sighed and said, "Well all I can say is there is going to be a lot more, fires that is." Irene agreed and that global warming is taking place.

I broke in. "The lake is in the Sierra Nevadas. You have been here before."

Freeda agreed.

Now we are going forwards, I stated. Last time we were going backwards. We saw the mountains first then we came backwards. Now we are in the desert going into the foothills and that is where the lake is and it is pine trees, but there is also deciduous trees. The lake is at the junction between the deciduous trees and the pine trees and there is cabins there. Not a lot of cabins, perhaps six, perhaps eight.

Irene interjected, no, it is not a built up area, just as Freeda remarked, "Bill, I have got your waterfall".

I replied, "I have not seen that yet. I am still high."

Freeda said that she had a river off one side of the lake and a waterfall.

Irene interjected, "Yes, discharging the water down into the lake."

Freeda agreed.

"It is not very high though," I replied. It is quite wide. There is a few rivulets. They are showing me Niagara Falls now. That is how much water we need in Australia. The Bridal Falls, the Seven Veils, the Horseshoe Falls.

Freeda remarked, "As I said before, there is going to be droughts and then there is going to be floods. There is going to be a bit of both, mind."

There is many animals, I offered.

Irene remarked that it is already happening, the worst flooding in places since records began; and in places that could do without it. The places that could do with it are not getting it. Well, what is the message they are trying to get to us.

Freeda agreed with this sentiment as they were going over it again, aren't they.

I broke in: "We have just had a bell. A very faint bell. We need to be, centred."

We want a balance, Freeda replied.

I continued, "We are drifting off. We need to be centred. We need to come together. We need to concentrate."

Freeda replied, "We want a balance though, don't we of, you know like the flooding and the drought. We need a balance. We have lost our balance. It is out of sync."

I remarked, *"I just have yellow orange. Very light orange in the centre. It is closing in. It has just closed the door. The yellow orange closing the door. It is not a door: it is like a porthole. Portal. It is purple inside and the cloud is closing it down. The energy is all over. It is like going into the energy and seeing it then the energy is parting. It is like looking at the sun through closed eyes, half closed eyes. Squinting and the sun is bleaching in and you see this reddy orange colour as if it was shining through your eyelids."*

Freeda said she had just had a snake with its tongue tasting the air, sensing what is going on by flicking out its tongue.

Why are they showing me a little transistor? I asked. A little transistor with three legs, a TO3 case. That is a funny thing to show me. No, they are laughing. The camera is not triggering. Did we not tell you about that, they stated.

Freeda interrupted and telling us that they were on about the
snake again sensing. The snake senses the moisture. You know I
suppose that it finds its prey by moisture around it. That is what
it is trying to say, you know it knows where to find it.

I added that it tastes the air and the electro-magnetic field of
the prey.

Freeda continued. It is just showing me that and it is
something to do with our weather as well. They are trying to tell
me. They are showing me you should be able to sense the dryness
and you should sense the moisture. You know it should be sensing.
There should be a sensor if you want to put it that way, pre warned.

I stated that I had only felt it once and that was coming back from
Canada when we landed. When you got out of the aircraft, you
could taste the water in the air. It felt as if you were drowning
because the air was that dry in the mountains. It took a while to
get used to it and then it went after a few hours. It was even worse
when we landed at Teesside, with more moisture in the air and
a hint of salt.

Irene said, "I wonder if they are trying to tell us, obviously
I do not know but it is just what is coming into me. My mind is
trying to tell us we are going to have to get used to the different
levels. Like you said, you felt as if you were drowning because of
the moisture in the air. As if they are trying to tell us there will
be lots and lots of water but we are going to have to try to get used
to it, to be able to live with it. I do not know."

Freeda replied that what she is keep getting is this.

I interrupted Freeda stating, "We Geordies can live anywhere".

She continued. What I am keep getting is to say we have a
moderate weather but it is going to the extreme, right. Australia
is going to the extreme and they are just trying to say something
about balancing it, balancing it. We are out of sync. You know
they are keep saying, we are out of sync. They are not saying it is
global warming, they are not saying that. They are saying we are

out of sync. We are out of the proper seasons you know, out of sync with everything, sensing stuff. It is just, ah. I cannot explain what they are telling me. I just want: our senses are not right. We are not sensing stuff right, we are out of sync. The global warming, oh, it is just a mess. For example, we do not need any more water; they do not need any more heat.

Yes. I replied. We need more cold.

Freeda said, "Bill, can I ask you something: are you feeling more of the vibrations around you? Not just the cold: but more of the vibrations around you."

I laughed. *"I cannot feel it. Feeling and sensing is two different things. I can sense. I feel the cold. It has gone really, really, cold. It has been over the last couple of minutes, really, really, cold around my feet and my legs. I can sense that it is slowly moving, but it is a vibration, I take as a constant at a frequency. It is not as it seems to be in waves. The frequency changes all the time so you would not get a pure tone or a pure vibration. It is up and down but it is not in tune because there is no tune. They are very low vibrations. If you want to call them vibrations, it is more a movement of air. The vibration is the frequency. The vibration is the result of creating the vibration.*

Do you hear it in your ears? Irene asked.

I replied, *"Yes, but the ears is a lot higher vibration than what the coldness is."*

Oh, I do not know, Irene replied. I always thought the cold was extremely high vibrations.

No. I replied. *Extremely high vibrations give you heat.*

No. Irene replied. Not what I understand so there you are.

I countered. *Well a microwave is 2.4 Gigahertz and that creates heat by vibrating the molecules. At a low vibration, it actually vibrates the substance itself rather than the molecules.*

Freeda asked, "So why do you get really freezing cold and then ice cold?"

Because it is heavy, I replied. It is a heaviness: it is a density.

Well I do not know about that, remarked Irene.

I replied, "As the temperature goes down the density increases so as you heat things up it becomes lighter and freer and more separated."

Freeda suggested, "So when we get really cold, Spirit is more close to us because it becomes denser."

Yes. I replied. They are denser than what we are.

They are denser than what we are? Irene queried.

I replied, it is denser energy than what we, our bodies, are.

Irene stated, "Oh no. I cannot agree with any of that, not over my years. When you do the healing, your base chakra is the slowest of the chakras: you have the other ones, but the main one that you do; that is vibrating at red and it is slow. It is wrong and as you go up the chakras the vibrations, the frequencies increase and as you get towards the top, you really get what they call the angelic vibrations; if you like, and that is what I have always worked off."

I was laughing. *"You do not know what the frequency of vibration is. You have just given an example of a scale."*

They have too, Irene replied.

I replied, *"But you do not understand where the scale is on the scale of every vibration: Yes it is high; but how high is high?"*

Irene replied, "Oh well that does not. I mean you just know that you can go off to infinity."

Freeda commented, "I always find that when I have got Spirit very, very, close or if you want to put it that way Spirit Guides and Helpers and everything, it is freezing. It goes really freezing cold."

Irene commented, "And would you think they are on a higher vibration or not?"

Yes, replied Freeda. I would say yes, they are on a higher vibration than we are. When it goes really cold when they come closer, they are coming more towards our energies but still on a high vibration. You understand what I am saying.

I do, I do, replied Irene. They must lower, for us to feel them.

Yes, replied Freeda. I do not think I am communicating very well today because I think I am still flat.

I said, *"What they are saying is if it was so, so cold, your body would say it is burning so you would get the sensation of heat although it is freezing, freezing cold because your body can only differentiate between certain ranges of temperatures. Once you go outside those temperatures, the body does not know and it can be easily confused. If it is very, very cold, you get the sensation of burning and your skin blisters, even though it is cold."*

Oh yes, I know that. Irene said. I just know in healing, I feel it and I hear it change in the frequency. I do know when I am working on somebody's head and it is purple, violet or whatever, and it is cooler vibrations. Beautiful. Sometimes it is the highest healing coming in. It is freezing and I will tell you what, I am talking about.

People who I have healed and they have had a miracle healing. One lady who was dying, she had leukaemia, she had a failed bone marrow transplant from her brother and she was given days to live. She came and as far as I know, she is still here.

Brilliant, remarked Freeda. Well, I am going to come out because I am not getting anything.

Irene commented, "There is nothing we can get. The reason we see things and that, there is no reason to it. I mean Shairi-Lah, yes, that was lovely what he was pointing to but apart from that, we have had no direction."

Freeda agreed unless Bill has some more.

I replied that I was coming backwards. *I am seeing little plates with little pictures on and just drifting away through this little tiny hole and it is all dark purple around it. Just these little plates with*

*children like sitting on these little small rocks as if they were playing.
Which I think is us. It is a sign from them. We are not into it today.
We were just like children playing.*

*They are not very happy, but we did not give them sufficient
notice. They are just showing us a storm cloud forming. Yes, very
sorry it has not worked out today.*

Freeda laughed as she was just hearing; "But it has". I do not
know why they are saying "but it has". We might find something
that we find out later on and it could be so small.

I commented, *"We might have been looking for something
different from something that they wanted to show us and they
have shown us what they wanted to show us."*

Irene broke in stating, "I know Shairi-Lah; I am over the moon
with that."

I continued, *"But we have doubted what we have seen."*

"Have you?" Irene said.

Once again I continued. *"But we have questioned what we
have seen."*

"You reckon?" Irene asked sarcastically.

I replied, *"We have questioned what they have shown us."*

"I haven't," retorted Irene.

Freeda said that she was still going to concentrate on what we
had, when she had a bit more time on that snake sensing, tasting
the atmosphere.

I said, *"They are saying disaster like Australia."*

Freeda replied, "That is hell. That is pure hell what they have
had, mind, isn't it."

I replied, *"We did have to shuffle things about to get here today.
We were not, really aware of the human illnesses that you were
carrying, because your Spirit, your light was not showing it."*

"Not today," remarked Freeda. Irene has been flat. I have been
flat and you have had an awful cold, Bill.

"They are still there," I replied. *"We have been rubbish."*

Freeda said that she would like to say thank you to everyone that has come along today and tried to communicate with us. Let us hope that our light shines better the next time we come and get some brilliant evidence and they have said we will not be disappointed with this but I do not know why. We will find out, right.

Freeda laughed as they were saying; perhaps this was one of the more successful ones. They are just saying that, right. I would like to say thank you to everybody that has come in to try to communicate with us. It is not your fault. That we are not up to it today.

I would like to say thank you to everybody that has come until we meet again. For everybody to go through the hatch and to your appropriate place and thank you so much for coming.

We did try. We were here for you.

It is just that our light was not shining as bright as it should have done today, right.

They said Bill's was. Freeda laughed at me. Yours was, she remarked through the laughter.

I replied, *"There is three jigsaw pieces just floating about and we have not got them together. The three jigsaw pieces lock together."*

Freeda said that she thought we would leave it for today as I said thank you very much.

Irene and Freeda argued over who would put the kettle on.

It is sad to say that for all the negativity in this session, it was in fact, one of our best. All three of us, privileged to share the same visions, at the same time. That is powerful evidence of a world beyond this Earth. We circled the Earth, were shown the ravages of man, climate change and the extremes of weather. We experienced the power of Spirit through the coldness we felt. Our beliefs in vibration, frequency and energy levels were challenged. Privileged to have the explanation from a far more knowing Spirit world of what scientists still do not understand. We must open our minds and our hearts. We must accept these truths to move on our path. Spirit is the best teachers we can have. In this world and the next.

Chapter Fourteen
– Unexpected confirmation

I know that Shairi-Lah, the hermit in the cave high in the Himalayas, Waa-Nee-Tah, Guy, who I understand is a Manchu and works so hard to coordinate our sessions and arranges everything for us so beautifully. Bella, burnt as a witch, who gave me so much peace, love and care; and the members of my family passed, are all helping me on my journey.

I thank Yellow Cloud, a Lakota Nation (Sioux) Chief, who gave us such a brutal description of what we, as the human race, are inflicting on our planet and thereby to ourselves.

Because of our treatment of the indigenous tribes of North America and the theft and destruction of their homelands, it is understandable that they do not like us. I feel privileged to work with these proud people, due to my love of nature and Mother Earth

I detest the ruins left by man's exploitation of nature's bounties, in North America, Canada and all over our World. I am on their side, as they have suffered greatly, and are still suffering today from the largest genocidal attack in written history.

These proud people have a deep spirituality: not completely erased from the few who remain. Their ancestors have looked for people like me, to be aware of their suffering and their proud traditions.

I have seen the spiritual place of Waa-Nee-Tah, a Pawnee medicine man; and been immersed in that spiritual water from the small waterfall where the ancestors appear to him. Tested by the Council of the Elders, they showed me the beginning of time. They have told me the history of our world through their eyes. I have ridden the Thunderbird and seen the place of the gathering.

I know that there is a subtle irreversible change to my thoughts and outlook on life. I know it is Spirit guiding and pushing me to where they want me to be. I am a willing pupil and forever grateful to all the people along the way who have perhaps, unconsciously guided me to this point in my life.

My thanks go to Bryner Ramsey, who saw my guide, Yellow Cloud, in the magnificence of his prime. A bare chested and proud Man standing beside me at a Divine Service on a Sunday evening at Horden Spiritualist centre. He would not let her go without mentioning that he stood beside me. Proof to the audience that, indeed, I had Spiritual guidance.

To Alison Jones, another Medium, who after a Divine service, also saw him standing with me, along with the pure orange white light of Shairi-Lah. I am truly blessed and privileged to have these wonderful Spirits to help me.

Lynda Bland, another Medium, who once again reminded myself and the congregation of the Spirits around me, at the divine service on the 1st March 2020 at Horden.

It is the more ironic that the promised big changes to my life in January 2020 would be the end of this phase of close meetings with Spirit,and our little group disbanded.

When I look back over the fifteen short weeks and the same number of months since Spirit collected me up, it seems to me, a lifetime away.

For Irene to disregard all the effort other Spirits had made, except for Shairi-Lah and his wisdom, is to deny all. Within these pages is a world of truth. Pearls of wisdom I still find I have missed, despite going through the tapes and videos, time and again.

Spirit informed me to plant a new crop and to store what I had harvested. Spirit has shown me peace and love that far exceeds all I have ever known. My heart filled with love, peace and knowledge from the wonderful Spirit Ladies and Gentlemen whom I have channelled. I thank them and bless them all.

A short time after our last session, I joined a new group with Freeda. This group is now six-strong. The next step of my journey with Spirit. They accept it is a partnership of respect between us. I will guide them as they guide me. We all have this capacity buried within our souls. You must look within to find your purpose. Spirit will show you if you ask.

Since the passing of Catherine, my beloved daughter-in-law in November 2018, there has been many dark times where grief darkened my being. You struggle to function and life loses any meaning. From somewhere in those dark recesses, that so often clouded my vision, there was a tiny spark of light. As the days passed, that spark flickered. Each of us in our close family felt her presence. Subtle yet persistent signs of something or someone around us. A tiny white feather, the sudden appearance of a robin, goose pimples for no apparent reason. A feeling that someone was beside or behind you.

These signs became more insistent for me. A new phone, two pop-ups on the screen to inform me of a meeting at Horden Independent Spiritualist Centre. A sudden urge to go there, less than an hour before the start of the meeting.

It reminded me of a spring morning, the dawning of a new day. The call of the first bird welcoming the hint of light from the darkness of the night. The first hint of the world awakening. My journey over the last twenty months has been like the slow motion beginning of a new day, the transition from darkness to light in an inexorable progression of awakening. Another bird song, another sign. More birdsong, more signs. As the daylight strengthens, so does my awareness of Spirit.

Sitting as one of the congregation of around thirty people on a Wednesday evening at Horden, was a means of slowly developing my connections with Spirit. I became more aware of the energies circulating in the room. I marvelled at how people could stand up and pass messages from Spirit to others in the audience. I would often see faces in my mind, as if they were looking for someone to bring them through but I was shy and afraid. If I stood up to speak, I would get nothing and make a fool of myself. I did not have enough faith to commit myself to a felt ordeal that I would face. I just sat dumb, observing and listening.

One Wednesday evening at the open circle meeting at Horden, I pictured two old women sitting in armchairs, talking. They looked up at me curiously. One of them asked, "Well, are you going to speak up for me? I can give you something if you will stand up." At a brief lull in the proceedings, I found myself standing and everyone was looking at me. My thoughts were racing, my legs felt like jelly. What could or should I say? I described what I had seen. I heard the name Edith and repeated it, although I was unaware of which of the two women in the chair had mentioned it.

I heard in my mind two sisters then no, three sisters. A woman in the audience said yes, I can take that but not Edith. The woman in the armchair I had seen closest to me stood up and said, "I will show you. Tell her what you see and she will know who I am." The scene in my vision, through my now closed eyes, opened up into a dance floor, the old woman stood up and morphed into a younger, taller woman, wearing a blue, flared, pleated dress with a high collar neckline and a thin waist belt. She gracefully took to the dance floor and slowly twirled around, as the bottom of the dress flared slightly as if dancing to unheard music. Her hair was dark and shoulder length with the edges curled in a forties style. I gave the description of what she was showing me. I repeated the words that she loved to dance and tell her I can go dancing every night over here. I am well and it is wonderful over here. You would love it but it is not your time yet. The woman in the audience said it sounds like my mother. The elegant dancing lady, smiled and said, "look at my face and tell her what you see", as she gave a little tinkling laugh. I saw bright red lipstick and said so aloud. She only wore lipstick to go dancing she told me and I repeated this aloud. She sends her love to you, I repeated to the woman in the audience. Oh, and by the way, Edith was my next-door neighbour who I used to go to all the dances with. You remember now, don't you? As I repeated those words, the woman in the audience bowed her head and shed a few silent tears. Those few words from her mother had flooded her mind with the happy times of her childhood but the absolute evidence was the bright red lipstick that she had watched her mother apply on dance nights. The only time she ever saw her applying makeup. With a wave and a mouthed, thank you from that elegant lady, my vision closed and I sat down, polite applause ringing in my ears. Still trembling from the experience.

Two further unexpected confirmations are stuck in my mind. The first one was my cousin Malcom's wife, Hazel, who had passed with cancer around the same time as Catherine. Just after breakfast one Monday morning, I had a vision of Hazel and she said to me, "He has not lit a candle for me", then it was gone. I thought about this and remembered we had a candle in the kitchen window. On the windowsill stood not one but two, a red one and a white one. Drawn to the white one, a Yankee candle. I picked it up, and placed it on our fireplace then lit it. I silently said, "There you are, Hazel, a candle just for you. I will find out why he did not light one." I rang Malcolm but there was no answer. I rang the next day and after exchanging pleasantries with Malcolm, I asked him to listen without interruption until I had finished talking to him. I recounted my experience.

He was amazed as he had to attend the hospital on Monday morning for a minor operation and would be out of the house all day. He had lit a candle for Hazel on the Sunday but her birthday was actually Monday. The tea light candle had burnt out but he had forgot to put it on a heat resistant pad and it had marked the sideboard next to her photograph. He had not wanted to leave a lit candle on the Monday, as he knew he would be out all day. Hazel's favourite candle was, yes, a Yankee candle.

The episode was a sign to Malcolm that Hazel was close to him, watching, but unable to communicate with him and evidence to me that I was indeed progressing and more open to Spirit.

The second episode came in three parts, the first two some six months apart and the third just a few days after the second, for the same person. Alice was the MC for most Sunday services at Horden. One Sunday evening while listening to the Medium passing messages to the congregation, I had the vision of a seated woman above Alice's head. She appeared to be playing an organ or piano. Every time I looked in Alice's direction, the woman appeared, until the service ended. At this point, I quietly drew Alice aside and asked if I could speak to her, to which she replied, "Yes". I asked about a woman who played the piano. She then said, you do not have to tell me anything else, as I know the person. Her brother's wife was a beautiful piano player and as she was in the middle of a house move, she had not spoken to him as she usually did each week. His wife had passed some time before. It was clearly a message to Alice to telephone her brother.

About six months after, I woke early and as I was shaving a voice said, "Phone Alice". I thought to myself, it is only six forty-five in the morning. I cannot phone Alice at this time. I forgot about it. Again, at ten a.m., a far more insistent voice came to me. "Phone Alice", it said. I could feel the urgency in the voice so I immediately telephoned Alice and with her permission, recounted what had happened that morning. Due to the Covid-19 virus lockdown, we had no real contact for a couple of weeks and I was unaware it was her brother's funeral that morning. She was waiting to go to the funeral but my contact was a help to her, hearing my voice after some weeks of silence. She said we have plenty of time as the funeral is at eleven a.m. and it is only eight twenty. This took me by surprise, as I knew it was ten twenty a.m. I told her so and she asked her husband, who confirmed it was eight twenty. I reiterated the correct time and please check the TV time for confirmation. I was correct. They would attend the funeral now at the correct time!

Three or four days after the funeral I had another vision. Sitting on the couch watching TV, I had closed my eyes. I saw a yellow path, winding gently up a shallow rise to a stand of trees at the top. Along the path were a couple of park benches. On the edge of my vision to my left, I saw a beautiful garden of flowers, all in bloom. The grass was a lovely, well-manicured carpet of green. On the path coming into view were a couple, arm in arm, walking slowly, as if the man was taking his time, like a person in recovery after illness. The first steps outside, on this warm summer day with blue skies and high, wispy white clouds. The man gave me thoughts about him. A private man, old fashioned and reticent to show emotion. His words to me were few, but profound. "Please tell Alice, thank you and I am reunited with my wife. We are both doing fine. It is a little difficult for me at present, but I am getting better all the time. Thank you for your help."

I telephoned Alice and told her what I had received. Everything I mentioned she could, and did, relate to her brother and his wife. Simple, yes. Profound, Yes. Reassurance of life after death? Definitely.

There are a few more episodes like this. The most compelling are in this little book about my journey. Freeda's mother and brother, the most powerful evidence for her and me.

This is truly our journey. We all have the capability. We will all go through this awakening of our soul eventually.

Whether in this life or the life beyond.

It is your choice when you start your journey.

Remember: LISTEN and OBSERVE.

The beginning of your journey is only a thought away.

God bless to all.

Printed in Great Britain
by Amazon